THE
$100M
JOURNEY

YOUR GUIDE TO GROWING THE BUSINESS OF YOUR DREAMS WITHOUT GOING OFF THE CLIFF!

JOHN ST.PIERRE

Advance Praise

"John & I both cut our teeth in business 30 years ago at College Pro Painters. His book is a must-read, packed with actionable strategies for entrepreneurs who want to sustainably build and grow a business without repeating the same mistakes we've both made. Every leader needs to devour this."

—Cameron Herold,
Founder, COO Alliance and
Author of Vivid Vision

"*The $100M Journey* is not just another business book. Having been both a witness and mentor to John's relentless pursuit of growth and success firsthand, his insights go beyond just theoretical guidance. It's humble, practical, personal—and it's proven."

—Charlie Chase,
CEO, California Closets

"An outstanding read that will help management navigate business obstacles and provide proven techniques to uplift Profit, Cash and Value".

—Alan Miltz,
Co-Author Scaling Up by Verne Harnish (Cash Component), and
Co-Founder Cash Flow Story used in 96 Countries globally

"Failure...it's such a harsh word that many of us seem to fear and avoid. The Author of *The $100M Journey* takes us on a personal journey showing that 'Failure' can be a momentary re-direction leading us to learn and grow, while providing an opportunity for greater success and satisfaction on our own personal journey."

—Jeff Wall,
CEO of Handyman Connection

"An incredibly valuable and inspiring resource packed with actionable strategies for successful business practices. An absolute must-read for anyone in the entrepreneurial space."

—Rande Somma,
Author of Leadersh!t

"You can't get to your destination without embarking on the correct journey. John's book provides a better than GPS guide to the promised land for every hopeful entrepreneur. John reminds us that if we fall flat on our face, then we are at least falling forward in the pursuit of our entrepreneurial dreams."

—Steve Cohen, Esq.
Devine Millimet

"The best lessons learned are those born out of failure. *The $100M Journey* is the perfect guide for entrepreneurs to navigate the difficult challenges and create a path for success."

—Vince Pastore, CPA
Partner, HBK Advisors

"If you're an entrepreneur looking to start a business or an executive looking to scale your company, *The $100M Journey* is a must-read."

—Ted Ma,
Leadership Strategist and
Author of High Performance Leadership

"This book is an essential read for any emerging business leader. It offers valuable lessons, real-life stories, and important strategies based on the author's experience in growing multiple companies between $50M and $100M."

—Jeffrey Unger,
Founder and CEO of G2 Capital Advisors

"John is a savvy entrepreneur, an intrepid adventurer, and a compelling storyteller. He has given us an inside look at the sometimes perilous and scary journey on the road of starting, growing, scaling, and ultimately conquering the mountain of the business visionary. If you want to grow your dream in the business sense, start here, and pay attention."

—Kellan Fluckiger,
10x Amazon International Bestselling Author,
Creator of *The Results Equation*

"John's entrepreneurial journey tells a powerful story that is rich with important learnings. His desire to help others avoid critical pitfalls echos throughout the book and translates into 7 battle-tested principles. This book is a gift to any entrepreneur looking to grow their business in a healthy and sustainable way."

—Ruth Lund,
Co-founder of True North Culture Advisors

"Too many aspiring entrepreneurs believe that high-growth entrepreneurship is all about finding the right idea at the right time and riding the ensuing rocket ship to the moon. Alas, most often, that's not how it works. For those who are willing to invest the time, effort, tenacity, and so much more into making their entrepreneurial dreams become real – despite the adversity and setbacks they'll inevitably encounter – there's no better guide than John St. Pierre and no better guidebook than *The $100M Journey*."

—John Mullins,
Author of Break the Rules! and The Customer-Funded Business
and Associate Professor, London Business School

THE $100M JOURNEY WORKBOOK

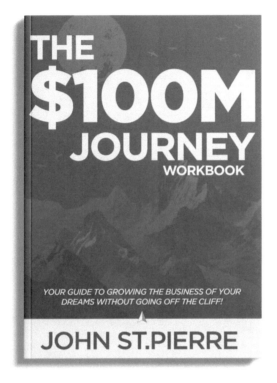

The $100M Journey Workbook is a guide with tools, templates, and other valuable resources to assist you on your entrepreneurial journey!

Scan the QR code above or go to
100MJourney.com/Workbook for access

THE $100M JOURNEY

*YOUR GUIDE TO GROWING THE BUSINESS OF YOUR
DREAMS WITHOUT GOING OFF THE CLIFF!*

ISBN   978-1-961098-25-1   *Hardcover*
        978-1-961098-26-8   *Paperback*
        978-1-961098-27-5   *Ebook*

*"You know who your true friends
are when the going gets tough."*
—Unknown

To the love of my life, Amy; our boys, Maxim and Danick;
my parents, Sandra and Armand; my sisters, Tracey and
Patricia; our extended families, and . . .

every single person that stood by me on my entrepreneurial
journey. You know who you are!
When I was down, you were there to inspire and motivate
me to get back up and Kick Some Ass!

Thank you!

TABLE OF CONTENTS

PATIENT & PERSISTENT AMBITION BY CHARLIE CHASE

"Ambition without a goal is just a dream. A goal without strategy is hope. Persistent, goal-focused strategies achieve ambitious results."

—Charlie Chase, CEO of California Closets

My relationship with John has spanned well over two decades. I've been along with him on his journey from his days as a young college student with big ambitions to the accomplished entrepreneur he has become. John's journey has been filled with hard lessons, growth opportunities, and an infectious drive to succeed. In my experience, success comes in one of two paths: "right place right time" and "hard-won." John's career follows the latter path. He possesses an unwavering persistence and a thirst for learning which are traits that not only define his entrepreneurial spirit but also inspire others to grow and dream big.

In my career, I have had the distinct pleasure of working with hundreds of amazing entrepreneurs. These "low-tech" businesses have spanned vast geographies where leadership of people was a key component of success. These entrepreneurs were building companies to scale either through franchising, company owned, or dealership relationships. In all cases these entrepreneurs had to master leadership skills that focused on goal setting, coaching, conflict resolution, problem solving, and financial management. Most importantly, these entrepreneurs had to live by an inspirational set of core values that influenced their teams.

In John's case, he was an ardent student of these leadership skills. John's ambition has always been tempered by his gap in knowledge; if he didn't know an area of study, he went and found the information. Anyone who knows John well knows how dogged he can be as a constant learner. This concept resonates at the core of John's entrepreneurial journey; he lived his core values through continuous improvement. His aspirations have always been grand, but it was not until he learned some of the hard lessons he shares within this book that he became grounded. He got to a place where he became ambitious yet patient, bold yet humble, assertive *and* persistent.

I distinctly remember the call I received from John after he had just been fired from the company he had nurtured for over 15 years—a company that he and his early partners poured their hearts and souls into patiently developing the relationships required to scale. During this humbling moment, he wanted to understand how it happened, where he failed, and how he could recover. At that moment, he was already prepared to introspectively digest my feedback and he was determined to not be defined by the setback. Fifteen years into this business, John knew that entrepreneurship is a long marathon and not a sprint: a game that is not for the faint of heart, but for those that have the grit to persevere, learn, and grow. He has learned that having patient and persistent ambition is the recipe for long-term success.

In this book, *The $100M Journey*, John shares his hard-learned lessons and strategies that entrepreneurs need to seriously consider to scale their ventures and achieve significant results. The chapters guide you through very important goals, concepts, and strategies that are foundational to building your success. This is not an MBA course, nor is it what invest-ment bankers want you to read. This book is a real-life narration of John's challenges, successes, and failures in his entrepreneurial journey, complete with a roadmap, grounding principles, and a workbook with actionable tools for achieving long-term business success—on your terms.

The $100M Journey is not just another business book. Having been both a witness and mentor to John's relentless pursuit of growth and success firsthand, his insights go beyond just theoretical guidance. It's humble, practical, personal—and it's proven. This book encapsulates his experience, learnings, and commitment that will resonate with entrepreneurs in their journey toward building businesses in a durable and significant manner.

I am honored to have mentored and advised John and various other extraordinary entrepreneurs on their business paths. *The $100M Journey* is John's story and your guide to hard-won lessons in each chapter. I hope his golden nuggets of entrepreneurship will guide, inspire, and catapult you toward amazing success.

- Charlie Chase

DEAR ENTREPRENEUR,

It's time to wake up and take control of your business and your life!

You wanted to become an entrepreneur because you dreamed of achieving financial success and freedom by running your own business. Still, here you are stressed out, overworked, sleep-deprived, out of shape, not spending enough quality time with your family, and paying yourself less than you're worth (if you are paying yourself at all).

What are you doing? The tail is wagging the dog. If this is what being an entrepreneur means, you would be better off getting a job. Maybe you were meant to work for another entrepreneur and help them achieve wealth and freedom. Many great companies are looking for talented people like you. You could get a very consistent and lucrative salary with several weeks of paid vacation (where you can entirely escape your responsibilities), and you could stop killing yourself trying to achieve your ambitious entrepreneurial goals.

Oh, so you do not think this letter is directed at you? Do you think you have this thing called business all figured out and that you are on the path to achieving all your business dreams? Yeah, I thought I knew it all as well! And guess what?!

Just when you think you have it all figured out, you get punched in the gut, or worse, experience a fatal business event because you are not as wise as you think.

Then you wake up in the aftermath only to discover that you were a complete idiot for thinking you knew everything! You didn't *know*. There is a big difference between *thinking* you know something and actually knowing it. You reflect on all the times people close to you tried to warn you and you shrugged them off with an air of overconfidence.

If you want to learn from others' experiences and have a burning desire to achieve all of your life and business dreams and goals, this is where you need to be. Right here, right now! It is time to gain a new perspective and make a paradigm shift.

Don't let yourself become another statistic, another entrepreneur who loses their business. Take the initiative to be bold and go after what you want. You can make a real difference in your life and the lives of those around you. It's time to stop being a business operator and become an actual business owner!

Don't wait. It's time to regain control of your business and life!

It's time to kick some ass!

Sincerely,

Your future self

START WITH "WHY"

"The most successful people and organizations are those who are clear about why they do what they do."

—Simon Sinek, Start with Why

Welcome to *The $100M Journey*, where challenges are overcome, failures are avoided, and dreams are accomplished. But let's not sugarcoat it—this journey is not for the faint of heart. It's a battleground where only the resilient survive, where the line between success and failure is often razor-thin. As an entrepreneur, you've undoubtedly tasted the bittersweet realities that come with building a business from the ground up. You've experienced the sleepless nights, the relentless pressure, and the countless obstacles that threaten to derail your progress.

But here's the unfiltered truth: the odds are stacked against you. The statistics are sobering, revealing a staggering number of businesses that crash and burn within the first few years. It's a harsh reality that many entrepreneurs choose to overlook. They dive headfirst into the entrepreneurial abyss, oblivious to the pitfalls that await them. They rely on outdated strategies, misguided advice, and blind optimism, only to find themselves teetering on the edge of disaster.

It's time for entrepreneurs to have a new perspective. It's time to shatter the illusions and embrace a bold, no-nonsense approach to building the business of your dreams. In this book, we will dive deep into the 7 Principles that will help you navigate the treacherous terrain of entrepreneurship. We'll examine the catastrophic mistakes that have led countless entrepreneurs, including myself, to lose everything they have built. But more importantly, we'll uncover the principles that will empower you to rise above the odds and create a lasting legacy.

The "Dear Entrepreneur" letter opening this book is what, in retrospect, I wish somebody had written to me a few years back. Unfortunately, I was probably too confident and too cocky to have learned from it anyway. Do not let that be you.

Prepare yourself. This is not your average business book. It's a wake-up call—a reality check designed to challenge your assumptions, confront your limitations, and ignite a fire within you. If you're ready to strip away the illusions that have held you back and embark on a journey of unparalleled growth and success—fasten your seatbelt. The path ahead won't be easy, but with the right guidance, a clear plan, a directional compass, and unwavering determination, you can defy the odds and build the business of your dreams.

Are you ready to embark on *The $100M Journey* with me? Let's dive in.

My entrepreneurial journey has been filled with an incredible amount of learnings from both my successes and my failures. The failures contained massive mistakes and great learnings that made me stronger and more committed to achieving my goals. As the saying goes: if it does not kill you, it will make you stronger.

Knowledge is power, and we can learn from others' mistakes to avoid making them ourselves. I hope this book can prevent you from making the same entrepreneurial mistakes I and others have made, save you from pain, and help you build the business, wealth, and freedom you dream of achieving.

Ok, enough dreaming about it. Let's go make it happen!

WHO IS THIS BOOK FOR?

If you are an entrepreneur seeking to take your business to the next level, are experiencing growing pains, and have a burning desire to achieve the ultimate business and entrepreneurial success, this book was written specifically for you! To be more specific, this book will help guide you in the next phase of your entrepreneurial journey if:

- you have been an entrepreneur running a business for 5+ years;
- you have grown your business to generate $1M+ in annual revenues;
- you are constantly working *in* your business, not *on* your business;
- you have not yet been able to create true wealth and freedom with your company;
- you have a burning desire to achieve success for your business, yourself, your family, and your team;
- or any or all of the above!

This book may benefit you as well if:

- you are in the startup years of building a business. There are great principles you can learn and keep in mind as you grow. I also have sprinkled learnings from other business books throughout and you may want to read those as well to help you on your own entrepreneurial journey.

This book is *not* explicitly written for you if:

- you are one of the minority who has built and sold your company and already accomplished your entrepreneurial goals. If this is you, congratulations! I invite you to continue reading to discover if the 7 Principles resonate with your journey. If they do, or if there are other principles that you applied in your entrepreneurial journey that would benefit others, I welcome your feedback so that we can incorporate it in the future. Find us at 100MJourney.com.

Of course, if you want to read about my entrepreneurial journey (hi, Mom!) and learnings (hi, Dad!), I welcome you to dive right in. I hope you enjoy the read and look forward to your feedback.

WHY DID I WRITE THIS BOOK?

Writing this book has been an enriching and challenging exercise for me. The decision to tell the story of my journey and learnings was driven by identifying my life's purpose in 2019.

After a massive business failure, which I will share about later, I took a sabbatical to find myself. Waking up each morning with an empty calendar and inbox was very foreign to me.

For over 25 years, I had worked tirelessly to become the best entrepreneur and leader I could be. I read hundreds of business books and soaked up knowledge from business mentors, motivational speakers, and anybody I could learn from. Although I had achieved some success in business, I found myself broken.

I had been told by several business mentors that one day, I would figure out what my deeper purpose was, but I never fully understood what they meant until I found myself lost. I needed to finally figure out my "why." I needed to find a new identity and a compelling future that was bigger than just me. So with intention, I dedicated some time to doing just that.

My favorite TED Talk is Simon Sinek's "Start with Why." Whenever I host a strategic business planning session, I play this video and ask the team to focus on the company's "why." "Everything must start here," I say. We then lay out a clear Strategic Plan aligning with that purpose.

Why had I never really used that same strategy for myself? Why did I never take the time for deep self-reflection to determine my "why"?

Self-reflection might be the most underrated process of one's life. If we don't know where we want to go, any path will do. Then we get stuck on the wrong road only to be hit by the proverbial bus years later and wonder, "WTF just happened?"

This was me! Having clarity on my life's big goals was critical to understanding what I should be doing and in exactly which direction I should be headed. This aha moment ignited a fire in me. I worked tirelessly to develop a process to find my purpose, my "why"!

It became clear that my professional purpose was to use my talents and learnings to guide entrepreneurs to achieve success for their businesses, themselves, and their teams while avoiding the many pitfalls of business growth.

I want to help you achieve your business dreams. I want to help you be successful and avoid the mistakes I have made that cost me dearly.

An overwhelming majority of companies and entrepreneurs are stuck. Unfortunately, only a small percentage of entrepreneurs survive the daunting task of transitioning their business from a small Lifestyle business to a successful and sustainable High Performance business that will create the true wealth and freedom they seek.

So, where are you in your entrepreneurial journey?

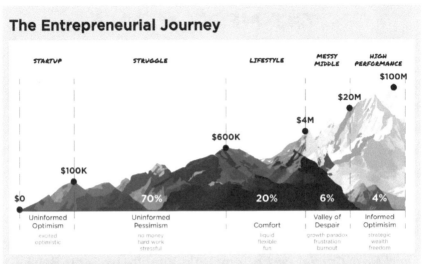

The Entrepreneurial Journey

STARTUP	STRUGGLE	LIFESTYLE	MESSY MIDDLE	HIGH PERFORMANCE

$100M
$20M
$4M
$600K
$100K
$0

70% 20% 6% 4%

Uninformed Optimism	Uninformed Pessimism	Comfort	Valley of Despair	Informed Optimisim
excited optimistic	no money hard work stressful	liquid flexible fun	growth paradox frustration burnout	strategic wealth freedom

Information on the above graph provided by https://www.dent.global/

"The Entrepreneurial Journey" chart was first introduced to me by Callum Laing. Laing is the CEO of MBH Corporation, Inc., a publicly listed company that aggregates small- to medium-sized businesses (SMBs), and the coauthor of the book *Agglomerate*. His book offers valuable insight into the entrepreneurs' challenges when transitioning from the Lifestyle to High Performance stage.

In an interview with me, Laing highlighted the problem we face as entrepreneurs: "Many entrepreneurs find themselves in *Groundhog Day*, running the same day over and over, not moving up the entrepreneur ladder. The first rung is a startup; the second is running the business; then the third rung is thinking like an owner. . . Part of the problem is that there is no roadmap about how they should take that third step."

Only 4% of companies achieve this High Performance level of business growth, so we know this is not easy.

Unfortunately, as entrepreneurs attempt to grow from Lifestyle to High Performance, they get stuck in the Messy Middle, the riskiest stage of the entire Entrepreneurial Journey.

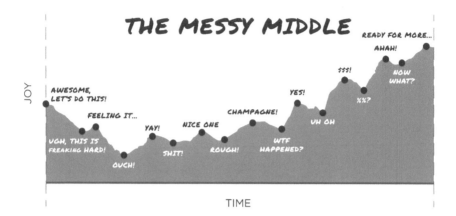

The Messy Middle: Finding Your Way Through the Hardest and Most Crucial Part of Any Bold Venture by Scott Belsky

The Messy Middle offers guidance on navigating the difficult and crucial stage of any ambitious project or venture. Belsky draws on his experiences as both an entrepreneur and investor and offers insights from other successful business leaders to provide practical advice and strategies for overcoming challenges and staying focused on the ultimate goal. The book is organized into three sections: Endure, Optimize,

and The Final Mile, each focusing on a different aspect of the journey. Belsky emphasizes the importance of embracing the messiness of the middle, staying agile and adaptable, and maintaining a clear sense of purpose throughout.

Key Learnings:

1. The middle of any ambitious project or venture is the most difficult and crucial phase, and it requires a unique set of skills and strategies to navigate successfully.

2. Embracing the messiness of the middle is essential for staying agile and adaptable and maintaining a clear sense of purpose.

3. Endurance is key in the early stages of the middle when progress may be slow and setbacks are common. Maintaining focus and momentum is essential for pushing through this phase.

4. Optimization is critical in the middle stage, as the venture takes shape and the team becomes more complex. Focusing on process improvement, team alignment, and communication is important.

5. The final mile is the last stage of the middle, and it requires a relentless drive toward the finish line. Leaders must stay focused on the ultimate goal, maintain a sense of urgency, and be willing to make tough decisions to ensure success.

"You survive the middle by enduring the valleys, and you thrive by optimizing the peaks. You will find your way only by reconciling what you learn from others with what you discover on your own."
—Scott Belsky, *The Messy Middle*

My goal is to help entrepreneurs grow their businesses beyond the Lifestyle stage and achieve their aspirations and dreams without getting stuck in the Messy Middle or, worse, losing their businesses through fatal mistakes.

So, how do entrepreneurs cross the chasm between a Lifestyle and a High Performance business without going off the cliff?

This is what I will answer in this book.

HOW TO READ THIS BOOK?

The entrepreneurial journey is challenging, lonely, demanding, and very stressful. This book is intended to help entrepreneurs create a clear plan for achieving business success while also recognizing many of the pitfalls we all face as entrepreneurs and providing ways to avoid those pitfalls.

I wanted the concepts and principles in this book to rise above core management philosophies flooding the market. This book is intended to address and attack areas of learning and opportunity that can help propel entrepreneurs to a higher level, help them avoid catastrophic land mines, and, most importantly, help them break through the Messy Middle to achieve ultimate success.

This book is divided into four sections. I would like to properly articulate each section's purpose and value so you can have the best experience.

Section I: My Entrepreneurial Journey

Much like all entrepreneurs, my journey is filled with challenges, adversity, failures, and successes. I look forward to sharing these with you, and I hope you will see similarities and common threads between your journey and mine.

Through my journey, you will understand how my learnings guided me to develop my True North Life Plan, a Strategic Business Plan, and the 7 Principles that ultimately helped me achieve the entrepreneurial success I was striving for.

Section II: Your True North and Strategic Plan

In this section, we review:

- Where are you on your Entrepreneurial Journey?

- What is your True North (your "why")?

- What is your Strategic Business Plan?

Knowing where you are currently and having clarity on your life's ambitions—your True North—is essential before you can design a Strategic Plan for your business. How can you create a plan for your business if you do not know what you are ultimately trying to achieve as a person?

Why did you become an entrepreneur in the first place? What does success look like for you? What is your "why"—your True North? These questions, and more, will help you develop a clear and concise Strategic Plan for your business that will align with your desired destination—your True North Life Plan. The Strategic Plan will help your company attain its short- and long-term goals while also helping you achieve your objectives as an entrepreneur.

Section III: 7 Principles of Entrepreneurial Success

With the clarity of knowing exactly where you are going both personally (True North) and with your business (Strategic Plan), the $100M Compass will guide you with 7 Principles that will help you grow the business of your dreams, without going off the cliff!

These 7 Principles have taught me valuable lessons and when appropriately executed, have helped me to break through the Messy Middle of high business growth and achieve outstanding results.

Each principle has been split into two parts:

- _**Why**_ the principle is crucial for entrepreneurial success (Theory)

- _**How**_ entrepreneurs can apply the principle in their businesses (Practice)

At the end of each principle, the entrepreneur is encouraged to take action and apply the learnings from that principle in their business. We have provided additional support and a workbook at 100MJourney.com/workbook. Use the resources provided to guide you and your company through each principle.

Principle I: Protect and Grow your Equity

Learn why and how entrepreneurs must grow and protect their equity so they remain in control of their own destinies.

Principle II: Build Your Own Capital

Learn why and how entrepreneurs must create their own capital through net operating cash flows rather than relying on bank debt or investment to grow.

Principle III: Reinvest Smartly

Learn why and how entrepreneurs must reinvest wisely and patiently in their growth to build a High Performance business.

Principle IV: Build a Culture of Intrapreneurship

Learn why and how entrepreneurs must fully engage their leadership teams and provide them the opportunity to participate in equity appreciation.

Principle V: Protect the House

Learn why and how entrepreneurs must strategically assess and manage internal and external risk factors that can harm the business.

Principle VI: Access Owner's Liquidity

Learn why and how entrepreneurs can build the strength of their balance sheet and access the liquidity within it.

Principle VII: Move from CEO to Chairperson

Learn why and how entrepreneurs must replace themselves operationally to strategically rise above the business.

Section IV: The Entrepreneurial Short Stories of Jekyll and Hyde

The short stories of two alter ego entrepreneurs, Jekyll and Hyde, will provide a fun view of two entrepreneurs taking different paths.

One of the entrepreneurs, Jekyll, had a clear Strategic Plan and followed the 7 Principles of Entrepreneurial Success. In contrast, the other entrepreneur, Hyde, took a more aggressive and careless path to grow his business. As you read about the outcomes of their decisions, decide which entrepreneur you want to be.

The differences in how these two entrepreneurs approach their business growth are drastic. You will see the power of the 7 Principles and how miscalculating their importance can lead to damaging results.

Epilogue: It's Time!

If you are not ready to grab the bull by the horns after reading this book, I did something wrong! It is time to create your True North Life Plan and your Strategic Plan, implement the 7 Principles, and build the business you always aspired to have.

It's time for you to take action!

LET'S GO!

After many years of trials, tribulations, failures, embarrassments, and disappointments, I finally found the 7 Principles of Entrepreneurial Success.

There is nothing quite like a sense of purpose and goal fulfillment that comes about when entrepreneurs achieve their goals. I hope this book will provide you with the confidence, clarity, conviction, and direction to help you achieve your wildest entrepreneurial dreams.

Let's get going!

DEATH IN THE BOARDROOM

"Success is not final, failure is not fatal; it is the courage to continue that counts."

— often attributed to Winston Churchill

"John, can you stay in the boardroom for a few minutes? I would like to speak with you."

My heart sank as I watched the five other board members hurry to gather their belongings to quickly exit the boardroom without a glance or goodbye. Trying to keep my composure, I knew what was about to happen.

A year before this board meeting, I had hired an executive to assist me in raising capital so that our company could continue its aggressive growth. Our 15-year-old company had grown from a hobby startup to over $50M in global revenues, achieving 400% growth over the previous two years.

After months of vetting suitable partners, we decided as a company to proceed with a private equity firm that this new executive had introduced to us. This new firm, along with other partners and I, invested significant capital in our business.

As the ink dried on the capital raise and the funds hit our company's bank account, I immediately felt a massive target on my back. Where was this coming from? How did this happen?

It was now seven months since the new private equity firm had joined the board, and it was painfully clear that they wanted to replace me with somebody they thought was better suited to lead the business to success.

"If the board does not believe that I am the right person to lead this business, then I will need to step down and support the new CEO as we grow the business to the next level," I told myself as I waited for the boardroom to empty. I had 15 years and significant capital invested in this business. As recently as the last capital raise, I had convinced my wife to invest a significant portion of our savings alongside the private equity firm's investment. I was all in!

"John, I asked the private equity firm if I could meet with you one-on-one before they return to the boardroom," said my partner Ron, who was the first investor to back our company years prior. "We have known each other for a while now, and I felt that you deserved to hear the news from me first."

The emotion in his eyes confirmed what I had thought was going on, but I was prepared. I saw this coming from a mile away and was ready to step aside to fulfill another role if that was what the board wanted. I loved this business, the brand, the people, and the culture.

Unfortunately, I was not prepared for what came next.

"The private equity firm will be coming back into the boardroom in a couple of minutes to terminate you from the company, effective today," he continued.

In complete disbelief, doing everything I could to control my emotions, I stared into his eyes, and all I could say was, "Ok."

What else was I supposed to say? I was floored! Being prepared to step aside and into a different role is one thing, but being terminated? How could this be?

I was not ok! I was being removed from the business I had cofounded with my best friends over 15 years prior. I had helped guide and build it from a hobby startup business to over $50M in global revenues. Why would the new investors want the cofounder and CEO of the company gone within seven months of having invested so much money?

The silence and tension were building. My partner, Ron, allowed me the time to think and let everything sink in.

"This does not make any sense," I said out loud.

"I cannot explain it, John, but they want a new CEO in place," he said.

"Bring them back in," was all I could say.

I looked away at the large painting of a beautiful golf course on the boardroom wall. Slowly analyzing the greenness of the fairway was all I could do to momentarily take my focus off what was happening. "I guess I will be spending more time improving my golf game soon," I thought, trying to distract myself from the moment.

The two private equity partners walked back into the boardroom, one of them holding a legal-sized envelope in his hand. That investor placed the envelope on the boardroom table right in front of me and remained standing in front of my chair, establishing a presence and position of strength over me.

"John, here are your termination papers; we are removing you as CEO and terminating you from the company, effective immediately," the investor said.

Having been on the delivering side of termination meetings countless times, I knew how all the parties in the room felt as they awaited my reaction. The tension in the room was very uncomfortable.

With an intense, targeted look at the envelope, I decided to not touch it. I slowly looked up at the investor and asked, "Who will replace me as CEO?"

It hit me as he paused, unsure if he wanted to answer the question. They were going to replace me with the executive I had brought on to help me raise capital. This is why the tide quickly changed. Unfortunately, this executive had controlled the relationship with the private equity firm from the onset and had placed a target on my back all along. How was I so blind and foolish as to let this happen?

"If he is going to be the new CEO of the business and the board believes that this decision is the best for all equity holders (including me), then fine, but why fire me?" I asked.

"This is a big mistake," I said, "I have led and helped build this company for over 15 years. I would give anything to protect this business and its people, and you are firing me?"

Without a valid explanation as to the exact reason for the termination, the meeting ended and the investors began to exit the boardroom.

I looked up at the high vaulted ceiling in the boardroom and shook my head in disbelief.

WTF just happened?

As I got into my car and exited the parking lot to begin my two-hour drive home, I did what any spouse would do and made the dreaded call to my wife to tell her what had happened.

"Hey," I said as she answered the phone, "I am not exactly sure what just happened, but I just got fired."

Over the previous few years, my wife had warned me about growing the business too quickly and raising large sums of money from private equity investors because we risked losing control of the company.

I do not know about your spouse . . . but unfortunately, mine is always right!

During what seemed to be the shortest two-hour drive I had ever had, I replayed the past few years' events and realized this would be a long, sleepless night.

Pulling past the golf course at the entrance of our neighborhood, I was reminded of what I thought about while looking at the painting on the boardroom wall: "I guess I will be spending more time on my golf game soon."

As I walked into our home, my wife was sitting on the couch with both of our young boys. She had apparently informed my 10- and 12-year-old sons that their father "had a bad day at work."

"I f**ked up, honey, and I am sorry," I said as she got up from the couch to give me a big hug.

SECTION I

MY ENTREPRENEURIAL JOURNEY

"Entrepreneurship is a turbulent ride. It's full of ups and downs, and it's not for the faint of heart. But if you're willing to put in the hard work and persevere through the tough times, it can be incredibly rewarding."

– Jim Collins, Built to Last

CHAPTER 1

THE AMERICAN DREAM

"What makes America great is the fact that anyone can take a risk, pursue their dream, and be successful."

—Anonymous

When I was three months old, our family moved from Sydney, Nova Scotia, into a small trailer park in a rural French city south of Montréal, Québec. My French-speaking father was a professor at the Royal Military College of Canada, while my mother, an Anglophone from Sydney, worked at home raising my two sisters and me.

In Québec, you can only send your child to an English primary school if one of the parent's first language is English. Otherwise, the law states you must send your child to a French school (see Canadian Charter of Rights and Freedoms, Section 23 in "References").

It's hard to believe in this day and age that this rule still exists.

Because my mother's first language, English, would dominate in the household, I would slowly learn to speak French from friends in the neighborhood, youth sports, and of course, from watching my beloved Montréal Canadiens on TV every Saturday night.

With a dozen highly populated French schools in our city, my small school was the only English one. Being known as the "square heads" or "tête carrée" (slang the French use for us English folks) was at times difficult. Being made fun of every time I improperly communicated masculine and feminine adjectives was not a laughing matter. I still get them wrong today. But the advantage of growing up bilingual in Québec would eventually become an incredible asset, making it easier for me to land summer jobs and become a conduit for communication with those that only spoke one language.

My entrepreneurial roots started in grade six when our small elementary school launched a chocolate bar sales fundraising campaign. I took the sales competition seriously and wanted to help support my school. After all, the first prize for the person who sold the most chocolate bars was a brand-new alarm clock! It was obviously not the prize that motivated me. It was the opportunity to win that drove my competitive spirit.

My best friend, Stefano, and I went door-to-door selling chocolate bars to our neighbors. As we expanded to streets further and further away from our home, our sales became harder and harder.

"Maybe I am not going to win this competition," I thought as I looked at the sales leaderboard in the school's main lobby each morning.

But things changed drastically when we discovered that an easier way to sell these chocolate bars would be to knock on the dorm room doors of student cadets at the Royal Military College where my father worked.

Even though there was tight security at the entrance gate of the Royal Military College, my father gladly drove us onto the campus so he could get some work done grading assignments while we sold chocolate bars. In hindsight, it was a good thing that we did not ask for permission. These cadets had strict diets and no access to comfort junk foods. Undoubtedly, the Royal Military College officers would not be pleased with our scheme to go door-to-door through the dorms selling chocolate bars to cadets.

Within 15 minutes on our first night at the Royal Military College, we sold out of our 2 boxes of chocolate bars (48 bars). The following day we returned to school, turned in the funds we had collected the night prior, saw our names rise on the leaderboard, and asked the teacher for 5 additional boxes each. The teacher looked at us puzzled but appreciated our enthusiasm, did not ask any questions, and handed over the boxes.

This was my first exposure to the fundamental economic concept of supply and demand.

The cadets would not purchase one chocolate bar; they would purchase several in our one stop at their door. Not only did each room have two cadets, but many wanted to purchase multiple bars to stash away because they did not know when they would have access to chocolate again.

The ease of walking five to ten steps to knock on another cadet's door made the process simple, effortless, and fun. As Stefano and I walked out of the cadet dorm building on that second night, we knew we would win the sales competition . . . and we did.

From that moment on, my entrepreneurial juices were flowing.

What else could we sell and make money on? Not for the school's benefit but for our own! Stefano and I would frequently discuss other income-generating opportunities in our teenage years. We cut lawns, did chore jobs, painted (not very well, I might add), and much more.

As a teenage Anglophone living in Québec and growing up a few minutes from the United States border, I could escape the French channels that dominated the television and tune into CBS, ABC, NBC, and other local U.S. channels accessible on our TV antenna.

After doing my homework each evening, my sisters and I would watch *Three's Company*, *Magnum PI*, *Knight Rider*, *Family Ties*, and many other classic American shows.

In the media and at school, I would learn all about American Capitalism. There was no doubt in my mind that I wanted to be an entrepreneur, and there was no doubt that the U.S. was the land of opportunity for me.

> **Capitalism:** An economic system characterized by private ownership in which the free market alone controls the production of goods and services.
>
> Revr. Andy Smith, Investopedia Team

Sensing my ambitions, my father strongly encouraged and assisted me in contacting U.S. colleges as I entered my senior year of high school. Although the opportunity to go south of the border was exciting, it was also very intimidating. I had traveled to the U.S. once in my youth for sports; however, most of my experiences had been through U.S. media (television, movies, magazines, etc.). Undoubtedly, the American media in the '80s and '90s did a phenomenal job of selling the American Dream.

My family's support in allowing me to attend college in the U.S. was a dream come true. However, my intention to major in business was not entirely to my father's liking. My father insisted that majoring in business was too general and not focused enough. He felt strongly that I needed to develop expertise in accounting so I could learn the numbers behind running a business.

I pushed back fairly aggressively and challenged his insistence to major in accounting. I did not particularly love math and was concerned that accounting would be both too hard and too boring of a concentration.

"I want to be an entrepreneur and lead companies," I thought, "not be an accountant."

His wise mentorship would prove me wrong (thanks, Dad!). An accounting education would prove to be an essential part of my entrepreneurial development.

After my first year of college in the New England region of the U.S., I returned to Canada because my friend Stefano had heard about an excellent opportunity to make a lot of money with a unique summer job.

"Let's go plant trees in northern Ontario," he said. "We can make up to $3000 in two months."

This job was located six hours north of any civilization in northern Ontario, it was freezing cold in the middle of summer, and black flies forced us to wear full-body suits all day. Going to the bathroom was no joke. This was not my idea of a great summer job, but we did it anyway.

After a month and a half, Stefano and I had had enough. Along with our long beards, backpacks, tent, and sleeping bags, we embarked on the fun mission of trying to hitchhike the 20-hour-long ride back to our homes south of Montréal.

To the shock of both of our parents, we showed up on their doorsteps a few days later, looking like hillbillies. My parents could barely recognize me. I had lost 15 pounds, had a long beard, and looked like I had lived in the wilderness for two months (because I had).

Although we did make good money, planting trees was the worst summer job ever.

The following year, I was committed to staying in the U.S. for the summer. No more planting trees for this guy.

There was only one problem: being on an international *student* visa in the U.S., I could not get a job and get paid because I did not have a *work* visa.

I only had two options:

> **Option 1:** Get an internship at a public accounting firm and work for them as an unpaid intern for the summer. Yuk!

> **Option 2:** Start my own business! "There's no requirement for citizenship to operate a business in the U.S., so long as it's the right form of business. This means that a noncitizen can operate a limited liability company (LLC) or a C corporation . . ." —Rona L. DeLoe, Esq.

How could I start my own business? My wheels were turning.

As fate would have it, one day, as I walked through my dorm building, I saw an attractive poster on the wall!

"Own A Painting Franchise With College Pro Painters!"

Not caring that my only painting experience doing small projects for neighbors with Stefano was nothing short of a disaster, I took down the number, returned to my dorm room, and called.

Within the next two weeks, I sat down for a face-to-face interview and meeting with the regional general manager of College Pro Painters.

"How does this work?" was my first question.

"Well, it's pretty simple," the regional general manager replied. "We are looking for college entrepreneurs to run their own businesses in the summertime. We will provide you with all the training and tools necessary to be successful," he continued.

All I kept thinking was how amazing this opportunity seemed. I could own a painting business for the summer and hire college students to do all the actual painting without picking up a brush myself?

Faced with the alternative options of going back to Canada to plant trees or participating in an unpaid internship at a public accounting firm, I followed through on the rigorous interview process and was awarded a franchise territory with College Pro Painters.

I registered a Limited Liability Company (LLC) in the U.S. and became a business owner.

Have you ever met a former College Pro Painting franchisee? If not, let me share the story of how I received an MBA of hard knocks.

Self-Reflection Zone

- Where did your entrepreneurial roots start?
- What risks have you taken or are willing to take to pursue your goals?
- Think about a time when you had to choose between following a traditional path or venturing into the unknown. How did you navigate that decision, and what insights did you gain from the experience?

CHAPTER 2

MBA OF HARD KNOCKS

"The only thing that beats getting an MBA the old-fashioned way is getting an MBA the new-fashioned way: through experience in the real world."

— Peter Drucker, The Effective Executive

Although my youth was filled with random entrepreneurial experiences, the opportunity to run a painting franchise for College Pro Painters was my first real business venture.

Franchising is known for its proven and easy-to-follow systems and processes. This made it possible for me to start a business with minimal experience and capital.

As I arrived at the College Pro franchisee training session, I found myself alongside other hungry entrepreneurial college students like me. It felt great being among other young, driven, like-minded individuals.

To make my dreams come true and learn what it meant to be an entrepreneur, this was the type of experience and group I needed.

After the first training weekend, we were off and running; green as could be, still unsure about how to properly paint, I began marketing exterior home paint jobs.

I spent my afternoons after classes driving through neighborhoods—placing lawn signs on every street corner and knocking on doors to cold-call homeowners and ask if they were interested in refreshing the exterior of their homes with a paint job.

It was the same process as selling chocolate bars at the Royal Military College to win the school fundraising competition. The only problem was my success ratio on cold-calling homeowners on a $3K paint job was much lower than selling chocolate bars to cadets.

Homeowners would answer their doors to find me asking them if they wanted to get their homes painted by a bunch of college kids. I received a mixture of responses from "I would never trust you to paint my house" to "I would love to help college students earn some additional income." If only the latter had known that I still did not know how to paint a home yet . . .

Using the sales competency model I had learned at training, I miraculously secured signed contracts and collected initial deposits from the homeowners.

With these deposits, I began purchasing ladders, a ladder rack for my red Ford Escort, and other necessary tools and materials to start my journey as a painting contractor. If this is not a "Ready, fire, aim" model, I don't know what is.

As the summer approached, I continued to sell more and more jobs.

This was working!

It would have been great if I had never had to paint the homes, but that was unfortunately not an option.

I was off to the second training session to learn how to hire, train, and manage a painting crew to professionally paint a home. The training was incredibly comprehensive and provided me much more comfort with exterior home painting.

At first, hiring painters was very easy because all my college friends were looking for summer jobs. At the time, working with friends during the summer days and partying with them at night sounded like a great idea and a lot of fun. This quickly became an issue as I realized my friends didn't like to work that hard (sorry guys!). It was even harder to hold them accountable since we partied each night in our college apartment complex, reminiscent of an MTV's *Real World* party house.

And then all hell broke loose. . .

As we painted the homes, homeowners started to call the national customer service center to express their disappointment with a particular aspect of their paint job. Collecting payments would prove difficult because the jobs were incomplete and had punch list items to correct.

It is easy to understand why homeowners should never fully pay a contractor until the job is 100% complete and perfect.

Finding myself in a jam, I would work long days and weekends, going to homes myself to fix problems. I needed homeowners to pay me because I had to pay my painters, paint suppliers, franchise royalty fees, and other business expenses.

I was learning how tough running a business really is and that things don't always go as planned. I was caught in my little version of the Growth Paradox.

The Growth Paradox

As a business grows (in my case, the more I sold paint contracts to home-owners), you need more employees, equipment, supplies, sales, and cash; more growth can sometimes equal more problems.

As a first-time entrepreneur, I needed to roll up my sleeves, get dirty, and work out of this problem. If I didn't know how to paint homes before I began training with College Pro, I would become very proficient within a few short months.

I became the lead foreman on every job to ensure everything was completed correctly and on time so I could collect the final check from the homeowner. This final payment from the homeowner became the most important thing to keeping the business running.

All my efforts in the trenches, overseeing the production crews myself, were still insufficient. Cash flow was tight, suppliers needed to get paid, and the only way to get more cash would be to do more estimates and sell more paint jobs. It was a vicious cycle.

Finally, I had come to realize that I was in trouble.

With the next payroll approaching, I knew I had insufficient cash to cover the employees' payroll and the upcoming monthly franchise royalty obligations.

I could do more estimates, sell more paint jobs, and collect more deposits. Still, the cycle would continue over and over again. I would be robbing Peter to pay Paul!

I would eventually come to find out that I was in a "Crisis of Intervention" on the Transition Learning Curve and I needed help getting out of the "Valley of Despair".

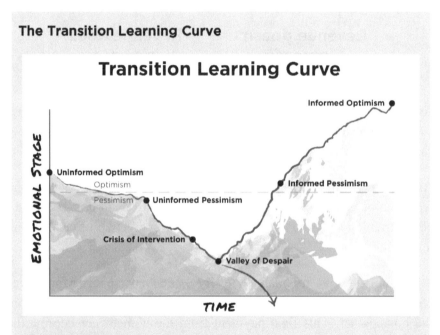

The Transition Learning Curve

Uninformed Optimism

In this state of mind, the entrepreneur is overly optimistic. They dream of the end result of their endeavors but have no fundamental understanding of the costs it will take; they are simply uninformed. Everything they see is exciting and positive, and they have yet to see or encounter any upcoming challenges.

Uninformed Pessimism

Uninformed optimism doesn't usually last that long. Entrepreneurs quickly will learn as they collect information that everything is not as rosy and straightforward as they once thought, and pessimism starts to set in. In this stage, entrepreneurs realize that their endeavors will not be easy. They begin asking themselves more pessimistically, "Is this really worth it?" They are still very uninformed.

Crisis of Intervention

As entrepreneurs ask themselves pessimistic questions, they, unfortunately, receive pessimistic answers. They will give up if they do not persevere through this emotional state. In this state, it is always best to seek help from mentors or trusted advisors to intervene and rewire your mindset.

Valley of Despair

This is the most dangerous area of the learning curve. To persevere through the Valley of Despair (and not fall off the cliff), one must deeply understand why they are here in the first place and have a strong passion for wanting to persevere and achieve their goals.

Informed Pessimism

The possibility of survival increases as the entrepreneur shifts their mindset to focus on why they are here and how badly they want to achieve their goals. They put actions in place to handle the areas they now understand (but still do not love), because the benefits of overcoming these pessimistic areas are worth it! The key is to persevere through these pessimistic areas until one has overcome them.

Informed Optimism

Achieving this final stage can only happen when the entrepreneur has processed the other four stages; they now know all the good, bad, and ugly of their undertaking. They can now achieve the success they originally dreamed of. The tasks that they were once pessimistic about are now comfortable. Everything was worth it!

Hoping I could convince my father to bail me out, I got in my red Ford Escort and drove six hours back home to visit my parents in Montréal.

I was scared shitless. If I couldn't figure this out, what would I do?

"Maybe being an entrepreneur is not for me."

"Should I just quit?"

All these thoughts and emotions were going through my head.

My parents were surprised and happy to see me when I showed up in the middle of summer. Not wanting to spoil their excitement, I waited until the following morning to schedule a meeting with my father. Yes, a meeting.

Throughout my youth, whenever my father wanted to have a serious talk, he would schedule an appointment with me. We had meetings to talk about getting summer jobs, we had meetings to talk about any of my discipline issues, and we had meetings to talk about the birds and the bees. My father would schedule meetings for all our serious conversations. He always came prepared with copious, illegible notes written all over his notepad.

In asking him for a meeting, I knew I would have to come prepared with my notes, a specific request for help, and a plan to get the business back on track.

The following morning, my father listened intently as I explained my business's cash crunch situation. I am sure he could tell from my nervous voice that I had gotten myself into a jam.

"What is your plan to get out of this situation?" he asked.

Over the next several minutes, I explained my half-baked plan to get the business back on track between that moment and the end of the summer.

I am not sure if I even believed I could make it through, but I did my best sales job to convince him I would.

And then I went in for the big ask.

"Dad, could you loan me $5000? I promise to pay you back by the end of the summer," I muttered nervously.

His quick response to offer me the help I needed surprised me.

"Sure, I will help you," he said instantly. "However, you need to execute your plan, and I want you to stick by your commitment to pay me back at the end of the summer."

In hindsight, I think I got a quick approval because my need for assistance probably paled compared to some thoughts that had probably been going through his head since I had requested an unexpected meeting with him in the middle of the summer.

The following day, before I departed to return to the U.S., my father presented me with a two-page legal loan document. I somewhat expected him to simply cut me a check for the loan and send me on my way, but not my father.

As I now have kids of my own, I've learned why having me sign an official loan document mattered greatly to my father. He wanted a formal arrangement for the loan, with interest and payback terms, so I would truly understand what it meant to get a loan. I signed the document and secured the loan I needed to get back on my feet, then raced back to deposit the money in the bank and ensure the payroll would clear.

I needed to prove to my father that my word (and loan document) were solid. I did not want to let him down.

For the remainder of that first summer as a College Pro Franchisee, I became the onsite leader with my depleted crew of painters, ensuring that all our jobs were completed properly, on budget, and on time.

Oh, and yes, I did pay my father back the loan plus interest at the end of the summer, and I vowed never to ask him for a loan again.

Surviving one's first summer as a College Pro Franchisee became a badge of honor. Those who were able to persevere through the Transition Learning Curve were then offered an option to sign up again for the following summer as a "returning" franchisee. This also allowed successful returning franchisees the opportunity to upgrade to larger territories with better demographics, providing the franchisee the potential to build a bigger business with the experience they gained during their rookie year.

And so, with the lessons of the first year, I committed to returning for a second year in a new territory that had done 3X the revenue I had done my first summer.

In lieu of waiting until the late spring to start marketing, estimating, and selling paint jobs, I began working on my new painting franchise region immediately to build up a book of business for the following summer.

The second year as a franchisee was dramatically easier. I had encountered so many of the issues in my first year and I was able to set up the business for success. I prebooked most of the contracts before the summer even started. I properly hired my staff, spent more time training my crew leaders, rewarded the team for completing jobs on time and on budget, and started to get a taste of what owning a business could be like.

That second summer, my painting business generated over $120K in revenue. The profits more than made up for the pain, sacrifice, and hard work of the first summer's learning curve. It also gave me a taste of what entrepreneurial success felt like. The income from the business provided me the opportunity to enjoy my last collegiate summer, as I purchased a boat with my college roommate and enjoyed the summer on the lake, all the while running a business.

The College Pro franchise experience was challenging. Many fellow franchisees would not survive the summer because they entered the Valley of Despair region of the Transition Learning Curve and could not get out. Much like the reality of entrepreneurship as a whole, traversing the Messy Middle is no cakewalk.

To succeed in any venture, you need to have the ability to persevere through the Transition Learning Curve. As entrepreneurs, we go through the Transition Learning Curve of ups and downs every day, every week, every month, and every year. The ability to self-regulate and persevere through the low, dark times of entrepreneurship is a skill set that is very difficult but necessary to master.

> "'Self-regulation is the ability to control one's behavior, emotions, and thoughts in the pursuit of long-term goals' (Gillebaart). More specifically, emotional self-regulation refers to the ability to manage disruptive emotions and impulses—in other words, to think before acting. Self-regulation also involves the ability to rebound from disappointment and to act in a way consistent with your values. It is one of the five key components of emotional intelligence."
> —**Arlin Cunic**
>
> Marleen Gillebaart, "The 'Operational' Definition of Self-Control"

The ability to regulate one's mood and have a positive growth mindset, even when the "sky is falling," is tough but also an incredible asset to entrepreneurs.

Reflecting on my lifecycle as an entrepreneur, my experience at College Pro thoroughly shaped my ability to self-regulate my emotions and mindset as an entrepreneur.

"If I can do this, I can do anything."

As a franchisee with College Pro, I gained incredible lessons about what it means to be an entrepreneur. I learned

- how to hire, train, manage, fire, and lose employees;
- how to market, cold-call, estimate, and sell;
- how to manage and resolve conflict;
- how to do accounting, balance my checkbook, manage suppliers, process payroll; and
- how entrepreneurs need to be incredibly persistent and resilient to be successful.

I got a real-world MBA with College Pro.

The lessons I learned through this experience have had a lasting impact on my entrepreneurial drive.

Self-Reflection Zone

- What were the 5 biggest learnings you developed in your first entrepreneurial venture?
- Have you ever been caught in the Growth Paradox? How did you get through it?
- Do you have mentors you can lean on for help and support?
- Do you remember the last time you were in a Crisis of Intervention or the Valley of Despair on the Transition Learning Curve? How did you get through it?
- How do you self-regulate your emotions (mood) through the ups and downs of entrepreneurship?

THE MENTORSHIP

"Mentorship is the bridge between potential and achievement."
—Ted Ma, author of *High Performance Leadership*

During my two summers of running a franchise for College Pro Painters, I experienced many obstacles, failures, and successes that helped form a solid entrepreneurial foundation. They prepared me for what was ahead in ways I could have never imagined.

With my college accounting degree in sight, I began to evaluate what I would do postgraduation. How could I use the entrepreneurial skill sets I had developed to launch my career?

As I began seeking opportunities, I was reminded that my options as an international student were limited. My only employment options were with private accounting firms willing to sponsor a work visa. These opportunities were scarce and of little interest to me.

I had a strong desire to continue my entrepreneurial development, but with my parents done supporting my education, I needed to earn a paycheck to live, and I lacked the financial capability to start my own business.

As if it were meant to be, the perfect opportunity came calling.

"John, we are very interested in interviewing you for a general manager position at College Pro; however, we do not have any openings in the New England market. We have an opening in Chicago. Would this interest you?" stated Ken, the president of College Pro U.S.

"Chicago?" I thought to myself.

All I could imagine was this massive U.S. city, and I was instantly intimidated. Chicago was a long way from my family in Montréal, I did not know anybody in the Midwest, and I had developed a strong base of friends in New England.

"I am not sure this is for me. I was hoping to stay in the New England market," I responded.

Ken responded in a manner that was hard for me to reject. "Look, I strongly suggest that you at least go interview. We will fly you out. You can interview with the Midwest vice president, get a feel for Chicago, and you can decide if it is a good fit. . . But you should at least go check it out."

The general manager's role consisted of recruiting, interviewing, hiring, training, and managing college student franchisees and mentoring them on how to run a painting business as their summer job. There were no better candidates for the general manager position than former successful franchisees who had gone through the process themselves. Because this was such a specialized role, and the only pool of candidates was former franchisees, College Pro U.S. was willing and able to sponsor my work visa.

As I pondered the opportunity, I was reminded why I had decided to come to the U.S. in the first place. This was the land of entrepreneurial capitalist opportunity. Why not go to the major metropolitan city of Chicago, expand my horizons, and evaluate the opportunity firsthand?

I will never forget that beautiful, sunny, 80-degree July day when I flew into O'Hare International Airport. It was one of my career's most pivotal and memorable moments.

As I arrived at baggage claim, a gentleman was waiting for me, holding a sign with my name on it.

I was glued to the window of the black town car as we drove down Lake Shore Drive along the incredible Lake Michigan toward my hotel on Chicago's famous Magnificent Mile. People were rollerblading, running, and playing beach volleyball on North Beach to my left, and incredible architecture and skyscrapers were approaching on my right. My perception of Chicago was quickly changing.

The driver dropped me off at the hotel to check-in, drop off my luggage, and quickly change my clothes because the Midwest vice president of College Pro, Jeff, was hosting an outdoor BBQ at his home with other members of the College Pro Midwest team.

The BBQ allowed me to meet the team in a very casual setting and as we all shared our best College Pro franchisee stories, it was clear we were all cut from the same entrepreneurial cloth. Any successful College Pro franchisee had a certain entrepreneurial je ne sais quoi about them.

This was not just a staff BBQ. We also had tickets to the Chicago Cubs game at Wrigley Field, a few blocks from Jeff's home.

Walking toward Wrigley Field, I was amazed at where I was and what was happening. Not only was it an incredible summer day but I was also going to one of America's most historic sports venues that I had only seen on TV when the Cubs faced my hometown team, the Montréal Expos.

As we settled into the Wrigley Field bleachers and sipped on the venue's popular mai tais, my jaw must have been visibly down to the floor.

We still had not sat down one-on-one for a formal interview, but I was sold. I had never been in such a dynamic and beautiful environment in my whole life.

Chicago was an amazing city, and this was a big opportunity for me. The job perfectly fit my skill set and was an amazing opportunity to expand my horizons and live in a big metropolitan city.

Two months later, I relocated to downtown Chicago two blocks from Wrigley Field. The decision to come work as a general manager for College Pro was based on my comfort with the company, my knowledge and confidence that I could excel at the role, the willingness of the company to sponsor my work visa, and the amazing experience I had in Chicago on that sunny July day. It was a perfect fit!

I quickly transitioned from being a student and learning how to run a business to becoming a teacher and leading other young entrepreneurs. I loved it!

I traveled with my two colleagues, Rich and Pete, to the Midwest colleges—the University of Illinois, the University of Iowa, the University of Wisconsin, and others—searching for the best entrepreneurial college students we could find.

Once candidates were identified, we put them through a grueling interview process to test them for all the values and abilities we were seeking. If they qualified, we would sell them on the benefits of becoming an entrepreneur while in college.

I knew firsthand that being a College Pro franchisee was very difficult and certainly not for everybody. Heck, I barely survived it myself, and I know how hard I had to work to persevere. In my role as general manager, if I did not perform a thorough interview and did not select students that could persevere through the Growth Paradox and Transition Learning Curve, I would not be able to achieve the objectives of my role.

Candidates had to have the fundamental ability to persevere through the learnings and pressures of running a business.

I needed to develop my leadership skills and lead these young college entrepreneurs to success. They were just as green as I had been when I started as a franchisee, and they needed to learn all the skills necessary to survive and succeed in running their own business.

Jeff, my boss, was only a few years older than me. He owned a nice townhome a few blocks from Wrigley Field, drove an expensive BMW, invested in stocks in his spare time, and, quite simply, had his shit together. He was an incredible role model for me and became a great mentor and friend.

At the time, I did not realize how critical it was to have such an impactful mentor and such amazing colleagues in my first job out of college. The support I received and the relationships we formed were amazing.

I had a mentor I admired and could watch and learn from daily. I became a sponge to everything he did and said. I wanted to impress him, just like I wanted to impress my father. Wherever Jeff went, I was right there with him. I even convinced him to let me join him in Las Vegas annually for his March Madness week with his college roommates. That is where one of my alter egos, "Johnny Vegas," was born, but that is a story for another book.

Rich, Pete, and I became lifelong friends. In addition to being the ultimate competitors trying to outpace each other in recruiting and leading our franchisees, we challenged each other to improve and grow every day.

It became clear that if I could continue to surround myself with people like Jeff, Rich, and Pete, I would learn a ton about becoming a strong entrepreneurial leader.

For two years, I led 40+ entrepreneurs in running their businesses. Some failed and could not persevere through the Transition Learning Curve, while most succeeded and were rewarded with the same feeling I had as a franchisee: "If I can do this, I can do anything."

I had developed incredible entrepreneurial skill sets through coaching young entrepreneurs to successfully navigate running their own small businesses, and I now had a burning desire to take my skills to the next level!

By this time (the late '90s), Internet businesses were booming. Many sought opportunities to leave steady corporate jobs to join the Internet revolution. The allure of stock options with the next dot-com company that was growing at record paces was enticing to all.

I had heard rumblings through the College Pro network about a highly successful former franchisee and general manager, Eric, who had recently founded an Internet company in Oregon called HandymanOnline.com.

Intrigued by what Eric was doing, many College Pro general managers, including me, started to reach out to Eric to learn more about what he was building.

After several discussions and interviews with Eric and his management team, I painfully met with my boss, mentor, and close friend, Jeff, to resign from College Pro. I joined Eric's exciting Internet startup as the branch manager for a new HandymanOnline.com sales office to be opened in Chicago. There was certainly a risk involved in leaving my position with College Pro. Still, the potential reward-to-risk ratio was very high. I had very little to lose and did not want to miss the opportunity to be part of a dot-com success story.

Self-Reflection Zone

- Who was your first mentor? What is one trait you learned from them that you display in your leadership style today?

- What mentor do you need today to help you achieve your entrepreneurial dreams and goals?

- Who do you mentor today? Who else could you mentor?

- Remember your first job out of college? What were your 3 best memories or learnings?

CHAPTER 4

DOT-COM BOOM & BUST

"You miss 100% of the shots you don't take. Don't be afraid to fail—the only way to truly learn is through experience, so take those risks and don't be discouraged by any failures along the way."
— Attributed to John Wooden, UCLA Basketball Coach 1948–1977

It was GO time! With College Pro, I gained an incredible repertoire of entrepreneurial skills, but there was a cap on my earning potential as an employee of the corporation. As an early employee of HandymanOnline.com, the potential felt unlimited. In addition to an increase over my prior compensation, there were strong bonuses and stock options to motivate us to drive the company as hard as possible.

My commitment, work ethic, and dedication to growing our HandymanOnline.com office in Chicago to become the country's best sales office was intense. I wanted to prove to Eric and other executives that I could do more for this fast-growing Internet business. In addition to building and growing the office in Chicago, I worked to develop companywide processes and manuals for other offices across the country. I was young and hungry. I put everything I had into this startup.

By the end of the first year, not only was our sales office in Chicago growing exponentially but the company had secured a large venture capital investment from a well-known firm in Silicon Valley. Within months, I was promoted to vice president of Sales for the entire company. This was a dream come true for me! As vice president of Sales, my role entailed opening additional company offices in all the major metropolitan cities in the U.S. and implementing our sales methodologies to grow our revenue streams as quickly as possible.

As you can probably tell from my journey thus far, this role inspired me. Flying to every major metropolitan city in the U.S., locating office space, hiring branch managers, training the teams, and setting the office up for success was a massive responsibility for a 24-year-old.

It was not long before we grew HandymanOnline.com from 5 to 25 sales offices nationwide as the business snowballed. Atlanta, Tampa, Philadelphia, Boston, Dallas, San Diego . . . you name it, we had an office there.

Armed with stock options and a robust compensation package for executives of my age, I was all in! I felt like all of my entrepreneurial dreams were coming true.

In reality, I wasn't an entrepreneur; I was an intrapreneur. But that is a topic for a later chapter.

As the company grew by leaps and bounds, I was asked to move to the corporate headquarters in Beaverton, Oregon. This would provide an opportunity for the executive management to be together on a more frequent basis and navigate the rapid growth.

Open to the challenge, I packed my belongings and moved to the West Coast.

What happened next has been well-known and well-documented. Everyone who left a safe and comfortable corporate job will never forget the dot-com crash of 2000.

Dot-Com Crash

The dot-com bubble (or dot-com boom) was a stock market bubble in the late 1990s. The period coincided with massive growth in Internet adoption, a proliferation of available venture capital, and the rapid growth of valuations in new dot-com startups.

Between 1995 and its peak in March 2000, the Nasdaq Composite stock market index rose 400%, only to fall 78% from its peak by October 2002, giving up all its gains during the bubble.

"Dot-com bubble," *Wikipedia*

Following the dot-com crash, the company's founder, Eric, requested a meeting with me in his office.

Within seconds of my sitting down, Eric said, "John, I'm very sorry, but we are going to let you go."

I was baffled and frozen, unsure what to say.

I had gone from feeling like I had this thing called "business" all figured out and dreaming that my stock options would make me a wealthy young man to losing everything I had poured my heart and soul into for over three years. I had committed everything to this company. I was all in. I had just recently moved to Oregon. I was devastated.

"I do not understand," I said to Eric. "Why?"

Eric proceeded to provide me feedback regarding my leadership style and how it rubbed others in the organization the wrong way. My positions were frequently black and white and I did not leave room for gray areas or the opinions of others to be considered. I will never forget his analogy of a rock dropping into the water. The bigger the rock and the harder it is thrown, the larger the wake left behind. This feedback forever changed my leadership style and was instrumental in changing how I wanted to be perceived by my peers.

I exited Eric's office, gathered my belongings, and left the building. I was numb.

Within 24 hours, I packed my Jeep Cherokee with all my life's possessions and began my journey back to Chicago.

The drive back to Chicago was one of my life's most impactful road trips. I wasn't sure what I was going to do next. I wasn't sure where I would live. But the three-day, soul-searching drive was what I needed to figure out where I would go and what I would do next.

Ironically, I had recently purchased Anthony Robbins's *Personal Power!* cassette tapes. There was no better time than during that drive to pop them into my Jeep's tape deck and listen.

Personal Power!: A 30-Day Program for Unlimited Success by Anthony Robbins

Anthony Robbins's *Personal Power!* tapes are a self-help program designed to help individuals achieve success, fulfillment, and personal transformation. The program consists of a series of audiocassette tapes that guide individuals  through various exercises and techniques to develop their personal power and achieve their goals. The program has been widely praised for its transformative impact and has helped countless individuals worldwide achieve greater success and inner fulfillment.

Key Learnings:

1. Take personal responsibility for your life and your results.
2. Establish clear goals and take consistent action toward them.

3. Learn to manage your emotional state to stay focused on what you want.
4. Find ways to challenge yourself and grow as a person.
5. Develop meaningful relationships with other people.

"The only way to get what you really want is to become the person who can truly have it."
—Anthony Robbins, *Personal Power!*

Halfway through the drive back to Chicago, I received a call from Steve, the West Coast director of HandymanOnline.com in San Diego, CA.

"John, you will not believe this, but somebody from corporate showed up at our office this morning and closed our office permanently. Everybody was laid off," Steve said instantly upon my answering the phone.

It must have been known that I had put so much passion and energy into these offices that I would have resisted and put up a big stink if I had known of the plan. Furthermore, my role would have been eliminated regardless.

The dot-com bust had come to haunt HandymanOnline.com. The venture capital firm funding the growth of the business was going to reduce or pull its investment if the company did not contract and lower its overhead expenses quickly!

To add insult to injury, not only was I let go, but the 25 offices we had set up nationally were being closed. I had hired branch managers and regional directors like Steve and convinced them to leave their steady and cushy corporate jobs to join a fast-growing dot-com with the promise of a great opportunity.

Specifically Steve, a former College Pro franchisee and general manager, had moved his whole family just six weeks prior, from Philadelphia to San Diego, for this opportunity.

What a mess! Three years of work down the drain.

Eventually, HandymanOnline.com officially closed down as a business. The company's assets would be sold to Service Magic, which was later rebranded to HomeAdvisor.com, which was then merged with AngiesList.com and rebranded as Angi.com.

I listened to the entire *Personal Power!* cassette tape series as I drove through the mountains of Idaho, Utah, and Wyoming. I was determined more than ever to intentionally go after my goal of being an entrepreneur. There was one big problem: I needed income for my basic living needs and I still did not have the capital to risk on a startup.

If now was a bad time to start my own venture, I wanted to find a small company where I could have a massive impact and make some money to pursue my dream of starting my own company someday soon.

Within a few hours of arriving in Chicago, I received another call from Steve about a possible opportunity. Charlie, the former CEO and cofounder of CertaPro Painters, was seeking to hire an executive for a startup e-commerce web platform he had invested in: WorldAtMyDoor.com. Like all Internet companies following the dot-com crash, WorldAtMyDoor.com needed help to scale and find a viable business model for long-term success.

The opportunity to become the president of WorldAtMyDoor.com was very intriguing, but even more exciting to me was the opportunity to partner with a highly respected business person like Charlie.

I spoke with Charlie and he invited me to visit him in Philadelphia to learn more about WorldAtMyDoor.com and interview for the role of president. I had great respect for Charlie and what he had built with

CertaPro Painters (at that time, a College Pro Painters sister company). Like my first boss and mentor, Jeff, Charlie was a perfect business mentor for me at the right time on my journey.

For two years, I worked with the WorldAtMyDoor.com team to pivot the business model as we found a niche for our technology platform within the professional photography industry. In the early 2000s professional photographers were converting from traditional camera rolls to digital cameras. Along with that transition came increasing customer demand for digital access to the photos being taken. The company, rebranded as PhotosAtMyDoor.com, was a pioneer in providing hundreds of professional photographers across the country with the technology to upload photos from weddings, sporting events, or other engagements to their own websites for their clients to view and purchase.

In 2003, we successfully sold the WorldAtMyDoor.com business and technology platform to a company in Michigan. Although small, it was my first ever sale of a business.

Upon exiting, I knew what I needed to do next: own my own business. I wanted to control my destiny and fully invest in being an entrepreneur.

My desire and need were further reinforced when I first read Robert T. Kiyosaki's *Rich Dad Poor Dad*. This book amplified everything I had always believed about entrepreneurship. I just did not know how to achieve the success I sought.

Rich Dad Poor Dad: What the Rich Teach Their Kids about Money - That the Poor and Middle Class Do Not!
by Robert T. Kiyosaki and Sharon Lechter

Rich Dad, Poor Dad is a must-read for entrepreneurs and all who seek financial freedom. In his book, Robert Kiyosaki talks about the owner versus employee mindset and how the American system is built to reward capitalism and entrepreneurship. The book is based on Kiyosaki's personal experience of growing up with two different dads: his biological father (the "poor dad") and the father of his best friend (the "rich dad"). Kiyosaki contrasts the financial advice he received from both dads and draws lessons about wealth creation and financial success.

Key Learnings:

1. The rich make money work for them, instead of working for money.
2. Focus on acquiring assets that generate income, not liabilities that drain your resources.
3. Financial education is crucial for making good financial decisions and achieving financial freedom.
4. Cultivate a mindset of abundance, take calculated risks, and work to create value for others.
5. Focus on learning new skills and gaining experience to achieve success in the long term.

"The mistake in becoming what you study is that too many people forget to mind their own business. They spend their lives minding someone else's business and making that person rich."
—**Robert T. Kiyosaki,** *Rich Dad Poor Dad*

Kiyosaki talks clearly about the four types of assets that you must build to achieve financial wealth:

1. Businesses
2. Real estate
3. Papers (bonds, notes, stocks)
4. Commodities (gold, silver, bitcoin, etc.)

Based on my background, it was clear that I needed to focus on building business assets. I did not have the knowledge, at this stage of my career, of how to accumulate real estate, stocks, or commodities.

Becoming a successful entrepreneur was more difficult than I had once thought. I wanted to achieve my dreams of being a successful entrepreneur, but I had built up some credit card debt and did not have the means to invest in a startup. I was starting from scratch.

Luckily, my wife provided much-needed financial stability to my weak financial situation. There is no doubt that it is very difficult to be an entrepreneur without the support of your significant other, family, and friends. Her entrance into my life and the stability she provided by having a well-paying career as an engineer allowed me to pursue my entrepreneurial dreams (love you, Honey!).

It was time to make a run at starting my own business and becoming the entrepreneur I had always dreamed of being. Not knowing where to start, I quickly found a couple of startup opportunities to invest my time and energy into.

Since college, I had been developing a strong network and expertise in contracting and project management through College Pro and HandymanOnline.com. During my search for an entrepreneurial opportunity, I had lunch with an executive from a partner company of PhotosAtMyDoor.com and discovered an interesting opportunity to form a commercial project management company that would assist with deploying and installing digital photo kiosks in retail locations across the country. Within a few months, and upon securing our first contract, we cofounded our project management company along with two other partners.

At the same time, a couple of close friends and I cofounded a small, hobby, youth sports business by coordinating sports tours, tournaments, and camps. This business was fun, rewarding, and in an industry I was very passionate about—sports.

I had very little capital to invest in one startup, let alone two simultaneously, so these opportunities needed to generate revenue and cash flow quickly.

As I began investing all my time into these two startup businesses, I remained dedicated to building something significant. Although still unsure what exactly I was trying to achieve, I was hungry for entrepreneurial success!

Self-Reflection Zone

- Have you ever spent a lot of time building something, only to end up with nothing? What did you learn from this experience?

- What books (or pieces of content) impacted your entrepreneurial development the most?

- Which of the 4 assets mentioned by Robert Kiyosaki have you built in your personal wealth portfolio?

CHAPTER 5

STARTUP MODE

"The way to get started is to quit talking and begin doing."

— Walt Disney

Startup mode can be very challenging; unfortunately, entrepreneurs tend to always pay themselves last because they lack cash flow in the early stages of their business. You need to generate enough cash flow to support the business and its employees, and if there is anything left, you get to pay yourself some as well.

Forced to be lean and mean, I worked hard to implement strategies I had learned from the book *The Millionaire Next Door* by Thomas J. Stanley and William D. Danko. While I called myself extremely frugal, my team called me a "cheap ass." Every expense, from office space and furniture to computers, was meticulously managed for cost.

The Millionaire Next Door: The Surprising Secrets of America's Wealthy by Thomas J. Stanley and William D. Danko

The Millionaire Next Door examines the lives of wealthy people and provides insight into how the wealthy live and become wealthy. It emphasizes the importance of living below one's means, creating wealth through frugality and thrift, and investing in one's future. The book also offers advice on becoming financially independent, managing one's finances, and planning for retirement.

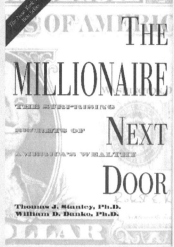

Key learnings:

1. Wealth is better reflected by a high net worth rather than a high income.

2. Many millionaires are self-made and have built wealth through hard work, discipline, and frugality.

3. Financial intuition and making sound investment decisions are more important than having a high IQ.

4. The wealthy tend to avoid debt and live within their means, prioritizing savings and investments.

5. Upbringing doesn't determine financial success; the millionaire mindset can be achieved through education, discipline, and long-term planning.

"Wealth is what you accumulate, not what you spend."
—Thomas J. Stanley, *The Millionaire Next Door*

Slowly but surely, both businesses grew and generated positive net operating cash flow. It wasn't long before I found myself with two Lifestyle-sized companies, and I could finally start getting paid for my efforts. Things were going great!

And then, BANG! I remember it vividly. As I prepared for work on October 6, 2008, NBC's *The Today Show* was playing on the TV in the background. Well-known TV personality and financial guru, Jim Cramer, was conversing with Ann Curry, and the tone and seriousness of the discussion caught my attention. I paused and listened intently:

"I thought about this all weekend," Cramer told Curry. "I do not want to say these things on TV. Whatever money you may need for the next five years, please take it out of the stock market right now, this week. I do not believe that you should risk those assets in the stock market right now."

As I got in my car to drive to the office, I contacted our financial advisor: "Should we pull our money out of the market?" I asked. Unfortunately, it was too late. That day, the DOW dropped 800 points, falling below 10,000 for the first time since 2004, and the markets panicked. By the end of 2008, the economy was officially in a full recession.

I could not believe this was happening again: first, the dot-com bust, and now, a massive recession. What would this mean to my two 5-year-old startups?

There was no way I would let this ruin what we had built. Unlike the dot-com bust, I now had more control over these businesses, and we needed to persevere. Thankfully, both businesses were being run frugally. Maybe being cheap was not a bad trait after all. My only other experience navigating a financial crisis was when I had to get a loan from my father to keep my painting business afloat in college. I had never managed through a recession as an entrepreneur.

How does a small-business leader react when facing an economic recession? If you do not move fast enough to cut overhead, you will burn through your cash and not have enough to weather the storm; if you stop investing in sales and marketing because you are scared, then you will lose market share and you will not be able to sustain your revenues. So much was going on in my head.

Charlie, an always-present mentor, taught me his learnings from prior recessions, learnings that I will never forget. These lessons would pay big dividends in my future. Unfortunately, recessions and other unforeseen economic events come around more often than we would like, but if you know what levers to pull, you can come out of them stronger than ever.

Lesson 1: Cash is King (and Queen)

Cash is always king (and queen), and when you have a limited bankroll, you need to conserve as much as possible. Ensuring that not one penny is wasted throughout the organization should be priority #1 (*save* cash). Then ensure that you are maximizing your margins on everything you do. Then ensure that you are invoicing and collecting quickly (do not let customers drag out paying you since they may be experiencing cash flow issues themselves). And lastly, renegotiate payment terms with your vendors to ensure you are not paying them before you get paid.

Lesson 2: Invest in Sales and Marketing

Charlie had just told me to save cash, but now he was saying I should invest in sales and marketing? What I quickly came to understand in the conversation was that 95% of companies are going to retreat during a recession. They will stop investing in sales and marketing and lay off their sales representatives. The 5% that have the foresight to know that a recession is a cycle and that the economy will come out of it will invest to gain market share, while others retreat. Be bold and let people know that you are not retreating.

Lesson 3: Upgrade Talent

Every entrepreneur can quickly differentiate who on their team is an A, B, C, or D player. In a recession, one of the unfortunate by-products is layoffs. Now is the perfect time to upgrade your team! Replace your C and D players with A players. You must challenge your B players to step up or face the same consequences. Undoubtedly, employees, especially those with families, will usually elevate their efforts during an economic recession because they fear losing their employment due to performance issues they control. Always take the opportunity to challenge and upgrade your team.

My respect and trust for Charlie and his experience were a huge asset, and I am forever grateful. These three recession tips I learned came into play again in 2012 and 2020, and surely will be helpful again in the future, but more on that in the coming chapters.

Over the next two years, as we navigated our way through the recession, both businesses experienced periods of being on life support. Every dollar coming in would first ensure weekly payroll and necessary expenses were paid. If there was any leftover, it would go to pay the other expenses building up. There was little room for error as we continued to confront difficult challenges that tested our resolve and ability to persevere.

The project management company's largest client did not survive the recession and went bankrupt, making it necessary for us to write off $225K in accounts receivables as bad debt. The company could not afford this massive hit. For weeks, I remained determined—and sleepless—as we ground away trying to keep the business alive. In addition to halting compensation to myself, we needed to resort to factoring the receivables from other clients, delaying all payments to vendors, and doing our best to generate more revenue to grow ourselves out of the problem.

The sports management company, although fairly unaffected by the recession itself, suffered a major blow when nature intervened. In 2010, the eruption of Eyjafjallajökull volcano in Iceland halted transatlantic air travel on the exact date the company had hundreds of youth athletes and their parents either already in Europe, already in flight to Europe from North America, or in airports throughout North America waiting to board their planes to Europe. Families had saved up thousands of dollars for these once-in-a-lifetime international tour experiences and our team had to jump into action. For days, all hands were on deck. This event could have crippled our company, but we were unwilling to throw in the towel. Ultimately, the international events were postponed. We shuttled all the stranded travelers back to North America once air travel was permitted and worked collaboratively with all families to reschedule the event for later that summer. We issued full refunds to those unable to attend the rescheduled event and turned a horrible situation into a badge of honor. We persevered through the crisis with determination and resolve.

The pride I had for both companies persevering through these tough years was enormous. Many companies would not have had the strength and ability to navigate these challenging moments.

Eventually (it felt like forever), both companies found their footing again. The project and sports management companies were producing $5M and $10M in annual revenues, respectively; however, both companies were still stuck in the Messy Middle. They were both operating to mild profitability, but the scars from the previous few years were real. Every time we set a goal to grow the businesses, something smacked us upside down. Growth beyond this point would not happen unless there was a dedicated focus on it, and there was no way I could continue to spread my focus to both businesses.

It was time to pick my horse and ride it. Although I had more years of experience in contracting, I had a stronger passion for the sports business. Hence, my decision was straightforward. I wanted to exit my role as CEO and president of the project management company and focus 100% of my time on the sports business.

I began a search for the right suitor to which I could sell the project management company. Through that effort, I was introduced to Ron, the owner of a large third-party logistics company based in the Boston region. Ron's logistics company had grown to $100M+ in revenues, and he was looking for strategic niche acquisitions. After several meetings and discussions, I believed this would be the perfect strategic purchaser that could take our project management business to the next level. We began negotiations to sell the project management company to Ron so I could exit that business and focus on building the sports company I had a strong passion for.

After one of our meetings and over a glass of red wine, Ron asked me to tell him more about the sports company. I gave him an overview of the hobby business we had grown from a grassroots effort to $10M in revenues. I was extremely passionate about what we had built, and he surely could sense it from my enthusiasm. Then he proposed something I was not expecting.

"John, what if I invest in both the project management and the sports companies, and we build your two companies and my logistics company as a part of a bigger holding company, with capital to invest in growing them all?"

As we discussed the opportunity further, Ron's desire for my role was to not focus exclusively on the sports company, as I had originally desired. The logistics company had a void in the executive leadership team he was looking to fill, and he wanted me to help oversee that business as its vice president of Operations.

"I do not know anything about warehousing or logistics," was the first thing out of my mouth when he first proposed his plan.

"That is ok. I am looking for an entrepreneurial leader like yourself. We have enough people that understand logistics, and you will learn. We specifically need a servant leader who can guide the business's operations.

We can insert new leadership in your project management and sports companies and oversee them together," Ron responded.

> A servant leader is a leader who puts the needs of their team and organization before their own, leading by example and empowering their team to reach their fullest potential. They focus on building relationships, listening and responding to their team's needs, and creating an environment of trust and collaboration.

This was a pretty big curveball.

Initially, I had planned to sell the project management company and focus exclusively on the sports company. I was now considering an executive-level job in a new industry while, alongside Ron, overseeing both of my companies within the larger private holding company.

Although I had never worked in logistics, nor for a company of that size, the opportunity fascinated me. My experience was with much smaller companies. In the role of vice president of Operations, I would have oversight of over 1500 employees throughout the organization.

"You can learn a lot from this new partner, specifically how a company grows to $100M. This experience will be great for you, stretching your belief in yourself. You will come to find out that you also have the skills and ability to build your own $100M business someday," I remember hearing from Charlie as I evaluated the opportunity.

After aligning the partners in both the project management and sports companies on the opportunity, we sold a majority stake of equity in both companies to Ron and the logistics company. Upon consummating the sale of the equity, all the partners in both the project management and the sports companies were diluted to a minority percentage of ownership.

"This is a great opportunity," I told my partners. "Even though we have a smaller percentage, we will be able to grow our overall equity value to be much higher with this new partnership and access to growth capital."

Having a new partner with capital to invest in our growth was very exciting. We were ready to join the large logistics company and grow all the businesses to the next level.

Self-Reflection Zone

- Remember your first startup? What skill sets did you develop?

- What are 5 things your business can be doing to be more frugal, like the "Millionaire Next Door"?

- How many recessions have you navigated as an entrepreneur? What advice would you give a young entrepreneur going through their first recession?

- Have you ever sold equity in your company to bring more capital to your business? What did you learn from that experience?

- Have you ever been in a role where you had to lead others in an industry you had very little knowledge of? What did you learn about leadership in this capacity?

CHAPTER 6

EXPLOSIVE GROWTH

"The belief is that as you scale the company—and increase your dream team, prospects, and resources—things should get easier, but they don't. Things actually get harder and more complicated."

— Verne Harnish, *Scaling Up*

For the next two years, I spent a significant amount of time learning the logistics industry and being a servant leader to the organization. I was learning how the company was built and managed, investigating how it had continued its growth from $100M to $300M since I'd joined the organization. The learnings and experiences were amazing, and my ambitions to someday build my own $100M company were stronger than ever.

Meanwhile, as the logistics company tripled in size, the project management and sports companies had plateaued. Neither company had grown since the investment and merger with the logistics company. Both companies' management teams, cultures, and finances needed more attention. Something needed to be done about them quickly, or both would be lost in the dust of this now $300M logistics enterprise. The project management and sports companies had, unfortunately, become distractions to the larger logistics organization; however, my passion for them was still strong. These were my two babies, now 11+ years old but on life support. I cared greatly for the businesses and the people within them and did not want them to fail.

My experiences with the logistics company gave me a lot of valuable insight into how a $100M+ company operates. And I had witnessed firsthand how the company had tripled in size (and saw the difficulty and risk of this growth). Through these learnings, I had built up the confidence that I, too, had the skills and ability to grow a company to $100M+, and ultimately, I knew that I wanted to be an *entrepreneur*, not an intrapreneur building value for somebody else.

Armed with this unwavering confidence, I was ready for my next move.

"I would like to resign my role in the logistics business, where I have no equity, and focus on growing our sports business to become a $100M company in the next five years," I blurted out to Ron, the owner of the logistics company and majority owner of the sports company.

"Over the past two years, I have learned a lot, and the experience has been invaluable. I can provide you and your investment in the sports company much more value if I can spend 100% of my time building that business," I continued. "Furthermore, the project management company needs attention or will suffer a slow death. I would like to purchase this equity back from you and remove it from being a distraction to the logistics business."

After several back-and-forth conversations, we eventually agreed on the terms of both proposals.

Mike, the general manager of the project management company, and I purchased the equity of the project management business from the logistics company with a loan from a small commercial bank. Mike immediately took the reins as the CEO and president of the business. Mike had started as a sales associate for the project management company 10 years prior and was always the top sales representative. As he continued to deliver for the company, he was eventually promoted to vice president of Sales, then general manager, and finally to CEO, president, and partner.

I knew the business would be in good hands with Mike leading the company, and there was nobody else I would have wanted to partner with. The project management company had been stuck in its Messy Middle stage for eight years. It was stuck between $3.5–$5M per year in revenues and barely making any money. Having Mike, the company's top salesperson, become the new leader of the business was the logical option for the business going forward.

I exited my role as the vice president of Operations in the logistics company to return to the sports company as its CEO and president full-time. I was now on a mission to prove to myself, Ron, and my partners that we could 10X the company from $10M to $100M. This idea to commit to growing the sports business by a factor of 10 was highly motivated by the book I read during this time, *The 10X Rule* by Grant Cardone.

The 10x Rule: The Only Difference Between Success and Failure by Grant Cardone

This motivational book emphasizes the importance of setting ambitious goals and taking massive action to achieve extraordinary results. Cardone argues that most people underestimate the effort required to succeed and urges readers to adopt a "10X" mindset, which means setting goals that are ten times bigger than what they initially think possible and putting in ten times the effort to achieve them. He shares practical strategies and mindset shifts to overcome obstacles, increase

productivity, and cultivate a relentless commitment to success, ultimately inspiring readers to take control of their lives and reach new levels of achievement.

Key Learnings:

1. Set ambitious goals and commit to taking massive action to achieve them.

2. Be willing to take risks and view failure as an opportunity to learn and grow.

3. Develop a successful mindset and build relationships to create wealth.

4. Believe in yourself and stay positive, no matter what.

5. Take ownership of your life, break free from your comfort zone, and live life to the fullest.

"Wake up! No one is going to save you. No one is going to take care of your family or your retirement. No one is going to 'make things' work out for you. The only way to do so is to utilize every moment of every day at 10X levels."
—Grant Cardone, *The 10X Rule*

I was back to where I had started but now armed with a wealth of knowledge and confidence. It was time for me to jump in and build the sports company from $10M to $100M in five years, as I had promised Ron. I had a plan of attack, and I was ready to execute it!

In addition to *The 10X Rule* and wanting to significantly grow the sports business, I was always fascinated with this lovely, high, rounded $100M number. I viewed it as the pinnacle of success for entrepreneurs. It's a lofty, Big Hairy Audacious Goal (BHAG) and a great badge of honor. Only 0.19% of U.S. businesses attain this level (NAICS), and I wanted to be a part of this $100M club.

The term "BHAG" was first coined by Jim Collins and Jerry Porras in their 1994 book *Built to Last*. The concept was meant to describe a stretch goal that was ambitious but achievable. Since then, the term has become part of the popular business lexicon and is often used by organizations to set ambitious, achievable, long-term goals.

Built to Last: Successful Habits of Visionary Companies by Jim Collins and Jerry I. Porras

Based on six years of research, the book comprehensively analyzes 18 well-known companies, including 3M, Boeing, Hewlett-Packard, and Procter & Gamble. By comparing these successful companies with their less successful counterparts, *Built to Last* identifies essential qualities such as a shared core purpose, long-term vision, and a commitment to growth and innovation. The book provides practical advice on creating a thriving, enduring company culture. It offers a blueprint for leaders to follow to build organizations that are truly "built to last."

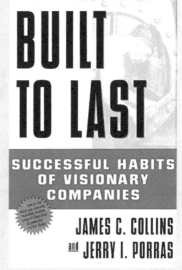

Key Learnings:

1. Visionary companies have a strong sense of purpose and values that guide their decision-making and direction.

2. These companies often have a culture of excellence and are committed to constantly improving and innovating.

3. Successful companies prioritize long-term goals over short-term gains and are willing to take calculated risks to achieve them.

4. They focus on building and maintaining strong relationships with

stakeholders, including employees, customers, suppliers, and community members.

5. Visionary companies have a flexible and adaptable structure, allowing them to adjust to changing market conditions and environments while maintaining their core values and purpose.

"Visionary companies are so clear about what they stand for and what they're trying to achieve that they simply don't have room for those unwilling or unable to fit their exacting standards."
—Jim Collins, *Built to Last*

To achieve the 10X mission of growing the sports company from $10M to $100M in five years, we needed to grow aggressively, both organically and through mergers and acquisitions (M&A).

Even though I was the CEO and president of the sports business, Ron was still the majority owner. As I presented the vision to him, the glaring question to answer was how we would fund such aggressive growth. The company had some access to bank financing, graciously backed by Ron, that would help us fund small, strategic, tuck-under acquisitions. We had a working line of credit, but that would not be enough to help us grow to $100M in such a short timeline.

We knew that to execute this plan to $100M, we would need to begin raising capital from other investors. Although HandymanOnline.com had raised venture funding, I had not been involved in the capital raise process. This was something I would need to research and learn about.

For months, I contacted everyone in my network to request meetings. I presented them with my vision of growing the sports company to $100M over the next five years. I was determined to find the investors to help us on this growth path and was unwilling to back down until I found the capital we needed.

Among many other presentations to investors, I will never forget the conversation I had when I invited my first boss and mentor, Jeff, to visit our corporate headquarters to pitch him on a possible investment in our company.

Jeff and I had always wanted to be in business together again, and I knew he had a deep passion for sports. Bringing him on as an investor would help surround me with people I trusted to guide me and help us grow the business.

As Jeff evaluated our business and offering, he asked a question that hinted as to why he was not sure this was a good investment for him.

"John, how much of this thing do you own?" Jeff asked.

"Around 12%," I quickly noted.

"So, how are you protected in this business?" he responded.

"I am the cofounder of the business. This is my strategy and plan. All my close friends work in this business. And the majority owner trusts me to run this business and execute this plan," I responded confidently.

"Yes, but what happens if . . ." and you know how the conversation went from there.

Jeff was genuinely concerned about me. He would have been interested in making a minority investment, but there was one big problem: he could not get comfortable investing in a business where the person he would really be investing in was at risk and not fully in control.

All strong and valid points, but my ability to hear them was handicapped. I felt invincible.

After months of research, we ultimately connected with a family office from Canada that had an interest in the sports space we were targeting and had an appetite to invest in our team and vision. Upon closing the $5M of growth capital, we were well on our way to achieving the first leg of our growth plan to $50M. We projected that the $5M capital raise would assist us in growing 5X—from $10M in revenues up to $50M—within a couple of years. Then we would need a more aggressive round of capital to reach our ultimate goal of $100M.

We began to grow the company aggressively: acquiring new companies, integrating cultures, hiring staff, building new processes and systems, and chasing new opportunities for revenue growth. We were moving very quickly. Sure enough, with a tremendous amount of effort by all to integrate great businesses and people into our company, the company grew to $50M in revenues within two years—right on target.

"We are on our way to $100M, and nothing can stop us now! All we need is the next round of growth capital to help us stabilize what we have built and take the next leg of our journey. We got this!" or so I thought.
. .

Self-Reflection Zone

- Does your company have a Big Hairy Audacious Goal (BHAG)?
- Have you ever tried to grow a business 10X? What did you learn?
- Have you ever brought investors into your company? How did it work out?
- What would you change the next time you raise capital?
- How would it make you feel if your business could organically build its own growth capital so that you never needed to dilute your equity to raise capital?

CHAPTER 7

THE BIG FAIL

"A funny thing happens once the business starts to grow. Instead of getting easier as you scale, it becomes a sort of waking nightmare. The Growth Paradox."

— Verne Harnish, *Scaling Up*

This was an exhilarating, challenging, and rewarding time for me as an entrepreneur. It was everything that I thought entrepreneurship was meant to be.

We had designed a plan to get to $100M in five years and were halfway there!

But things were getting harder and harder.

The company had grown 5X in two years, and we were experiencing significant growing pains. As the company grew, so did its overhead expenses, cash strains, bank loans, corporate overhead staff (accounting, marketing, executive team), number of employees . . . you get the idea.

The Growth Paradox

The only thing that did not grow as quickly was our net operating cash flow. We were reinvesting so heavily into our growth that it ate up all our cash. Worse, some of our investments were not making money. Instead, they were losing money and sucking cash out of the business. We were trying to grow the company so quickly that we deployed all of the cash flow we had generated from successful divisions into new expansion opportunities, trying to expand our footprint, services, and products simultaneously. With the company growing and a lack of net operating cash flow being generated, the balance sheet was getting heavier and heavier with the leverage from bank loans.

To escape this Growth Paradox, we attempted to grow *more*, diversifying into new verticals and developing new revenue streams to generate more profits.

We were growing for growth's sake!

As you can probably imagine, that just amplified the problem. We were stuck.

The more rapidly you rise, the harder it is to control: more money, more problems. In Jim Collins's book, *Good to Great,* the author argues that great companies are built slowly, over time, in a disciplined and consistent manner, ensuring that they can maintain excellence as they grow.

Good to Great: Why Some Companies Make the Leap . . . and Others Don't by Jim Collins

Jim Collins's advice in *Good to Great* is to avoid growing too quickly. He asserts that companies should focus on building a great foundation and only grow as fast as they can maintain excellence. He emphasizes the importance of finding the right people to ensure the company can grow without sacrificing quality. He also suggests that the company should create a culture of discipline and consistency to handle expansion pressures.

Key learnings:

1. Find the right people and put them in the right place.
2. Create a culture of discipline and consistency.
3. Focus on the core values that make you great.
4. Have a clear vision and strategic plan for the future.
5. Focus on sustainability and long-term success.

"When [what you are deeply passionate about, what you can be best in the world at and what drives your economic engine] come together, not only does your work move toward greatness, but so does your life. For, in the end, it is impossible to have a great life unless it is a meaningful life. And it is very difficult to have a meaningful life without meaningful work."
—Jim Collins, *Good to Great*

We had grown too fast, burned through too much of the capital we'd raised, and chased new avenues to grow even more.

The only way to get our company through this phase would be to accelerate the timing of raising the next round of capital to help us get to $100M. I presented a plan to the board and pushed for a new capital raise of $20M to pay down the bank debt we had amassed from the acquisitions, properly de-lever the balance sheet, and get the fresh powder needed for our continued growth to $100M.

I began to research potential prospects for our next funding round. We needed to expand the field of potential investors to more sophisticated private equity firms to raise the capital we needed and take the company through its next growth phase. I had never raised this much capital before and had no experience with private equity firms. I thought seeking support and advice in this area would be prudent.

As I began networking throughout our organization, one of our division leaders introduced me to an "angel" investor he had met in the industry who was looking for sports-related investment opportunities.

For months, I met and spoke with the potential investor and introduced him to several of our board members. Due to our rapid rise, our company was an attractive opportunity for this individual. He had a passion for sports and business and a résumé that *appeared* to have the exact experience I felt we needed at this growth stage. I needed a running partner to assist me in raising the necessary capital to help grow our business to $100M and beyond. He *seemed* to be the perfect candidate to join our company (or so I thought) and lead these efforts.

A CEO and president of a $50M company with hundreds of employees makes many decisions daily and must make those decisions quickly and decisively. I have come to understand that certain choices, termed "one-door" decisions, are regrettably irreversible. Therefore, they should be approached with extreme caution and care. Bringing on this new executive would become a pivotal choice, and regrettably, it wouldn't be the sole one-door decision I'd make.

We worked closely to build the company's confidential information memorandum to educate private equity firms on our business. We researched the private equity candidates and set up meetings to introduce our opportunity to them.

One of the private equity companies that joined the process was a private equity firm this new executive had invited. This seemed to be a great fit. After all, it was great that this executive had a working relationship with this private equity firm in the past, and they were interested in investing in the sports industry.

After meeting with several private equity firms, we decided to proceed exclusively with the private equity group the new executive had introduced to us. After six months of exhaustive financial and legal due diligence, the private equity firm invested, and their investment, added to what the other partners and I had invested, got us to our capital raise goal of $20M.

I had convinced my wife to invest everything we had alongside the new investors. We now had extensive financial backing from a private equity firm. "This is it," I thought to myself. "Next stop, $100M! Let's go!"

The capital raised was earmarked to pay off *all* the bank loans, *reset* our balance sheet, and provide us with *ample* capital to invest in both organic and acquisitive growth opportunities. We were armed and ready with a plan to clean up certain segments of our business and become the global leader in our industry.

The ink was barely dry on the closing paperwork when the tide changed.

Within a month of the new capital being raised, it was apparent that the executive I had hired had been undermining me with the new private equity firm and other executives throughout our company.

The vibe was getting awkward throughout the company. Here I was, edifying and promoting this new executive as being a big part of helping us on the next leg of our journey; meanwhile, he was throwing me under the bus to everybody that would listen.

I was oblivious to it all.

I wish I had read the book *Snakes in Suits* by Paul Babiak and Robert Hare, *before* the events I recounted in this chapter, but unfortunately, I had not.

Snakes in Suits: Understanding and Surviving The Psychopaths In Your Office by Paul Babiak and Robert Hare

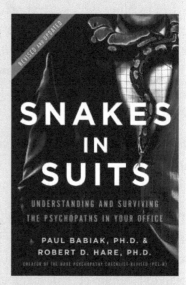

Snakes in Suits is a groundbreaking book that explores the dark world of corporate psychopathy. It examines how psychopaths lack conscience and empathy and can infiltrate and wreak havoc in the corporate world. The authors detail the different strategies psychopaths use to manipulate and deceive those around them and how their lack of conscience allows them to take advantage of those in positions of power. They also examine how to identify and deal with these psychopaths and protect yourself and your organization from their destructive behavior. The book is a must-read for anyone in a leadership role or who works with or around people in leadership roles.

Key Learnings:

1. Psychopaths can be highly successful in corporate environments.

2. Psychopaths have the ability to manipulate and deceive those around them.

3. It is crucial to identify and deal with psychopaths to protect yourself and your organization.

4. Understanding the strategies that psychopaths use to gain power and influence can help you defend yourself and your organization.

5. It is important to be aware of the warning signs of psychopathy and seek help if you suspect someone is a psychopath.

"First they assess the value of individuals to their needs, and identify their psychological strengths and weaknesses. Second, they manipulate the individuals (now potential victims) by feeding them carefully crafted messages, while constantly using feedback from them to build and maintain control. Third, they leave the drained and bewildered victims when they are . . . through with them."
—Babiak and Hare, *Snakes in Suits*

"Psychopaths have a great sense of superiority and entitlement . . . Their grandiose sense of self-importance leads them to believe that other people exist just to take care of them. Because they see most people as weak, inferior, and easy to deceive, psychopathic con artists will often tell you that their victims deserved what they got."
—Babiak and Hare, *Snakes in Suits*

I had made one-door irreversible decisions. I needed to try and navigate my way through them, but I was stuck. Not only did I hire this executive, but he also introduced us to the private equity firm that had just invested in our company. To make matters worse, the new private equity firm had negotiated strong management controls over our company based on the size of their investment.

I have learned through this experience that an entrepreneur should limit, at all costs, making one-door decisions that they cannot reverse. For example, my decision to hire an unvetted executive and then allow him to bring in a private equity firm with which he had a prior relationship resulted in my irretrievable loss of influence within my company.

Conversely, when entrepreneurs make "two-door" decisions, they can simply open the back door and get out if they make a mistake. For example, if you beta test a product or service and place a small bet, you can quickly reverse the decision with minimal damage and impact if that product or service does not work. My decisions were irreversible. I wish I had learned, before this moment, that one-door decisions can lead to devastating results, or worse, a business mortality event.

Within a month of the private equity firm investing in our business, they insisted that the company's finance division report to the executive I had hired. A few short weeks after that, I was being questioned on every single aspect of the business. Finally, within seven months, I was fired after a board meeting. The executive I had hired to help me build this business was appointed to become the new CEO and president of the company.

After investing 15 years of blood, sweat, and tears into growing the hobby business I had started with my best friends to over $50M in global revenues, I had lost it all.

I had invested all of our money, all of my time, and my love and energy into this venture! Worst of all, I was leaving the company, the people I loved, and the amazing culture we had created in the hands of an executive I did not trust—a snake in a suit. To say I felt defeated would be an understatement.

Self-Reflection Zone:

- Have you ever experienced the Growth Paradox in your business? What actions did you implement to overcome these growing pains?

- Have you ever made irreversible, one-door decisions? What was the impact of these decisions on you and your business?

- How has a bad hire or business partner hurt you in the past? How do you vet the people you bring into your business and life?

- Have you ever lost a business you poured everything into? What did you learn from that experience?

CHAPTER 8

IT'S TIME TO KICK SOME ASS!

"At some point, everything is going to go south on you. You're going to say 'This is it. This is how I end.' Now you can either accept that . . . or you can get to work."

— Matt Damon as Mark Watney (*The Martian*)

What was I to do now?

The embarrassment, devastation, disappointment, frustration, sadness, and depression were difficult to digest.

Most of my close friends over the last 15 years were still in this business I was no longer a part of. I had invested all my blood, sweat, and tears (and wealth) into this business and had nothing to show for it.

What had I done?

When dealing with a massive failure, the search for meaning is complicated because there is an intense desire and need to stay strong in the face of your family and friends.

For me, perspective became a major thought enlightener. My family was healthy, we had a great home, and I had the love of our family and friends. Although horrific for me, this situation paled compared to the daily issues millions of others around the world face. To any entrepreneur facing a challenging business situation, I recommend keeping this perspective while considering the personal and professional growth you stand to gain in facing that challenge.

Years before this traumatic experience, my good friend Ruth introduced me to the book *Necessary Endings* by Dr. Henry Cloud. I have subsequently recommended this book to others facing a business or personal situation where something has come to an end: a business partnership, employment, a marriage, and the like.

It was time for me to reread this book. Maybe this was a necessary ending for me. Perhaps this was meant to be, and there was a reason this happened. I needed perspective.

Necessary Endings: The Employees, Businesses, and Relationships That All of Us Have to Give Up in Order to Move Forward by Henry Cloud

In *Necessary Endings*, psychologist and leadership expert Henry Cloud explores the importance of letting go of relationships, behaviors, and beliefs that no longer serve us. He argues that endings are a natural and necessary part of life and that by embracing them, we can create space for growth and new beginnings. The author offers practical advice and tools for identifying what needs to be ended, how to end it effectively and with compassion, and 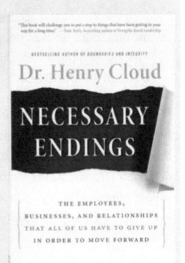 how to move forward confidently and purposefully. The book highlights the importance of self-awareness, courage, and resilience in navigating the endings necessary for personal and professional growth.

Key Learnings:

1. Endings are a natural and necessary part of life; we must learn to accept them and embrace them as opportunities for growth and development.

2. We often hold on to relationships, behaviors, and beliefs that no longer serve us, out of fear, complacency, or a sense of obligation. Recognizing when an ending is necessary and having the courage to follow through is essential.

3. Endings can be painful and complex but are also a source of liberation and new opportunities. It is important to grieve the loss of what is ending and focus on what is coming next.

4. Successful endings require clarity, communication, and boundaries. It is important to be clear with ourselves and others about what needs to be ended, why it needs to be ended, and what the process will look like.

5. Endings are about letting go of what is no longer working and making space for new growth and possibility. We can create a more fulfilling and purposeful life by leaning into necessary endings with an open mind and heart.

"Getting to the next level always requires ending something, leaving it behind, and moving on. Growth demands that we move on. Without the ability to end things, people stay stuck. Never becoming who they are meant to be, never accomplishing all their talents and abilities should afford them."
—Dr. Henry Cloud, *Necessary Endings*

Yes, I lost a company after 15 years, but I had much to be thankful for. Throughout those 15 years, I built friendships with amazing people and enjoyed incredible experiences with them. I gained valuable learnings while building that company. And after losing my place in the company

I helped build, I had opportunities for personal and professional growth that are often only recognizable on the other side of a failure.

Wanting to demonstrate my self-regulation ability and strength to my spouse, children, parents, and friends, I worked extremely hard to regulate my emotions and thoughts to keep a positive mindset whenever I inevitably started reflecting on what had transpired.

The world was trying to tell me something, and I needed to figure out what it was.

I had heard that failure is a prerequisite to success, but it is a lot easier to talk about the benefits of failure when you are not dealing with the heartache of it. Failure can be an extremely powerful and emotional experience. When entrepreneurs fail, they only have one choice if they want to keep striving for entrepreneurial success: face their truth!

In addition to self-regulation, another incredible skill I learned and developed from my College Pro roots was the power of introspection. Introspection is the ability to look inward and examine one's thoughts, feelings, motivations, and contributions to a situation to learn from what you should have or could have done differently.

As easy as it could have been to blame everybody else for how I felt wronged, I needed to spend my time evaluating the massive learnings that had just taken place that were well within my control. At the root of everything that happens in your business are choices you've made that have affected the outcomes. You need to know what your contributions were! Entrepreneurs need to take responsibility for what transpires, good or bad; otherwise, how will they ever move forward, learn, and succeed?

For the first time in 20 years, I was waking up every morning with an empty calendar, no emails in my inbox, no meetings or calls, and no voicemails to return. It was eerie.

I wasn't ready to start a new venture while I was processing what I had just experienced. I needed time to heal and to properly assess what I should learn from what had happened. As I reflected on the situation, I was determined to turn the negative situation into a big positive.

I needed to be humbled.

At the height of our growth from $10M to $50M, I thought that we were unstoppable. I believed we could build the company way beyond $100M.

I continued to feel that this incredible team, business, and culture was the best business I had ever been a part of. There was no other company or team in the world that I wanted to lead.

Unfortunately, when you get too cocky and confident, life has a funny way of punching you in the gut and knocking you down to send the message, "You're too full of yourself!" There is no doubt that this message was sent to me, and I needed to grasp it, pick myself back up, find my purpose, and get going again!

So that is what I did. I spent months figuring out how to find my purpose in life and business. I needed to find my True North and figure out who I wanted to be. It was time to grow up!

Every dark room has a light switch. The power of perspective, self-reflection, introspection, and a positive mindset always led me in the right direction. Under the theory that everything happens for a reason, I aimed to turn these "lemons" into the best-tasting ~~vodka~~ lemonade ever! I was on a mission to find my purpose and passion for my life and career and make it happen!

Years prior, I had heard about the diagram some call "What Success Looks Like." It's from the book *Good to Great* by Jim Collins, and in his book, this Venn diagram is referred to as "The Hedgehog Concept."

Hedgehog Concept (aka: "What Success Looks Like") by Jim Collins

The "What Success Looks Like" Venn diagram is the intersection of three circles:

a) What are you the most passionate about?

b) What can you be the best in the world at?

c) What can drive your economic engine?

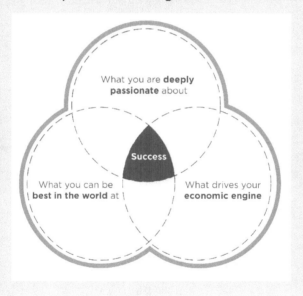

Unfortunately, this exercise was also a reminder that the sports company had fit perfectly in this Venn diagram intersection. No wonder I loved everything about that business! It had *everything* I had ever wanted!

Ok, no more crying over spilled milk. I needed to find this center and purpose again.

After several months of soul-searching, reading, listening, thinking, and every other possible mode of bringing my thoughts to light, I developed my own "What Success Looks Like" diagram.

Once I put this on paper for the first time, I knew that this was a success diagram I could get behind!

"What Success Looks Like" —My Version

Passion:

Entrepreneurship, Leadership, Growth, Family, and Fun—these all drive and excite me. I want an abundance of these items in my life.

Best:

Leadership Development, Communication, and Sales—I can be the best in the world in these areas with continued education and focus.

Economic:

Grow Business Assets, Build a Private Holding Company of Small Businesses, and Mentor/Coach other entrepreneurs—these would combine my passions in the areas I know I can excel.

This self-reflection, introspection, and thought development would only be worthwhile if I put *into action* what I had developed with all my learnings and skill sets.

I now needed to figure out exactly how I would do that.

The book *The One Thing*, by Gary Keller, would provide much-needed clarity.

- What is the One Thing I ultimately want to accomplish in my life?

- What is the One Thing I need to do in the next 3 years to be on track to achieve the ultimate goal?

- What is the One Thing I must do next year to be on track to achieve the 3-year goal?

- What is the One Thing I need to do this month to be on track to achieve the 1-year goal?

- What is the One Thing I need to do this week to be on track to achieve the goal this month?

- What is the One Thing I need to do today to be on track to achieve the goal for the week? . . . NOW GO DO THAT!

I used *The One Thing* model to create my True North Life Plan. What did I really want to accomplish in all segments of my life: career, family, relationships, finances, and health? My True North clarity and direction would now guide my daily, weekly, monthly, and yearly actions.

It was time to Kick Some Ass!

Armed with a clear purpose and a True North Life Plan, I was ready to relaunch myself.

I purchased the domain, TimeToKickSomeAss.com. This website, supported by a social media blitz, took me out of the dormant state of hiding I had been in for over a year and brought me out of my comfort zone. I wrote an EBook, *You 2.0*, and hosted a webinar to relaunch myself to over 50 close friends and family.

You 2.0: Find your Purpose & Kick Some Ass
by John St.Pierre

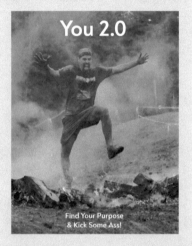

The Ebook walks readers through the power of self-reflection and provides a clear and detailed process on how to find one's true purpose.

I knew that if I committed and communicated to the world that I was ready to get off the bench and start kicking some ass, I would have to show up every day, stop feeling sorry for myself, and make things happen.

I had found my purpose, created a True North Life Plan, and relaunched myself publicly. It was time to show up and make it happen!

Self-Reflection Zone:

- How have you learned to process "necessary endings" in your life and business career?
- Do you have a True North Life Plan that guides all of your actions?
- What is your "One thing," your True North?
- Draw your own "What Success Looks Like?" Venn diagram.
    - What are you most passionate about?
    - What can you be the best in the world at?
    - What drives your economic engine?

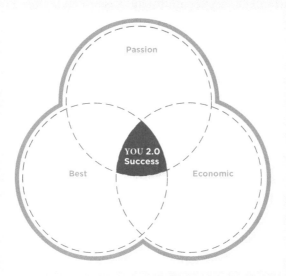

PROJECT 100

"When defeat comes, accept it as a signal that your plans are not sound. Rebuild those plans, and set sail once more toward your coveted goal."
— Napoleon Hill, *Think and Grow Rich*

Part of the problem with publicly declaring that you are going to start kicking some ass is that you have to wake up each day ready to do just that. After suffering the biggest failure of my business career, not following through on my commitment was *not* an option. I had a burning desire to prove to myself (and others) that I could succeed as an entrepreneur. I was ready. I had a renewed purpose and life plan!

In the background, Mike Hersh, the CEO of the project management business, had focused on steadily growing the business's revenues. The company's profitability, net operating cash flow, and balance sheet were getting stronger each year.

Since purchasing the equity of the project management company back from the logistics company, Mike, as its CEO and leader, led the growth of the business from under $5M in revenues to over $15M. Things were going very well for the company. Mike and I would meet every fall to carefully lay out the short-term and long-term goals of the business. The 1-page Strategic Business Plan we created provided Mike and his team with a clear plan for the year ahead: a plan to remain disciplined and focus on the business's quarterly actions, annual objectives, key performance indicators (KPIs), long-term big hairy audacious goals (BHAGs), and other strategic planning elements.

Mike—having been a close witness to the rise and fall of the sports company, my ups and downs as an entrepreneur, and my recent pronouncement that I was going to get back out there and "Kick Some Ass"—posed a question that provided me with additional clarity.

"John, I know that things didn't work out as you had planned with the sports company, but why don't we focus on growing this company to $100M?" Mike boldly asked.

As I paused to think about what he was proposing, he continued: "You have learned a lot about what to do and what not to do. Our project management company has a solid foundation, and we can grow this company substantially if we invest smartly in its growth. Why spend your time elsewhere? Let's build this company and implement your learnings right here!"

As I reflected on Mike's question, my wheels were spinning.

Could the project management company break through the Messy Middle of business growth and become a High Performance business? A $100M company, grown the right way?

He had a good point: why invest my time in any other business? The project management company had a 15-year track record, a solid leadership team, a growing customer base, positive net operating cash flows, and a healthy balance sheet.

"Let's do this!" I said to Mike.

We set a goal to grow the business to $100M. Our Strategic Business Plan stated clearly:

BHAG
Big Hairy Audacious Goal

To be the premier provider of world-class, high-touch project management services for large, direct customers, generating revenues of $100,000,000+.

With great learnings from the past, I needed to ensure we did not make the same mistakes I had made with the sports company. "This time will be different!" I said to myself.

Through a heavy dose of introspection and reflection on my entrepreneurial journey and incredible learnings, I developed some core strategic principles that I firmly believed were essential to ensuring success.

The journey of the two companies reminded me of *Aesop's Fable*, "The Tortoise and the Hare." The sports company had been the company that had grown much faster—it was far ahead of the project management company on almost every metric—yet the project management company stayed in the race and had developed an incredible foundation for long term sustainability.

"The Tortoise and the Hare" by Aesop

The story is about a hare who brags about how fast he can run. He challenges a tortoise to a race. The other animals in the forest laugh at the tortoise, knowing he will never be able to catch up to the speedy hare. The hare quickly runs out in front and takes a nap, thinking he has plenty of time to spare. The tortoise, on the other hand, steadily plods along, never giving up. Eventually, the hare wakes to find the tortoise has passed him and is close to the finish line. The hare races to the end, but it's too late. The tortoise wins the race.

Key Learnings:
1. Don't underestimate others.
2. Slow and steady wins the race.
3. Confidence can lead to complacency.
4. Hard work pays off.
5. Focus on your own race.

"Slow and steady wins the race!"
—Aesop

With the sports company, we tried to grow too quickly (the hare), carelessly diversifying into many different business lines. The revenue streams, pricing, and costing models were all different. These created massive distractions and complications in our financial systems. It was tough to scale and we needed too many resources and too much capital. By not generating enough free net operating cash flow, we did not build our own capital to finance our continued growth, and it caused us to make poor one-door decisions by bringing new investors into the business.

Our project management company had taken the slower, wiser growth path (the tortoise). It had all the components of a company that could take the next step in its journey. Unlike the sports company, where I did not protect or build my equity position, Mike and I had grown our equity interest in the project management company over time. Since cofounding the business, I had increased my initial equity interest from 25% to a majority position. Mike and I entirely owned this business together and wholly controlled its destiny. We generated our own capital through free net operating cash flow from operations. We reinvested this capital into the company to take advantage of additional strategic growth opportunities in a systematic and controlled manner.

Our Strategic Plan did not include raising capital from outside sources. We made a conscious decision to grow the business without diluting our equity. If we could not afford it, we would not do it. We had no interest in diluting ourselves. We believed in ourselves and wanted to invest in our skills and abilities.

Over the project management company's first 15 years, we found one thing that worked and stayed focused on growing that one business line. We encountered many challenges along the way and persevered through them all. We built a profitable pricing model that was simple and duplicable. As we started to generate strong net operating cash flow, we began to reinvest in sales and marketing to grow. We grew the team in a systematic and controlled manner, focused on rewarding the top performers, putting people in roles to succeed, and eliminating bad apples.

As we started to scale, we provided the key leaders in the business with long-term value appreciation rights so that they could participate in the company's growth in value. They were treated like entrepreneurs—expected to manage and deliver upon their division budgets. They were intrapreneurs within the company, truly vested in caring about the business.

> A value appreciation right is a form of a phantom equity agreement between a company and its employees that allows employees to receive future rewards based on the appreciation of the company's value.

We protected the business with all our might. We started our own captive insurance company and purchased extraordinary liability insurance coverages for the business. We had professional advisors looking over every single inch of the business.

A captive insurance company is a type of insurance company that is owned and controlled by its insureds. The primary purpose of a captive is to insure the risks of its owners and affiliates, allowing them to manage and reduce their total cost of risk. Captive insurance companies are typically structured as either single-parent captives (owned by one company) or group captives (owned by multiple companies).

As we began to generate strong net operating cash flows, we tapped into specific tax-beneficial vehicles—which I had never even heard about previously—to access the owner's liquidity. It may have taken over 15 years, but we could finally pay ourselves our full value. We had unparalleled confidence. We continued to build and follow our Strategic Plan, which we would refresh and update each fall for the coming year.

Everything became clearer and easier when the project management company attained $1M in free net operating cash flow for the first time. We had built our own capital to invest in furthering our growth.

An opportunity then presented itself to acquire BrandPoint Services, a synergistic, strategic competitor in our industry. This acquisition would double the business, provide some missing elements we needed to mature our company, and get us closer to our $100M objective.

"Should we reinvest our free net operating cash flow to make a strategic acquisition?" we asked ourselves in our strategic planning meeting.

Having completed several strategic acquisitions with the sports company, the idea of leveraging our balance sheet with bank debt to acquire a business caused me to pause.

"Mike, I am willing to do this under a few conditions," I proposed. "If we make this acquisition, we need to commit to each other that we do not make any other big financial decisions until we pay off the banknote and return the company to 'debt free' status."

Don't get me wrong. I am all for utilizing proper bank leverage to help grow your business. Unfortunately, I learned the hard way that if you take on too much leverage, you can lose complete control of your business. I was not going to let that happen here. If we were going to take on bank debt to make an acquisition, we needed to structure a good transaction and, more importantly, pay off the loan as soon as possible.

Steve Hearon, the former HandymanOnline.com West Coast director from San Diego, was now the CEO and president of BrandPoint Services. Ironically, within his organization, Steve had also launched an internal goal to grow his business to $100M.

Through our pre-acquisition diligence conversations, Steve, Mike, and I knew that bringing our two companies together would propel us to achieving our desired growth goals. And so Mike and I made our first acquisition, applying a portion of our free net operating cash flow, in addition to a banknote and a seller note, to purchase the business.

On the day of the announcement of the merger between the two companies, Mike and Steve prepared signage, t-shirts, and pocket compasses with the BHAG of the company: Project 100!

From my experience, most mergers of companies result in less-than-stellar outcomes. The expected outcome of 1 plus 1 equals 3 is often superseded by the more disappointing, yet standard, result of 1 plus 1

equals 1.5. Integrating cultures, teams, customers, processes, and systems causes incredible disruption and loss of synergy.

Thankfully, we structured and integrated these two businesses very successfully. In the first year, 1 plus 1 did, in fact, equal 3. The two companies, originally producing combined annual revenues of $35M (approximately $17.5M each), generated over $50M in the first year of the merger.

With one significant strategic move, we had grown our business from $17.5M to over $50M in revenues! And we did so very profitably! We were able to pay off the bank and seller notes within the first two years of the merger, and our business was back to being debt free.

A certain magic happens when a business attains what is called the "core capital target." This is when the business is debt free and has built up significant cash reserves. When a business attains this target and continues to generate strong net operating cash flow from operations, its ability to invest in growth is very strong.

Mike, the CEO, and Steve, the president, continued building the business in partnership, continually refocusing and implementing the annual 1-page Strategic Plan with one major goal: Project 100!

With the merger of the two companies completed and the loan from the bank paid off, we followed our Strategic Plan and identified another synergistic, tuck-under opportunity that would add new customers and project management talent to the business. The acquired revenue, along with strong organic growth from the existing customer base, further propelled the business forward.

With patient ambition—protecting and growing our equity, building our own capital, reinvesting the free net operating cash flow in a smart, systematic manner, building a culture of intrapreneurship, and protecting the business's vulnerabilities—we successfully grew our project management company to $100M in annual revenues, growing from $17.5M to $100M in four years (500% growth). The right way!

We had finally broken through the Messy Middle, and at last, the 20-year-old "tortoise" finally crossed the finish line. The BHAG we shared as entrepreneurs—of building a $100M business—was attained. It was time to celebrate! All 150 employees, key vendors, and advisors descended on Atlantic City for the annual company summit. This event had become a tradition for the company for over 10 years, but this one would be extra special!

We set a goal to achieve a significant milestone and we attained it. Watching Mike, Steve, and the whole team celebrate this amazing accomplishment brought tears to my eyes. Like a proud father watching his kids accomplish a major feat, I could not help but think about the long, 20-year road this business had taken; how Mike, who joined the company 15 years prior as a sales representative, led this company as its CEO to $100M; how Steve, whom I had met 30 years earlier as a fellow College Pro alum and hired years later at HandymanOnline.com, joined forces with us and propelled incredible energy into Project 100 as our president.

Celebrating a 20th business anniversary and the attainment of our $100M goal was an extraordinary moment and the pinnacle of our collective entrepreneurial careers . . . thus far.

The champagne popped, the celebratory cake was eaten, and the teams rejoiced. I began reflecting on my journey: all the ups and downs, the pain of my prior mistakes, the relationships I had formed, and the learnings I had gained. . . It was all worth it to experience that moment!

Self-Reflection Zone:

- Does your business have a product or service and a proven pricing model that is ready to scale?

- Does your business have a 1-page Strategic Plan?

- Is your Strategic Plan revised and updated annually? Does it provide your team with quarterly objectives?

- What is your company's BHAG? Is it big enough to motivate you daily?

CHAPTER 10

"OH, SHIT!"

"The weather today is sunny skies with a chance of TORNADO."

— Brian Stevenson, Wells Fargo Advisors

"John, we have a big problem!" Mike immediately stated as I answered the phone. "We need more cash!" he continued.

"How is this possible?" was my only response.

The company had just attained the highly coveted mark of $100M in revenues. Our profit and loss (P&L) statement indicated that we had done so very profitably. How could we not have cash?

Although we had generated a lot of cash on our journey to $100M, maintaining a business at this level seemed to consume more cash than planned.

What were we missing? Something must be seriously wrong here. My mind started wandering with all the things that could have happened to our cash.

"Oh shit! There must be some cracks in the foundation!" I thought to myself. Faced with the scars of past failures, I immediately started to question everything. What had we missed here, and how bad was it? All

I could think about was the message articulated by Alan Miltz, coauthor of the "Cash" section of the book *Scaling Up* and founder of CashFlowStory™: "Revenue is Vanity, Profit is Sanity, Cash is King . . . and Queen."

We had set our goals on building a $100M business and chased vanity! We had a good sense of sanity while reviewing our profitable net income statement, but we lost track of our cash! We were consuming more cash than we were making. We were growing cash poor! All the disciplines we had in place, which provided us the foundation to grow the business from $17.5M to $100M, were being stress tested. Like water finding its way through any crack in your foundation, we had found ourselves up to our noses in bills to pay and not enough incoming cash flow to pay them.

"Mike, we are not going down this way! We will figure this out and put action plans in place!" I said toward the end of our call. "We worked so hard to get the business to this level. Now we must focus on tightening all our financial controls and driving cash flow! Only one thing matters from this point forward: cash is king and queen!" I ended.

It was time to jump into the trenches with Mike, Steve, and their teams to help figure this out. It was time to work *in* the business. A few days later, I boarded a plane and headed to our corporate headquarters to meet with Mike, Steve, and the executive team. I asked them to remove everything from their calendars and join me for a three-day intensive deep dive into the cash flow problem we had found ourselves in.

Mike, Steve, and I—along with the CFO, COO, VP of Finance, director of IT, Operations manager, a hired financial consultant, and other executives—gathered in the "war room" (aka conference room) and quickly jumped into action.

I started the meeting with, "Team, let's brainstorm. What are all the levers in our business that drive cash? And what are all the levers in our business that eat cash?"

I'm not one to leave a whiteboard untouched, and the moment had come to put everything on the wall and understand what was happening.

The list on the board was long and somewhat overwhelming. No wonder we were bleeding so much cash; we had grown so quickly that all our controls had been thrown out the window.

The brainstorming list included items like these:

- We were making large prepayments of supplies and equipment before starting jobs.

- Customers were not paying us on agreed-upon terms.

- We were not always invoicing our customers accurately, which caused payment delays.

- Our overhead had grown too big.

- We were paying many vendors before their payment terms were due.

- Certain programs were operating at very low margins.

- We did not have terms with suppliers—we were paying upfront with credit cards.

- We were taking too long to invoice customers for projects once they were completed.

- We were not asking customers for deposits or progress payments on large projects.

- We lacked financial and operational controls (checks and balances).

- There was no procurement process, so we were not getting volume discounts.

- We lacked standardized processes companywide.

- We overused credit cards (exceeding limits and approvals).

- Our team lacked negotiating skill sets.

- Our sales representatives were not negotiating for better terms with customers.

- Our sales representatives were selling low-margin work because it was easier to make commissions.

- We had no incentives for anybody in the company to drive cash.

- Our customer credit risk was neglected and created large write-offs.

- We were performing a lot of costly warranty work.

- We had no aggressive AR collection process to catch issues with customers early.

"Of course we do not have any cash!" we all thought as we saw the extensive list of issues on the wall. We knew that we needed to take swift action.

Our president, Steve, introduced a great solution on how to proceed. "There are 10 of us in this room, but we have 100 of our team members out there. We are all in this together, and our ability to improve our cash flow touches everybody in the organization. Why not include the whole company in helping us solve this problem?"

With this suggestion, we divided the brainstorming list into eight buckets, with eight team captains, and we launched an eight-week project called "Cash is King and Queen."

Cash is King and Queen Teams:

Team 1: Financial controls, checks and balances

Team 2: Corporate overhead and customer credit analysis

Team 3: Customer Cash Flow Ladder (customer margin and cash conversion analysis)

Team 4: Development of operational standard operating procedures (SOPs)

Team 5: Procurement process, supplier terms, supplier rebates

Team 6: Improve speed and accuracy of the invoicing process and days to collect AR.

Team 7: Review and renegotiate all customer terms and push for more deposits and progress payments.

Team 8: Review subcontractor terms and improve gross margins with better team training.

Once the teams were formed, we hosted a draft. In what felt like a fantasy football draft (and was just as fun), the team captains selected leaders from each organization's division to join their teams on the project.

With the teams formed, each captain was asked to meet with their team once per week (minimum) for eight weeks, develop a project deck of everything they were going to tackle, and ultimately provide the company with

- 3 things we needed to start doing,
- 3 things we needed to stop doing, and
- 3 things we needed to continue doing.

The team and individuals that made the most impact on improving the organization's cash flow would be rewarded with a golden "Cash is King and Queen" crown at the company's next annual summit.

As the project manager, I was responsible for launching the eight-week project, coaching the team leaders, and providing Mike with reports of the actions being taken.

This was an all-hands-on-deck effort. We had done so many things right in building this company to $100M, but we chased vanity, and in doing so, we took our eyes off the most crucial aspect of any company: *cash*!

We were doing work for customers at low margins, paying for all their supplies and equipment upfront with our cash, paying vendors up front, invoicing our customers late, invoicing them incorrectly, not actively chasing AR, and wondering why we had no cash.

Running a business is very difficult, to begin with. Growing a company to $100M is an incredible challenge, and we were discovering that maintaining a large business can be even more challenging.

The Surge-Explode-Plateau graph immediately came to mind. It was first presented to me by my mentor, Charlie.

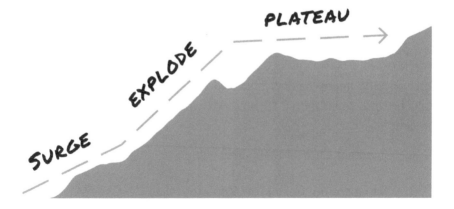

The Surge-Explode-Plateau graph reminded me that a business cannot explode continuously; it must plateau, catch its breath, correct its flaws, build up its cash position, and stabilize the foundation before surging anew.

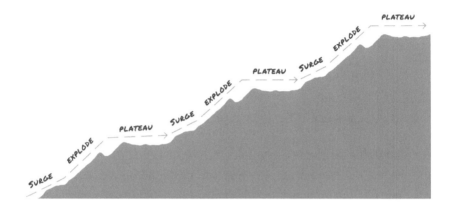

We had just exploded. There was no better time for us to take a breath, stop chasing the vanity revenue number, improve all our processes, and focus on cash.

From this moment forward, every decision the company would make would be through the lens of cash is king and queen.

From the eight teams, the ideas started flowing rapidly. Every single improvement, whether big or small, contributed to the project's overall success. The improvements completely changed the company's cash flow position and prepared it for its next surge.

Three specific improvements enhanced the company's cash flow position. They became foundational to how we would manage cash flow going forward:

1. Customer Cash Flow Ladder

2. Net Operating Cash Flow Report

3. Cash Controls

1. CUSTOMER CASH FLOW LADDER

In my attempt to seek solutions to our cash flow dilemma, I contacted Alan Miltz to ask him for guidance.

Alan's online webinar in March 2020, "The #1 Method to Boost Cashflow, Value, and Profits," hosted by the Growth Institute, was the most impactful one hour of content I had ever watched as an entrepreneur. Alan's mastery of cash flow and its importance in business health was something that we needed to master.

During our call, I shared with Alan the impact his message had had on my entrepreneurial journey and the problem our company was now facing with cash flow.

Alan's insight during our call was incredibly impactful. It provided us with a new framework to scorecard our business and customers moving forward.

The Customer Cash Flow Ladder!

Cash Flow Ladder Example (By Segment)

Segment	1	2	3	4	5
Revenue	4,960,000	3,589,800	1,547,700	159,500	306,090
COGS	3,135,000	2,667,400	1,029,000	122,500	241,370
Gross Margin $	1,825,000	922,400	518,700	37,000	64,720
Gross Margin %	36.79%	25.70%	33.51%	23.20%	21.14%
Overhead Costs	302,000	219,200	268,000	9,700	18,690
Net Gross Margin	30.71%	19.59%	16.20%	17.12%	15.04%
Accounts Recievable	697,000	835,000	149,982	25,830	7,184
Prepaid Expenses	0	250,000	0	0	0
Accounts Payable	269,000	123,000	167,500	11,560	9,924
Working Capital	428,000	962,000	(17,518)	14,270	(2,740)
Average AR Days	51	85	35	59	9
Average AP Days	31	17	59	34	15
Working Capital Days	20	68	-24	25	-6
Working Capital %	8.63%	26.80%	-1.13%	8.95%	-0.90%
Marginal Cash Flow %	22.08%	-7.21%	17.33%	8.17%	15.93%

> The Cash Flow Ladder provides the analysis of a segment (customers, industries, divisions, or products or services) of your business by providing a Marginal Cash Flow %. This percentage shows the effect this segment has on your cash flow. It should indicate whether a segment is driving positive cash flow to the business (GREEN if greater than 10%), negative cash flow to the business (RED if less than 0%), or in the middle (YELLOW if in between 0% and 10%).
>
> You can build your own Cash Flow Ladder by downloading *The $100M Journey Workbook* at 100MJourney.com/workbook.

Upon building our Customer Cash Flow model, we were alarmed to find that some customers we thought were our best were consuming all our cash and growing us poor! The more business we did for them, the more cash they consumed. We needed to start evaluating our customers differently. We would stop measuring success based on customer revenues or gross margins and start measuring success by each customer's marginal cash flow.

The Customer Cash Flow Ladder provided a view of our customers on the following levels:

- Customer Revenue and Gross Margin %
- Allocation of overhead to determine customers' Net Gross Margin
- Working Capital %
- Marginal Cash Flow %

In several cases, specific customers were generating negative marginal cash flow! For example, with one customer, for every $1 in business we were getting from them, it cost us $1.25 of our cash flow to perform the service. What were we doing?

Over the years, we had created scorecards for customers to determine who were A, B, C, or D customers, but we had never evaluated them based on cold, hard cash flow facts. By force ranking our customers on the Customer Cash Flow Ladder, we could mathematically see which customers were eating our cash. Using simple data formatting, we created a Red - Yellow - Green visual scorecard by customer and reviewed it monthly.

Alan's words rang in my head: "Your job is to provide your management team with the tools to win the game of making more cash for the company!" With this Customer Cash Flow Ladder, the management team knew where to focus and take action.

We either needed to:

- figure out how to improve the marginal cash flow through better performance internally,

- renegotiate terms with the customer, or

- fire the customer.

2. NET OPERATING CASH FLOW REPORT

Like most entrepreneurs, I had fallen into the trap of chasing vanity (again!). . . Monthly, I would receive P&L and balance sheet financial statements along with a write-up on the company's financials, but it was missing the most critical analysis: Did we make cash last month or not?

Why had it taken me so long to figure this out?

According to Alan, very few CEOs, if any, know their net operating cash flow because the finance industry has made the cash flow statement so complicated to figure out.

So as a default, beginning entrepreneurs measure their success by the P&L statement. As they get more sophisticated, they graduate to measuring the business performance from the balance sheet statement. All the while, the most critical model to measure and manage is the net operating cash flow of the business.

Net Operating Cash Flow Report Example

Cash Flow		Variance	
Cash from Customers	9,600,000	-400,000	●
Cash to Suppliers	6,500,000	-500,000	●
Gross Cash Profit	3,100,000	-900,000	●
Overheads excl Depreciation	3,500,000	-	
Operating Cash Flow	-400,000	-900,000	●

Net operating cash flow is determined by analyzing the change in certain balance sheet accounts over two periods and providing a clear view of the cash being generated by the business.

You can build your own Net Operating Cash Flow Report by going to CashFlowStory.com.

The Net Operating Cash Flow Report would become our most important monthly report. Did we make positive net operating cash flow last month, quarter, and 12 months? That is what matters!

3. CASH CONTROLS

Let's face it, we had gotten sloppy!

Yes, you are right—I should have known better from my prior experiences. My eye was on the ball, but I was watching the wrong game.

The P&L and the balance sheet looked solid; everything looked in order. "We are killing it," I thought.

But I was blind to the cash flow problems that were building up and the underlying reasons our financial controls were outdated. The rapid growth in the number of employees increased the vulnerabilities. The training was not done appropriately, controls in place were being worked around, credit cards were being handed out like candy at Halloween, and the checks and balances between operations and finance had been thrown out the window.

We needed to pump the brakes and step back, take a breath, and get the train back on the tracks by implementing the proper cash controls for the business. We needed a plateau year to catch our breath.

As a result of the "Cash is King and Queen" project, we implemented company-wide SOPs, a procurement department, and tighter checks and balances throughout our monthly close processes.

The company's leadership team pulled together to focus on the most important metric: making CASH! Before this project, everybody in the company had been focused on attaining the vanity revenue of $100M. This was a wake-up call, and the call came in just in time!

As the company's chairperson, I was able to strategically jump into the trenches with the executive team to help overcome the cash problem while they continued to run the business's day-to-day operations. "Never again," I kept saying to myself.

For now and the rest of my entrepreneurial journey, "Cash is King and Queen!"

Self-Reflection Zone:

- Do you know your net operating cash flow from the last 12 months?

- What are the 5 things that eat your cash flow?

- What are the 5 things that drive your cash flow?

- Do you have a Customer (or Segment) Cash Flow Ladder?

- What are 3 things you need to do to improve cash controls in your company?

CHAPTER 11

RETRACING THE JOURNEY

"I won't see you at the top, I will see you over the top!"

— Zig Ziglar

My entrepreneurial journey has been filled with incredible opportunities, experiences, relationships, learnings, mistakes, failures, successes, and celebrations! The turbulent emotions of being an entrepreneur aren't for everybody and at specific points during my journey, I wasn't sure they were for me either.

Throughout our entire existence, we're taught that failure serves as a necessary condition for achieving success. Narratives recounting Thomas Edison's thousands of unsuccessful attempts prior to creating the light bulb are endearing, yet they differ significantly from the profound anguish associated with the failures inherent in entrepreneurship.

All the steps I took, books I read, people I met, mentors I had, and learnings I gained helped shape and prepare me for this journey. They helped form the foundation for finally achieving the level of entrepreneurial success that I always aspired to achieve. Every action and every decision, regardless of its outcome, have formed who I am today.

That first experience of learning supply and demand by selling school fundraiser chocolate bars to cadets in a military dorm taught me more than I realized then. My early years back home in my small French town, dreaming of being a successful entrepreneur, led me to pursue the American Dream south of the border. I have often wondered how different my life would be if I had not made that big move. What if my parents had not supported my ambitions? What if I had stayed in my small town and not pursued my entrepreneurial dreams in the U.S.?

My father requiring me to study accounting in college instead of a general business course load was instrumental in my understanding of business finance. Running a painting business with College Pro could arguably be the best business decision I have ever made. It prepared me for how hard it is to build and manage a business. This real-world MBA "program" was and still is the biggest learning environment I have ever experienced.

Moving to Chicago, having the amazing fortune to be mentored by Jeff—the best first boss I could possibly have had—and cultivating relationships with many impressive entrepreneurs (many of whom also became lifelong friends) provided me with an incredible development platform that increased my skill sets, confidence, and desire for more!

Being an early team member of a venture-funded Internet startup company in the dot-com era provided me with an amazing opportunity to prove my skill sets, travel the country, grow a business at a rapid pace, and acquire a taste of American capitalism and how businesses can be built, valued, and lost. Of course, the ending of that job and the dot-com crash taught me incredible lessons about life, economics, recessions, venture-backed companies, and how life tends to knock you down when you feel invincible.

I also developed as an entrepreneur and leader through my experiences cofounding two startups and seeing the companies rise rapidly, go through major recessions, and take two different paths to their growth to over $50M in revenues over a period of 20 years. As I led these companies, I developed operational systems and implemented various technologies to help the companies grow.

And then, of course, the biggest failure of my life was a direct result of the decisions and mistakes I made growing a business too carelessly without generating enough net operating cash flow, bringing on too much leverage, making a horrible hire, and losing my equity and my decision-making authority in the business by bringing on investors. It's a failure that hurt me and the people I cared deeply about in ways that are still very painful to discuss.

Building a company you love, with people you love, for over 15 years, and seeing it all taken away from you and subsequently watching from the sidelines as the culture crumbles and the business is ultimately driven into the ground, is a painful experience.

When experiencing a failure like this, you start doubting yourself. Am I an imposter? Do I have what it takes to build a successful business? And then you snap out of it. Yes, of course you can learn from your mistakes, pick yourself back up, and move forward, but vow to never let something like this happen again.

I needed clarity. I needed to have a purpose bigger than myself. I needed to know what I was trying to accomplish in my life: not just for this year or next year, but overall—forever. I needed to find my True North and develop a 30-year plan for each segment of my life, providing clear direction on what actions I needed to take daily to build the life of my dreams and aspirations.

The pain and embarrassment of failure ignited a burn so powerful that I needed to consolidate all the learnings from my entrepreneurial journey and prove that I could build a successful business the right way. In many ways, I hope this book will prevent similar failures and embarrassment from happening to other entrepreneurs and companies in the future.

With the project management company, we took a slower, steadier, and smarter approach. We protected our equity at all costs, built our own capital to prevent the need to seek outside cash to sustain the growth of the business, reinvested smartly in the proven areas that we knew we could scale, created a culture of intrapreneurship within the organization, and protected our business with everything we had. And for the first time in my 25-year entrepreneurial journey, we were able to access the owners' liquidity that we had built within our strong balance sheet. As chairperson of the project management company, I was able to be a true business owner for the first time in my career. I was not the best person to lead and grow the business operationally, but I could execute and influence at a more strategic level, making sure to implement the learnings of my past. The company had great leadership in Mike, Steve, and the entire team of intrapreneurs and they achieved amazing results by following the clear, 1-page Strategic Plan we refined annually.

It is very powerful when you realize you are *not* the best person to *run* your business. Somebody else is! You might be the best person to guide strategic direction and mentor the leadership, but you do not need to run the daily operations of the business. Getting to a level with your business where you can extract yourself to a more strategic level is not easy, but once you can attain it, everything changes.

We do not become entrepreneurs and business owners so that we can work 80 hours a week and experience constant stress. Yet, that is what I thought being an entrepreneur was!

As our company's chairperson, I could stay at a strategic level and best support the company's long-term objectives by continually assessing business vulnerabilities from above the trees. My mindset as chairperson shifted from an operational mode to a strategic and protective mode.

Then, of course, "Oh, shit!"

With success came complacency, and in the blink of an eye, the business was vulnerable to a big risk: lack of cash flow. Although the business had grown to the $100M revenue mark, it needed to be reset. It needed a plateau year to assess its new vulnerabilities, get back to basics, and ensure the principles that got us to this level were not overlooked.

Ironically, the "Oh, shit!" moment happened *after* I had distilled my learnings into the 7 Principles of Entrepreneurial Success that you will learn about in this book. As I jumped into the trenches with the team to solve our cash crunch, I found that we had violated 4 of the 7 Principles. No wonder we hit a problem zone.

This further reaffirmed that knowing your True North, having a clear Strategic Business Plan, and following the 7 Principles are critical for entrepreneurial success.

YOUR TRUE NORTH AND STRATEGIC BUSINESS PLAN

Your Entrepreneurial Journey

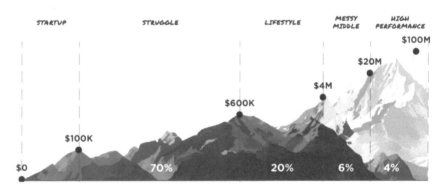

Where are you on your entrepreneurial journey? Just getting started? In the Struggle Zone? Comfortable in a Lifestyle business? Seeking to grow your business to become a High Performance business asset?

To design a plan for your journey, we must seek to understand where you are and the strategies and pitfalls associated with where you are versus where you want to go.

Your True North

There is nothing like a big failure to help you reassess where you are going, but why wait for that to happen? I have always been very goal-oriented; however, I never really took the time to design a comprehensive life plan. I figured that if I kept working hard and doing the right things, good things would also happen to me.

Without knowing what I was truly trying to accomplish, I made some fatal mistakes. Today, I know exactly what I want out of my life: 30 years from now, 10 years from now, 5 years from now, this year, this month, this week, and today. I have complete clarity, and this strategic clarity on my life's plan drives the strategic decisions of my businesses. They must be in sync; otherwise, there is imbalance and risk.

What is your True North? What are you trying to accomplish in your life, and how can being an entrepreneur help you achieve your desired goals?

Your Strategic Business Plan

A 1-page Strategic Plan that *aligned* with my True North objectives was missing for most of my entrepreneurial journey. Without adjoining these two, the decisions I made in my business were misguided and led to pain and failure.

This alignment and knowing exactly what I am trying to accomplish in my life and as an entrepreneur drives every strategic decision our company makes. Our Strategic Plan ensures that we protect the integrity of the 7 Principles of Entrepreneurial Success.

7 PRINCIPLES OF ENTREPRENEURIAL SUCCESS

Principle I: Protect and Grow Your Equity

As basic as this concept sounds, entrepreneurs mistreat and misvalue their equity way too often. I know I did.

I didn't safeguard my equity; I distributed it freely in exchange for partnerships, friendships, or necessary capital. Instead of owning 100% of a company, I would start at 25–50% ownership interest and, over time, dilute myself to a point of diminishing returns.

Once I learned to protect and build my equity properly, I focused on growing the equity percentage I would own and the ultimate dollar value of such equity in my businesses. This is where the magic happens.

Principle II: Build Your Own Capital

When you chase revenue (vanity) without a pure understanding of net operating cash, you will hit a wall, seek cash alternatives, violate Principal I, and dilute (or lose) your equity. That is what happened to me. We grew ourselves cash poor and needed to seek high amounts of bank debt and bring on investors—and it all went downhill.

For entrepreneurs to master Principle I: Protect and Grow your Equity, they must build their own capital for growth, or they will be forced to either slow down their growth or get diluted as they bring new capital into their business to fund the growth. In either scenario, they cannot appropriately grow the ultimate value of their equity.

"Cash is King and Queen" will forever come out of my mouth when talking to entrepreneurs. This is the most important factor driving your business to success or failure. Once I figured this out and respected it, everything changed for me as an entrepreneur. Once your business can achieve $1M+ of net operating cash flow, everything becomes clearer and easier. You get out of the rat race, you do not need to seek investors, you can reinvest into the proper growth for your business yourself, and *yes*, you also get a chance to pay yourself for once. That feels good!

Principle III: Reinvest Smartly

 Isn't it fun to chase shiny objects? Do this with your business and you will pay the price, just like I did. Without a clear Strategic Plan holding them accountable, entrepreneurs engage in wild goose chases and violate Principle I: Protect and Grow your Equity and Principle II: Build Your Own Capital.

Once more, I exemplified a violation of the initial three principles. Initially, I embraced a "spray and pray" approach, thinking extensive expansion across verticals was key to growth. Attempting to excel in numerous areas drained resources, time, money, and focus without yielding benefits—instead, it proved detrimental.

The way to build a strong company is to find a product or service you can be the best in the world at producing or selling and maximize its potential by reinvesting in its growth. You can focus on your pricing strategies and high-margin customers or industries, become the best in your space, own a market segment, and create a sustainable, long-term company with incredible value.

Almost weekly, I hear from entrepreneurs about how they want to develop a new service line or product when they have yet to master and monetize their current business lines. We need to stop this nonsense. The riches are in the niches and so is the growth of your ultimate equity value. Entrepreneurs must become the masters of their primary business lines and not attempt to be everything to everybody.

Principle IV: Build a Culture of Intrapreneurship

Instead of giving up equity in exchange for bringing high-end talent (or friends) into our businesses, there is a much better way that will respect Principle I: Protect and Grow your Equity. Create a culture of intrapreneurship. Provide key members an environment where they can be entrepreneurs (or intrapreneurs) inside your company.

Allow your team to run their own divisions and budgets, empower them to make decisions, provide them compensation plans that motivate and drive them, and invest heavily in their mentorship and advancement opportunities. Show your team that they can be successful within your organization and that you are invested in them as much as they invest their time in your business.

Allow key team members to participate in growing the value of your company without giving up your equity.

Building a culture of intrapreneurship has helped me be successful in all the principles before it:

- Principle I: Protect and Grow Your Equity was protected as we did not need to give key team members real equity to participate in the business's success and value growth.

- Principle II: Build Your Own Capital was protected as the intrapreneurs in the organization were just as motivated to create net operating cash as the owners. Their compensation and management objectives were in line with the company's.

- Principle III: Reinvest Smartly was protected because the intrapreneurs of the organization had shared incentives to ensure that the company was investing wisely and in alignment with the shared Strategic Plan.

Intrapreneurs feeling and acting like business owners have led our business to incredible heights, and they are the future of the business for the long term.

Principle V: Protect the House

Even if you think you have Principles I–IV locked in, make one mistake here and you can lose everything quickly. If you do not protect your equity and if your business is not generating its own capital, then you cannot reinvest in the business, it is harder to build a culture of intrapreneurship, and you will be incredibly exposed.

Even once our business attained the highly coveted $100M mark, we were vulnerable—maybe even more vulnerable than ever before. We took our eyes off the ball, and had we not jumped into action, I could be here telling you about the second time I tried growing a company to $100M and lost it.

Entrepreneurs must protect the business's vulnerabilities with all their might. With growth and success, the target on the back of your business will widen and your exposures will become larger. If there are 100 possible vulnerabilities, and you plug 99 of them, guess what? Yes, water will come bursting through that one last hole you did not plug. And it will *suck*!

Principle VI: Access Owner's Liquidity

What is the point of this whole thing anyway? I had grown a business for 15 years and was left with nothing to show for it. Our cash was being reinvested carelessly into chasing shiny objects and furthering our growth. We never were able to reward ourselves with the business. When did you last get a nice, large profit distribution from your business? I had rarely received one during my entire entrepreneurial journey.

It was only when our business started to make $1M+ in net operating cash flow that I could both continually reinvest smartly into the business and finally start getting access to the liquidity we had built in the business. Why is this? Well, a problem occurs when you start making real money: if you do not spend it, you will be taxed on it.

When we started working with the most sophisticated advisors, I started understanding how to make owner distributions in tax-advantaged and legal ways that benefited both the company and the owners. This changed everything! Prior to working with these advisors, I had no clue these tools and vehicles existed. Furthermore, my businesses had never made enough cash profits for these opportunities to ever be considered.

Principle VII: Move from CEO to Chairperson

For the majority of my entrepreneurial journey, I was the operating leader of the business. I believe that I am a strong operational business leader, but as soon as the businesses grew too quickly, I became a daily problem solver. I would spend 80% of my time operationally solving business problems, jumping from one to the next. I needed more time to think strategically and work on strategic initiatives.

I was working *in* the business, not *on* the business. Most entrepreneurs fall into this trap. They are the "chief cook and bottle washer." They do not hire people to replace them because they believe "nobody can do it as well as me," or they hire people to replace them, then jump to the next problem area and do not adequately develop their intrapreneurs to grow the business.

As a CEO, your job should be to replace yourself in every role you fulfill and either put people in those roles who exceed your talents or invest in mentoring and developing them to fulfill those roles.

Once I figured out that I wanted to be a business owner, not a business runner, I was able to be incredibly strategic, support the CEO and president, help the company attain its Strategic Plan, and by default, get closer to my True North goals.

—

Section II will guide you to understanding where you are on *your* Entrepreneurial Journey and how to look ahead to the next steps on your journey; how to find and create your True North Life Plan to ensure you are heading in the right direction; and how to design a Strategic Plan for your business that aligns with your True North so they work in harmony with each other.

Self-Reflection Zone:

- Retrace your entrepreneurial journey.

    - Where did you start?

    - What were your top 3 successes?

    - What were the top 3 failures you learned the most from?

    - Who were your top 3 mentors?

- Are you clear on where you are on your entrepreneurial journey?

- Do you have a True North Life Plan providing you with clear direction on what you are trying to achieve?

- Do you have a 1-page Strategic Business Plan guiding every decision your business makes?

- Which of the 7 Principles of Entrepreneurial Success do you want to learn more about? Why?

YOUR TRUE NORTH AND STRATEGIC BUSINESS PLAN

"Most people overestimate what they can do in one year and underestimate what they can do in ten years."

– Commonly attributed to Bill Gates, Cofounder of Microsoft

CHAPTER 12

YOUR ENTREPRENEURIAL JOURNEY

"The messy middle is when you have to prove your mettle. It is when you have to focus on the details, stay committed to the mission, and push through the challenges."

— Scott Belsky, The Messy Middle

Where are you on your Entrepreneurial Journey?

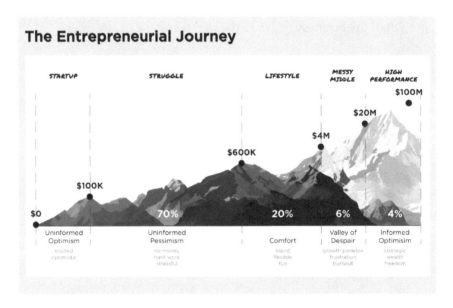

Startup

In the Startup stage, the entrepreneur is in a state of uninformed optimism. They have incredible excitement and optimism for their new venture and hit the ground running. The entrepreneurs are typically bootstrapping their businesses, meaning they are self-funding their operations. They put all their energy into the business, working long hours and wearing many hats. The biggest challenge in this stage is to reach a point where the company generates sufficient revenue to cover its expenses and begin paying the entrepreneur a consistent paycheck.

Struggle

In the Struggle stage, entrepreneurs enter a state of uninformed pessimism. Their business is still so young that there are many unknowns, and they realize that growing a business is much more challenging than when they first began. They are still working very long hours and starting to see some revenue growth. However, they also face significant challenges and early growing pains, such as cash flow problems, employee turnover, a lack of processes, etc. The entrepreneur must persevere through the obstacles and maintain momentum to continue the growth of the business to get to the Lifestyle stage.

Lifestyle

In the Lifestyle stage, entrepreneurs are starting to make a good living from their businesses. They have persevered through the first two growth stages and can now come up for air and take a deep breath. Now that they have a team and consistent revenues, they can work fewer hours and focus on other aspects of their lives, such as family and hobbies. For many entrepreneurs, this was their desired final destination: to build a nice-sized Lifestyle business for themselves and their employees. Others, who had original ambitions to build a larger business, are exhausted by the first 5–10 years of growth in the Startup and Struggle stages and remain trapped in the Lifestyle stage. And then there are the entrepreneurs who desire to continue on their journey in their ambition to build a more significant business. These entrepreneurs will now face more complex challenges.

Messy Middle

The Messy Middle is a stage of rapid growth and change. Entrepreneurs face similar challenges to the Struggle stage, but this time with more complexity and risk as they try to overcome the Growth Paradox. How to scale their business without sacrificing their lifestyle, how to protect and grow their equity, how to build their own capital to self-finance their growth, how to reinvest smartly, how to build a culture of intrapreneurship within their teams, and how to protect the business are all at the core of the challenges the entrepreneur will face in the Messy Middle. The biggest challenge in this stage is to stay focused and make the right decisions that will set the business up for long-term success.

High Performance

In the High Performance stage, entrepreneurs have built a company generating significant revenue, profits, and, most importantly, net operating cash flow. They can finally promote themselves from a day-to-day operational role to a more strategic level where they can continue to refine, improve, and protect all aspects of the business while evaluating new strategic initiatives. In addition to maintaining the momentum and growth of the company, the entrepreneur can now, with the help of professional advisors, access the owner's liquidity within the balance sheet and move from CEO to chairperson, turning their business into a passive business asset.

The road from Startup to a High Performance business is not an easy one. Entrepreneurs are very good at starting new companies but face a daunting task as they transition from being a small Lifestyle business to a successful and sustainable High Performance business that will create wealth for its owners.

Many entrepreneurs work on their business around the clock, endure the stresses and pressures of being responsible for everything, and often end up either highly undercompensated for their efforts or, worse, empty-handed. An alarming 65% of small businesses fail within 10 years (Delfino, LendingTree), only 4% grow to become High Performance businesses ($20M+), while only 0.19% of companies in the US reach annual revenues of over $100M (NAICS). This leaves most 10-year-old businesses somewhere between the Lifestyle and Messy Middle stages.

Meanwhile, private equity firms target these 10-year-old companies that are stuck in the Messy Middle stage. They sweep in to relieve the challenged and stressed entrepreneur and are significantly rewarded by helping the business break through the Messy Middle stage. What is going on here? Why are entrepreneurs unable to cross the chasm to become High Performance, cash-generating machines while retaining all of their equity and control?

In the book *Agglomerate*, Harbour and Laing ask, "How do you go from a business runner to a business owner?" and they highlight that many entrepreneurs don't know how to take the important step of thinking like an owner. This question hits at the core of what I am answering in this book.

Agglomerate: From Idea to IPO in 12 Months
by Jeremy Harbour and Callum Laing

This is a revolutionary book that debunks the myths around entrepreneurship and proposes a disruptive new collaborative model for rapidly growing small- to medium-sized enterprises (SMEs). While the world obsesses over big, multinational corporations and the "unicorn" tech startups, real small businesses, led by talented entrepreneurs, have been allowed to starve. In response, serial entrepreneurs and SME experts, Jeremy Harbour and Callum Laing, have developed a revolutionary new model, Agglomeration™.

Agglomerate
from idea to IPO in 12 months

JEREMY HARBOUR and CALLUM LAING

The model was created to democratize wealth and solve the problems entrepreneurs face in growing their businesses and creating value. An Agglomeration™ combines the best parts of a traditional M&A roll-up with the benefits of an initial public offering (IPO).

Key Learnings:

1. What is wrong with the entrepreneurial dream?
2. Why your business is a success but still not worth anything?
3. The big problems facing small businesses
4. How to unlock your value and access the liquidity you hold in your business
5. How to create the ultimate platform for growth and exit

"How do you go from being a business runner to a business owner?"
—Jeremy Harbour and Callum Laing, *Agglomerate*

This is a struggle I am familiar with. In my earlier entrepreneurial years, I focused my attention and expertise on the Startup stage of business. Startups are exciting, challenging, and extremely rewarding. Entrepreneurs who can successfully get through the initial Startup stage come to realize that their business must mature, and in maturing their business, they enter the dreaded Struggle Zone.

Seventy percent of entrepreneurs are stuck in this Struggle Zone and are challenged to grow their businesses with limited financial and human resources. They exert blood, sweat, tears, and countless years of grinding through this Struggle Zone to progress along the Entrepreneurial Journey to become a profitable and sustainable Lifestyle business.

In the Lifestyle stage, entrepreneurs can take a breath, get paid, and be proud of building a nice company for themselves. Unfortunately, this Lifestyle stage is also a zone of comfort and an entrepreneurial trap.

Consider this scenario: the entrepreneur spends the first 5–10 years getting their business off the ground. This takes a lot of resources—energy, cash, time away from family, and more. We all know that the first few years of a startup are tough. The entrepreneur works long hours, encounters a lot of stress, and is paid last (if at all). As the business enters the Lifestyle stage, it finally has an established base of revenues and employees. The entrepreneur can finally pay themselves a decent salary and take a deep breath.

More often than not, entrepreneurs start their business in their mid- to late-20s, and by the time their business escapes the Struggle Zone and becomes a Lifestyle business, other aspects of life have started happening around them. Relationships, marriage, starting a family, buying a dream home, and wanting a nice lifestyle all come into play. After all, you are an entrepreneur, aren't you? You should be able to afford a nice lifestyle, right?

Entrepreneurs get into the Lifestyle comfort zone that thwarts any attempts to take their business to the next level, and they become trapped.

As entrepreneurs contemplate ways to grow their businesses, they realize that growth can be risky and disruptive to their current comfortable lifestyle.

- Suppose you hire more employees or invest your earnings into increased sales and marketing. In that case, growth might pose a significant risk to your annual income.

- Suppose you bring new partners into your business to access growth capital. In that case, you give up equity and control in your business. That's not good.

- Suppose you get bank financing to invest more capital in your company's growth. In that case, you are adding leverage to the business, signing personal guarantees, and putting your family's lifestyle on the line. That's not ideal, either.

Then how can entrepreneurs grow from a Lifestyle business to a High Performance business? How can they cross this bridge to create true wealth and freedom for themselves?

This is the dreaded Entrepreneurial Dilemma!

Unfortunately, as entrepreneurs attempt to grow from Lifestyle to High Performance, they get stuck in the Messy Middle, the riskiest stage of the entire Entrepreneurial Journey. If the entrepreneur does not break through the Messy Middle, they are then forced to retract to a comfortable, Lifestyle-sized business, or they risk losing control of their business.

If you are not careful in the Messy Middle, you risk losing everything you have built, just like I did.

"Entrepreneurs are always unprepared for the exponential amount of things that can go wrong as they attempt to grow their business beyond a comfortable Lifestyle-sized business," Callum Laing told me. "Part of what gets us entrepreneurs out of bed in the morning is our collective delusion that the next deal will solve everything. . . And, of course, it never does."

Growing a business can be very tricky. Employees and customers come and go, and unexpected disruptions continually pose new challenges. When you attempt to invest in the growth of your business beyond the Lifestyle stage, you will encounter the Growth Paradox.

The Growth Paradox

Ask yourself these three questions:

- As the business grows, am I working longer and longer hours?
- Does every employee hired and customer acquired actually add more work and stress to my life?
- As my team grows, does it feel like I am doing more, not less?

Did you answer "yes" to one or more of the above questions? I'll bet you're wondering what's happening. What you're experiencing is the Growth Paradox.

If you can identify yourself in this situation, you are in good company.

My goal is to help entrepreneurs grow their businesses beyond the Lifestyle stage and achieve their aspirations and dreams without getting stuck in the Messy Middle or, worse, losing their businesses through fatal mistakes. As you grow, your Strategic Business Plan and the 7 Principles of Entrepreneurial

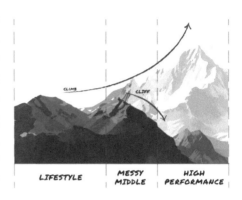

Success will help you overcome the Messy Middle and the Growth Paradox.

During my entrepreneurial journey, I frequently believed I had a handle on things—"I got this! This business thing is easy!"—only to be knocked on my ass several times in defeat and failure. It is not easy.

Through many failures, heavy doses of introspection, and my desire to finally break through the Messy Middle of business growth to achieve my entrepreneurial dream, I developed the 7 Principles.

I guess in my case, failure was, in fact, a prerequisite for success. I needed to learn these lessons to develop the framework for success that I am now sharing with you.

Entrepreneurs must learn, master, and implement the 7 Principles to build a High Performance business that will grow, thrive, and create incredible value.

Self-Reflection Zone

- Which stage of The Entrepreneurial Journey is your business in now?

    - Startup, Struggle, Lifestyle, Messy Middle, or High Performance?

- What 3 results does your business need to achieve to reach the next stage of The Entrepreneurial Journey?

- Do you want to build a High Performance business? If so, why?

- What 3 roadblocks might prevent you from growing your business to the High Performance stage?

Scan the QR code below to get access to *The $100M Journey Workbook* and other valuable resources to assist you on your journey!

CHAPTER 13

YOUR TRUE NORTH

"Whatever the mind can conceive and believe, it can achieve."

— Napoleon Hill, *Think and Grow Rich*

Why did you decide to be an entrepreneur in the first place?

This question must be answered before you can outline a clear and concise plan for you and your business.

I'm not asking you what your business does or why your business exists. The mission of your company may be a deep passion of yours, and that is very important. What exactly are you trying to achieve by being an entreprener? And do you have the grit necessary to accomplish these goals?

Without grit, you'll lack the passion, perseverance, and resilience needed to reach your desired destination. While I can equip you with a compass and principles, your capacity to persist through setbacks, obstacles, and even failures is paramount for success. If this resilience isn't within you, that's absolutely ok! It's crucial for us to ascertain this upfront, before delving into goal-setting, to ensure you possess the determination necessary to achieve the success you envision.

Before we chart a Strategic Plan for your business, we must grasp your ambitions. What are your personal entrepreneurial aspirations? What are your True North life objectives? It's essential for us to understand your motivations.

In his enduring self-help classic, *Think and Grow Rich*, Napoleon Hill unveils a secret that has driven remarkably successful individuals for generations:

"Whatever the mind can conceive and believe, it can achieve."

This statement was intended to emphasize the power of positive thinking and belief in oneself. Hill believed that our thoughts and beliefs greatly influence our actions and abilities and that if we can conceive an idea and truly believe in its possibility, we can work toward achieving it. Essentially, Hill meant that achieving success is a mindset and that anything is possible if we can conceive it in our minds and truly believe that we can achieve it.

Well, what have you dreamed of achieving? If you can be specific with what you are trying to accomplish and you can visualize it happening, it may just, in fact, happen.

***Think and Grow Rich: The Landmark Bestseller —Now Revised and Updated for the 21st Century* by Napoleon Hill**

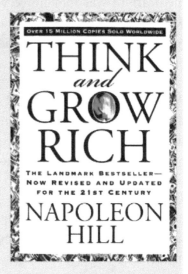

In the best-selling self-help book of all time, Hill emphasizes the importance of having a positive mindset, developing a clear plan, and taking massive action. He also discusses other topics, such as persistence, decision-making, and the power of imagination. The book has hugely influenced the self-help and per-sonal development industry, inspiring people worldwide to pursue their dreams and achieve their goals.

Key learnings:

1. Believe in yourself and have faith that you can achieve your goals.
2. Take action and don't be afraid to take risks.
3. Develop a strong work ethic and stay focused on your goals.
4. Develop a positive attitude and surround yourself with positive people.
5. Don't be afraid to ask for help and learn from others.

"The starting point of all achievement is DESIRE. Keep this constantly in mind. Weak desire brings weak results, just as a small fire makes a small amount of heat."
—Napoleon Hill, *Think and Grow Rich*

As entrepreneurs, we frequently schedule planning sessions with our leadership teams in an effort to develop a strategic plan for our business, yet we fail to spend the proper time to develop our own personal life plans.

I made fatal mistakes in my quest for business success because I did not have a solid personal life plan. These mistakes cost me and those around me dearly. I was running very hard in the wrong direction and for the wrong reasons. I lacked patient ambition and was unclear on what I was trying to achieve in my life and why I was trying to achieve what I was chasing.

"Patient ambition" is the art of accepting delayed gratification instead of the addiction to needing instant gratification for your efforts. It's about foregoing the allure of quick gains in favor of a calculated approach that builds a solid foundation for lasting success.

I had way too much careless ambition. I so badly wanted to achieve entrepreneurial success, and quickly. Unfortunately, I learned the hard lessons associated with running too fast without a proper plan directing my actions.

I never really spent the time to develop my personal life plan. I believed good things would happen if I kept working hard and growing.

Now, I am on a mission to help entrepreneurs avoid these crucial mistakes and help them achieve their entrepreneurial dreams.

Entrepreneurs are very impatient. We strive to achieve our desired level of wealth and freedom as quickly as possible. In chasing business success and growth, we make careless mistakes—sometimes really bad ones. This burning need to grow and achieve our goals as quickly as possible, without following a specific plan with patient ambition, has been the source of many entrepreneurial failures.

Having the discipline and patient ambition to finally create and align a clear plan for both my personal life and that of my business is at the core of how I ultimately broke through the Messy Middle and achieved the entrepreneurial success I was striving for.

Do you know what you are trying to achieve in all aspects of your life? What is your True North?

The simplest method for creating your True North Life Plan is to borrow the straightforward methodology from one of my favorite books, *The One Thing*, by Gary Keller and Jay Papasan.

In *The One Thing*, the authors teach us how to prioritize and achieve our life goals by continually asking ourselves one question: "What is the One Thing that will lead to the best outcome and make everything else easier or even unnecessary?"

The One Thing: The Surprisingly Simple Truth Behind Extraordinary Results by Gary Keller and Jay Papasan

The One Thing is a practical guide to achieving success in any area of life. Keller and Papasan offer a simple framework for getting the most out of life by understanding what matters most and focusing your resources and efforts on that one thing. The authors teach readers to prioritize, eliminate distractions, and take action to achieve their goals. The book begins by discussing the concept of "The One Thing"—a single activity or goal that will have the greatest impact on your life.

Key Learnings:

1. To achieve extraordinary results, focus on one thing at a time. Identify the most important thing that will make the biggest difference and prioritize it.

2. Schedule your day by blocking out specific times to work on your one thing. Eliminate distractions and stick to your schedule.

3. Set specific, measurable goals for your one thing and break them down into smaller, achievable tasks. Celebrate your progress along the way.

4. Adopt a growth mindset and believe that you can achieve your one thing with hard work and dedication. Surround yourself with positive influences and seek out mentorship and guidance.

5. Hold yourself accountable for your progress and results. Continually evaluate your actions and adjust your approach as needed. Seek out feedback from others and learn from your mistakes.

"Extraordinary results aren't built solely on extraordinary results. They're built on failure too. In fact, it would be accurate to say that we fail our way to success. When we fail, we stop, ask what we need to do to succeed, learn from our mistakes, and grow. Don't be afraid to fail. See it as part of your learning process and keep striving for your true potential."
—Gary Keller, *The One Thing*

I have used "The One Thing" method to form a simple, 5-step process for developing your True North Life Plan. These steps provide clarity to help you identify your True North and then make it your priority. This is the direction your compass should guide you every day.

1. Know your True North: Identify the most important thing you want to achieve in your life. Then create subcategories for the most important segments of your life and identify the most important thing to achieve in each area; for example, family and relationships, health (mental and physical), finances, business, and any other area of specific focus and interest.

2. Set goals: Set SMART (Specific, Measurable, Attainable, Relevant, and Time-Bound) goals related to your True North goal. Break down goals for each subcategory in 30-year, 10-year, 5-year, and 1-year increments.

3. Prioritize: Prioritize your quarterly, monthly, weekly, and daily activities to focus on the 1-year goals for all your subcategories.

4. Take action: Take consistent daily, weekly, and monthly action toward achieving your 1-year goals. Ask yourself, "Am I doing something that is helping me achieve my True North Life Plan right now?" If not, stop doing that thing and start doing what is necessary to achieve your True North plan.

5. Track progress: Track your progress and make adjustments as necessary.

I strongly encourage you to use the 5-step process to create your True North Life Plan. This will guide your daily actions toward your ultimate goals in life. In completing this exercise, it became very clear to me what I wanted out of my life in all the critical areas. I now had a plan in front of me every day that guided my actions.

John Mitchell, an entrepreneur and success mentor, provided the best articulation of Napoleon Hill's secret:

"What you envision in detail with emotion on a daily basis is what shows up in your life."

Many studies suggest that 95% of our daily actions are driven by our subconscious mind. These actions, habits, and behaviors occur automatically, often without conscious thought. This means that we have the potential to harness the power of our subconscious mind and train it to work in our favor. By understanding and reprogramming our subconscious patterns, we can enhance our effectiveness, unlock new performance levels, and achieve greater success in various aspects of life.

With a True North Life Plan, you can envision where you want your ultimate destination in life to be, every single day. By doing so "with emotion on a daily basis," your actions will be guided naturally.

Before developing a Strategic Plan for your business, you must clarify your True North objectives, as these two must work in sync.

What is important to you? Don't wait to start working toward it! If you do not have a plan like the True North Life Plan, stop here, go to 100MJourney.com/workbook, download the workbook, and put your True North Life Plan together today!

True North Life Plan

True North Life Plan

What is the One Thing you ultimately want to achieve in your life: your True North?

30 Years	What do you want to achieve 30 years from today?

Family: _____

Health: _____

Financial: _____

Business: _____

10 Years	What do you want to achieve 10 years from today?

Family: _____

Health: _____

Financial: _____

Business: _____

5 Years	What do you want to achieve 5 years from today?

Family: _____

Health: _____

Financial: _____

Business: _____

1 Year	What do you want to achieve 1 year from today?

Family: _____

Health: _____

Financial: _____

Business: _____

Self-Reflection Zone

- What is the ultimate One Thing—your True North—that you would like to achieve in your life?

- Do you have a clear and detailed True North Life Plan? Broken down by time periods and segments important to you? With S.M.A.R.T. goals?

- How can being an entrepreneur help you achieve your ultimate True North Life Plan?

Scan the QR code below to get access to *The $100M Journey Workbook* and other valuable resources to assist you on your journey!

CHAPTER 14

YOUR STRATEGIC BUSINESS PLAN

"Entrepreneurs struggle to cross the chasm from a Lifestyle business to a High Performance business because they do not know there is a specific roadmap that they need to follow."

—Callum Laing, CEO of MBH Corporation

Unfortunately, most entrepreneurs do not start their ventures with a pre-determined, desired, final destination. Instead, they navigate their business without a roadmap, driving aimlessly in circles, hitting bumps, landing in ditches, and going up and down the financial hills until they run out of gas, hit rock bottom, get flipped upside down, and wonder, "WTF just happened?!"

Once you have your True North Life Plan in place and know what you are ultimately trying to achieve through entrepreneurship, you must develop a clear Strategic Plan for your business. This 1-page Strategic Plan has been instrumental in helping me build a business that, in turn, has helped me accomplish the goals in my True North Life Plan.

What is strategy anyway? It is a highly overused word in business. The best definition I have ever heard that crystalized this for me was:

"Strategy is about deploying *limited* resources to maximize an *unlimited* amount of opportunities."—Unknown

Think about it. We are faced with numerous opportunities within our businesses every day. Those who win in the long run stick to their defined Strategic Plan and say "no" to these unlimited opportunities because they realize they have limited resources (people, money, time). The best entrepreneurs protect their businesses—and their resources—from these unlimited opportunities by being disciplined in sticking closely to their Strategic Plan.

As entrepreneurs, we are inherently challenged by the proverbial "Shiny Object Syndrome." This can be controlled and eliminated with clarity, focus, and patient ambition.

Developing a 1-page Strategic Plan for your business can be very rewarding. It is amazing to see and feel a team's clarity when, after a full 8-hour-day session, they have an entire Strategic Plan for the next 3, 5, and 10 years of the business—right in front of them. It's magical!

Entrepreneurs use several formats to develop strategic plans for their businesses. Over the years, I have borrowed principles from Simon Sinek's *Start With Why*, Gary Keller's *The One Thing*, and most notably, Verne Harnish's One-Page Strategic Plan (OPSP) method, from *Scaling Up*, to develop a Strategic Plan that has worked exceptionally well for me and my businesses.

Scaling Up: Mastering the Rockefeller Habits 2.0— How a Few Companies Make it ... and Why the Rest Don't by Verne Harnish

This is a comprehensive playbook for successfully scaling up a business. Harnish explains the four areas companies must master to scale up: people, strategy, execution, and cash. The book provides seven steps to follow to become a successful "Gazelle" (a company that excels in scaling up). Harnish outlines key lessons to ensure success when scaling up, such as focusing on scalable solutions and building a team of passionate and loyal people who will take the company to the next level.

Key learnings:

1. Develop a strategy to achieve long-term sustainability.
2. Cultivate an environment that supports scaling up.
3. Make decisions around people, strategy, execution, and cash.
4. Build your own cash and learn the Power of One changes.
5. Become a successful "Gazelle" by focusing on scalable solutions and building a team of passionate and loyal people.

"If you want to teach people a new way of thinking, don't bother trying to teach them. Instead, give them a tool, the use of which will lead to new ways of thinking."
—**Verne Harnish,** *Mastering the Rockefeller Habits*

The Strategic Business Plan consists of the following components:

A. SWOT analysis

What are the business's Strengths, Weaknesses, Opportunities, and Threats? The information gathered from a SWOT analysis, especially when completed in advance by an executive team, can clarify actions the business needs to take in the Strategic Plan.

B. Core values with behaviors

Clarifying a company's core values and corresponding behaviors is essential because it helps create a shared understanding and a common language for alignment within the company's culture.

C. Mission, vision, and BHAG

What is the mission and vision of the business? Why does this business exist, and what is the most ambitious, long-term (10+ years) BHAG that inspires and motivates everybody in the organization while providing constant direction for all the decisions made in the business?

D. 3-year strategic plan

Where must the business be in the next 3 years to be on track for the BHAG? What specific actions need to be taken over this period for the business to be on track for its goals?

E. 1-year strategic plan

Right here, right now—what are the 5 most important goals your company needs to accomplish this year to put the business in a position to achieve its 3-year goals?

F. Quarterly plan

Determine 5 specific goals and actions for each quarter that will help your business make progress toward achieving your 1-year plan.

With this plan in front of you and your team, you now have a fantastic sense of clarity on what you are trying to achieve and what you must do in the present to start making it happen.

Once this Strategic Plan is completed for the first time, it must be updated and revised annually, ideally a few months before the new annual budget year begins.

The yearly process becomes easier for the business as it simply asks its executives:

- Have our strengths, weaknesses, opportunities, or threats changed?

- Have our core values changed? Do we need to modify the behaviors?

- Is this still our long-term mission, vision, and BHAG?

- Have our 3-year goals changed?

- What are 5 critical goals we need to accomplish this year to help us accomplish the 3-year goals?

- What 5 different goals must we accomplish each quarter to attain the yearly goals?

SWOT ANALYSIS

STRENGTHS	WEAKNESSES	OPPORTUNITIES	THREATS
1	1	1	1
2	2	2	2
3	3	3	3
4	4	4	4
5	5	5	5
6	6	6	6
7	7	7	7
8	8	8	8
9	9	9	9
10	10	10	10

IDENTITY (WHO) FOREVER

CORE VALUES/BEHAVIORS

1
2
3
4
5
6
7

PURPOSE (WHY) 10 YEARS

MISSION

VIVID VISION

TO LIVE VALUES, PURPOSE
1
2
3
4
5

BIG HAIRY AUDACIOUS GOAL

BRAND PROMISE

TARGETS (WHERE) 3 YEARS

FUTURE DATE
REVENUE

MARKET

KEY THRUSTS/CAPABILITIES
3-4 Year Priorities
1
2
3
4
5

SMART NUMBERS/KPI's

GOALS (WHAT) 1 YEAR

YEAR ENDING
REVENUE

THEME

KEY INITIATIVES
Annual Priorities
1
2
3
4
5

CRITICAL NUMBERS/KPI's

ACTIONS (HOW) QUARTERLY

QUARTER 1 GOALS
1
2
3
4
5

QUARTER 2 GOALS
1
2
3
4
5

QUARTER 3 GOALS
1
2
3
4
5

QUARTER 4 GOALS
1
2
3
4
5

The process just keeps repeating itself over and over again. Soon your business and key executives will have a history of Strategic Plans, and they will be able to see the progression of thought processes and attainment over the years.

The annual Strategic Plan must be crystallized annually with the team's complete commitment. Speak now or forever hold your peace! If anybody disagrees or has a challenge to the Strategic Plan, hash it out as a team *before* it is finalized. Once everyone is in agreement, finalize the Strategic Plan, and get behind it!

Once finalized, the business must not deviate from the Strategic Plan unless there is an extreme case for a massive change, in which case the Strategic Plan should be formally revised with the whole team's buy-in.

Inevitably, an opportunity will arise that is not a part of the Strategic Plan. This is the time for extreme discipline on behalf of the entrepreneurs and executives running the business. The business has limited resources, and the team has finalized a Strategic Plan for deploying these resources. Taking on another opportunity will either take additional resources or cause other initiatives to be missed.

It is vital to create a culture within the business to frequently ask each other: "Is this opportunity, new idea, or shiny object in the Strategic Plan?" If the answer is "no," the team should plan to bring up this new great concept or idea at the next annual strategic planning meeting to discuss and review it, and if it makes sense, then incorporate it into the following year's Strategic Plan. Then get back to focusing on the current, approved Strategic Plan.

Entrepreneurs are very opportunistic by nature, so if there is a game-changing opportunity for the business and a decision must be made immediately, get the team together and revise the entire Strategic Plan accordingly. However, I have found that "great" opportunities are not usually urgent, *game-changing* opportunities. Any great opportunity is better approached slowly and more strategically—annually—with patient ambition. If it *is* that great of an opportunity, it can probably wait for the proper investment of resources to be made in the next Strategic Plan.

As an entrepreneur, you will know if your Strategic Plan is working when you and your team start saying "no" a lot more than "yes"; when you start screening customers and your team executes with more patient ambition.

For over 10 years, my business partner, Mike, and I have met annually to work on our Strategic Plan. He commented on its impact: "Our Strategic Plan kept us on the straight and narrow and did not allow us to chase shiny objects. As you grow, you will be presented with many distracting opportunities. Our Strategic Plan held us accountable."

Having a Strategic Plan that provides both short-term and long-term clarity for the business is essential to getting your entire team on the same page as you drive your business to reach its goals.

Self-Reflection Zone

- Do you have a 1-page Strategic Plan for your business?

- What is the BHAG of your business? Do you know what specific actions are needed to achieve your BHAG?

- Is the Strategic Plan for your business clear to your management team?

- Do you have an internal process to evaluate opportunities that are not in your current Strategic Plan?

- When scheduling a Strategic Plan planning session, who are the top 3 people in your business and the top 3 people *not* in your business that you would want in the room to help guide and challenge you?

> To get assistance in creating a Strategic Plan for your business, visit us at 100MJourney.com and request a free consultation.

Scan the QR code below to get access to *The $100M Journey Workbook* and other valuable resources to assist you on your journey!

7 PRINCIPLES OF ENTREPRENEURIAL SUCCESS

"It takes 20 years to build a reputation and 5 minutes to ruin it. If you think about that, you'll do things differently."

—Warren Buffett in *Corporate Survival*

In this section, we review the Entrepreneur's Compass and the 7 Principles that have taught me valuable lessons and, when appropriately executed, have helped me to break through the Messy Middle of high business growth and achieve outstanding results.

Each principle has been split into two parts:

- ***Why*** the principle is crucial for entrepreneurial success (Theory)
- ***How*** entrepreneurs can apply the principle in their businesses (Practice)

At the end of each principle, the entrepreneur is encouraged to take action and apply that principle in their business. If you are serious about building the business of your dreams, you will implement these principles in your business. If you need assistance implementing these principles, we have additional support for you and a workbook for you to download at 100MJourney.com/workbook. Throughout my journey, I have relied heavily on experts from different fields to help me learn and implement these principles. The more you desire to grow, the more support you will need. We are here to help.

7 PRINCIPLES OF ENTREPRENEURIAL SUCCESS

Principle I: Protect and Grow your Equity

Learn why and how entrepreneurs must grow and protect their equity so they remain in control of their own destinies.

Principle II: Build Your Own Capital

Learn why and how entrepreneurs must create their own capital through net operating cash flows rather than relying on bank debt or investment to grow.

Principle III: Reinvest Smartly

Learn why and how entrepreneurs must reinvest wisely and patiently in their growth to build a High Performance business.

Principle IV: Build a Culture of Intrapreneurship

Learn why and how entrepreneurs must fully engage their leadership teams and provide them the opportunity to participate in equity appreciation.

Principle V: Protect the House

Learn why and how entrepreneurs must strategically assess and manage internal and external risk factors that can harm the business.

Principle VI: Access Owner's Liquidity

Learn why and how entrepreneurs can build the strength of their balance sheet and access the liquidity within it.

Principle VII: Move from CEO to Chairperson

Learn why and how entrepreneurs must replace themselves operationally to strategically rise above the business.

PROTECT AND GROW YOUR EQUITY

"Equity is the one thing that is always very hard to ever get back!"

—Anonymous

This first principle emphasizes the importance of protecting and growing one's equity in their business. Equity is the vehicle through which entrepreneurs will ultimately build the wealth and freedom they seek through ownership of a business asset. The more ownership (equity) an entrepreneur has in their company, the more opportunity they will have to create value and maintain control of their future.

Key learnings:

1. Equity is the most important factor for building wealth through a business.

2. Invest in yourself; don't give away equity loosely.

3. Have a clear strategy for allocating equity to partners or key team members that will also protect your interests.

4. Develop a long-term plan to increase your equity ownership and value.

5. Have the proper legal agreements to protect your equity and the business's decision-making mechanisms.

CHAPTER 15

WHY PROTECT AND GROW YOUR EQUITY?

"Never sell your soul."

— Laura Schlessinger (aka Dr. Laura) in *Take My Advice*

For the first 20 years of my entrepreneurial journey, I worked my ass off. I was driven by such a passion to be successful. I wanted to prove to myself and others that I could build and grow successful companies, but equity was not the first thing on my mind. What a dumbass!

I did not pay as much attention to protecting myself, my equity, or my investment. I put myself in vulnerable positions, which ultimately cost me everything. I was naïve, uneducated, and blinded as to why equity is the single most important thing in business. I needed a wake-up call, and I got it—the hard way.

Entrepreneurs must protect and grow their equity in their business at all times and at all costs! It is critical to understand that the more equity you have in your company, the more opportunity you will have to create value and maintain control of your future. This is why we are entrepreneurs.

If your goal, like mine, is to achieve wealth and freedom through building a High Performance company, that will be achieved through one primary mechanism: the equity in your business!

After failed attempts with a venture-funded company during the dot-com era and then being terminated from the company I cofounded—after 15 years of building it—I refuse to get involved in any venture where I do not have significant equity and decision-making authority. It is simply not worth it.

I want to fully invest in myself and other entrepreneurs I trust and believe in!

As my business mentor, Charlie, often reminded me, "The best person to invest in . . . is yourself." I wish I had taken that road earlier in my entrepreneurial journey and stuck to it with confidence.

There is a reason we become entrepreneurs to begin with: we believe investing in ourselves will be more rewarding than creating value for somebody else's business. Otherwise, we would just go get a job for another entrepreneur. We are very confident by nature.

Well, if we are that confident, why invest in anything else? Why not fully invest in yourself by accumulating more equity at every opportunity, never selling your equity, and focusing on building the company's overall value? Doing this will ultimately position you in a much stronger and more stable spot, which will be well worth the effort, even if it takes longer (have patient ambition!).

Unfortunately, some entrepreneurs do not fully commit to investing in themselves, and they throw in the towel due to a heavy dose of self-doubt. The lack of short-term compensation, fear of failure, stress from turbulence, imposter syndrome, business cash-flow issues, and other limiting beliefs creep into our minds.

So what do we do? We drag others into our business alongside us and call them partners. We give them equity to give us a sense of security that we are not alone. We sell equity the first chance we get to "take some chips off the table." We do not appropriately protect and grow our equity as we build our business.

If you do not believe that investing in yourself is the best investment you will ever make, this book is not for you. Entrepreneurship may not be your best route forward either.

Protecting your equity starts on day one! When forming a company, entrepreneurs are immediately faced with a dilemma. Often intimidated by the thought of starting a company alone, most entrepreneurs quickly surround themselves with partners.

Growing up as an athlete, I always loved being part of a team and as an entrepreneur, I have wanted to surround myself with like-minded individuals to form and build companies. But unlike sports, where teams evolve and change each season, business and business partnerships operate less cyclically.

Bringing partners into your business is much more like a marriage. Everybody hopes it will last forever, but if it doesn't, you end up with a big mess to untangle as your business evolves and changes.

Jeffrey Unger, Founder and CEO of G2 Capital Advisors, has seen this repeatedly. He told me in an interview, "Entrepreneurs always have the best of intentions in parsing out equity to others, but then find themselves dealing with a big mess after the business experiences success."

The equity you did not protect at the onset and the corporate documents you failed to ensure fully protected your rights can and will return to haunt you. Imagine losing everything you have built because you did not fully protect your equity stake in the business.

The structure of the operating agreements typically provides decision-making authority for the business based on equity ownership. If you did not protect your equity, you most likely also did not protect your influence over the governance of the business. This leads to partner conflicts or, worse, your termination from the business you have poured your heart and soul into for years. Unfortunately, this happens all the time!

If you do not own 100% of the equity in your business, do you feel that your percentage of ownership is *fair* compared to the other partners' percentages and what they originally contributed to the business or what they are currently contributing to the business's continued growth?

More times than not, the answer I had was: *no*! Maybe I simply overvalue myself compared to the contributions of others. Still, in many instances, I felt I deserved more equity than my partners based on my contributions. I am sure you have felt this way before as well.

"Then why did you put yourself in that position?" you ask. Great question!

- I did not believe in myself enough;
- I did not have enough money to invest 100% of the needed capital;
- I wanted to be on a team versus being a sole entrepreneur;
- it was more fun to build a company with others; and/or
- I did not appreciate the principle of protecting and growing my own equity!

The reasons for protecting and growing your equity are so easy to see. Yet, I found myself in many situations throughout my entrepreneurial journey where I owned a minority of the business I cofounded. I could have started, built, and controlled the entire business on my own and retained most of the equity, but I chose not to.

I always believed the business would grow faster and be more enjoyable with other partners involved. Maybe I lacked the confidence to go for it on my own, or maybe I lacked the capital to fund the business myself, but one thing is certain . . . I did not have any foresight into what I was trying to accomplish for myself or my business and how critical it was to protect and grow the equity I had in the business.

It is easier to give equity away and disregard the importance of proper operating agreements in the earlier stages of the business because, frankly, the business is not worth anything yet.

Then as time goes on, your business grows, and the value of each percent of equity in your business begins to grow with it. The partners' motivations begin to change, the company's direction evolves, and then you realize that the business you have sunk every day of your life into, the business you built, is really not fully yours.

The law of diminishing returns must be evaluated in all equity decisions, especially when equity is handed out at formation. Once you provide an individual with equity, it is very tough, if not impossible, to get back.

Your business must be X percent larger to compensate for the equity you give out carelessly. You will need to work X percent harder to build the ultimate value you are trying to create.

If you are a partner in an entity today where you own less equity than you desire or feel like you deserve, then you need to do something about it. As you go through the entrepreneurial journey, you will either bet on yourself or you won't.

Equity can be costly to purchase (another reason that you should never give it away). In many cases, even if you desire to own more, you may not have enough capital to purchase it, or your partners may not be willing to sell their equity. This is why you must protect your equity at every stage of your business's growth. It is your equity that will be the source of your ultimate success.

When should you sell your equity?

Only when you have accumulated the wealth and value you desire to achieve through that business and are ready to move on should you consider redeeming your equity for cash and exiting. I have learned that the time to sell your equity is only when you are 100% getting out of the business.

If you are selling equity for any other reason—you need cash (capital), you're afraid the company has reached its maximum potential, or you simply just want to take chips off the table to purchase material objects—you should rethink your entire position.

Don't get me wrong; if it is time for you to monetize all of your efforts, go ahead and sell your equity to protect yourself and your family. But the moment you sell your equity, you should fully exit the business and do something else. Maybe even start a new business! This is important for the following reasons:

1. If you sell a majority interest in your company and you become a minority partner, you might as well exit. Did you not believe in yourself? Did you lack capital (Principle II)? Did you not reinvest properly in your business over the years (Principle III)? Do you not have a strong enough team (Principle IV)? You get the idea . . . something is not right. Or . . .

2. If you think the equity value has been maxed out, exit and do something more rewarding in your life. Do not devote your time and attention to a company you no longer believe in.

———

Equity was something that I took for granted. I gave it away loosely upon founding my companies. I didn't protect it. I sold parts of it to take chips off the table, which cost me decision-making control in my company. I did not protect myself in the legal agreements governing the business. These are things I will never do again, nor should you!

As an entrepreneur, we aim to build the value of our equity in our business assets because that is how we will create wealth! You should not tie your success to how fast you grow or how much capital you raise from investors because, ultimately, these will mean very little compared to how much your equity in the company is worth.

The most sophisticated investors and entrepreneurs understand the power of equity and prey on taking advantage of small- to medium-sized business entrepreneurs who repeatedly make the same mistakes. Nothing is more important than equity. Start taking it seriously! Have a plan in place to protect and grow your equity over time by fully investing in yourself and your business!

Self-Reflection Zone

- Have you ever regretted giving away equity in your business? Why did you do it?

- Have you ever purchased more equity from a business partner to grow your interest in a business you were involved in? Was it worth it?

- Do you have an operating agreement that sufficiently protects your ownership rights?

Scan the QR code below to watch a supplemental video about why this principle is so important!

CHAPTER 16

HOW TO PROTECT AND GROW YOUR EQUITY

"Too many entrepreneurs give equity away loosely without calculating the terminal value of such equity."

— Jeffrey Unger, founder and CEO of G2 Capital Advisors

In this chapter, we cover four strategic equity factors that, when not addressed carefully, can cause major issues for entrepreneurs:

1. Allocation of equity to partners

2. Growing your equity interest and value over time

3. Protecting the power of decision-making control

4. Proper legal agreements in place to protect your equity

----

1. ALLOCATION OF EQUITY TO PARTNERS

An entrepreneur must consider the potential consequences of giving away too much equity too early. The biggest mistake an entrepreneur can make is bringing their friends or family along for a ride with the business.

Even with the best intentions, this can become a personal and professional disaster in the long run.

I love Jeffrey Unger's quote that opened this chapter: "Too many entrepreneurs give equity away loosely without calculating the terminal value of such equity." If your goal is to create wealth and freedom from your business asset, then you should have very solid mathematical reasoning as to why you would give away or sell the equity in your company to anybody!

For example, you plan on building a company that you aspire to be worth an exit (or terminal) value of $10M in the future. This might be far from where you are today, but stick with me. Then you give a partner 10% equity in your business as an incentive to accompany you on the exciting journey. Mathematically, you are placing the value of this new partner's contributions at $1M. Is that what you meant to do? Will this new partner provide $1M of value to the business? In some cases, this answer might be a resounding "Yes!" and if so, that is great! But unfortunately, entrepreneurs tend to overallocate equity to others and end up regretting it later in the lifecycle of the business.

This is an example of not understanding the value of the potential equity you have allocated so loosely to this partner and not protecting the ultimate exit value of your equity in the future. It happens all the time. I have done it, you have done it, and we must stop it!

To be clear, I am not suggesting that having equity partners is a bad idea. However, we must clearly understand what they are contributing to the business and how much that needs to be valued in terms of actual dollars before allocating equity to them loosely and without logic.

Entrepreneurs need to determine the right amount of equity to allocate to each partner based on each partner's contributions to the business. There are three types of contributions typically made into a business in exchange for equity: capital (cash), intellectual property (asset), and sweat equity (time). In a perfect world, the partners would all contribute equal capital, intellectual property, and sweat equity and receive equal equity ownership of the business. Simple, right?

Inevitably, one partner will contribute more capital than the other, or one partner will invest more sweat equity into the business without getting paid, and the original portions of equity become disproportionate and unfair. This then leads to conflicts, misunderstandings, and a partner overvaluing their contributions over others'. How many times have you seen this?

Remember, equity is very hard to get back once allocated. The number of partner conflicts I have witnessed over the years because one partner was not contributing their fair share is very discouraging. This happens because entrepreneurs jump into partnerships without fully understanding the ultimate contributions of others. Then as time goes on, life happens—people evolve, change, lose interest, get distracted—and an ultimate conflict appears.

This can be avoided by diligently allocating equity within your business. Protect it with everything you have.

Let's review in depth the three forms of contributions in exchange for equity.

Capital (cash):

If you need to bring an investor into your business because you do not have the capital to fund the business yourself, you may be forced to allocate or sell equity to an investor. Before doing this, the entrepreneur should consider how they can minimize or eliminate the amount of equity they need to provide to investors.

- Build your own capital (See Principle II): By running a frugal business and maximizing net operating cash flow generation, the entrepreneur can reduce or eliminate the need for external funding and maintain the highest level of equity ownership for themselves.

- Debt financing: Entrepreneurs can explore opportunities for debt financing. This involves borrowing money from banks or other lenders with the promise of repaying the loan with interest. Bank loans, government programs, and friends and family loans do not involve giving up the equity interests in the company.

- Convertible debt: This form of financing allows investors to access capital as a loan or debt instrument, with the option (usually the lender's option) to convert the loan and interest into equity in the company at a future date and presumably at a higher valuation. This can be a good option for entrepreneurs who want to maintain as much equity as possible but still need capital today to grow their businesses.

- Revenue sharing: Entrepreneurs can provide investors a percentage of the company's revenue (instead of or in addition to equity) until the investors have received their desired return on investment (ROI). This can be a good option for entrepreneurs who want to keep the equity of their business while still providing investors with a great opportunity. Kevin O'Leary, "Mr. Wonderful" from *Shark Tank* on NBC, presents this option to entrepreneurs in scenarios where he would need too much equity in the business for the requested capital. It provides an option for the investor to get a strong return and for the entrepreneur to retain as much of their equity as possible.

- Negotiation: Entrepreneurs can negotiate with investors to find a middle ground where the investor might be willing to combine some of these methods or present more creative ones.

Overall, entrepreneurs should carefully consider their options for raising capital and seek professional advice to determine the best approach for their business.

Intellectual Property (assets)

Intellectual Property (IP) is typically contributed at the formation of a company. Valuing the IP can be extremely complex and must be agreed to by all partners. Small businesses typically see four types of IP being contributed in exchange for equity.

- Trade secrets: A trade secret is any confidential information that gives a business a competitive advantage over its rivals. In most cases, this is exchanged for equity when a partner brings essential trade secrets to the company.

- Patents: A patent is a government-granted right that gives the owner the exclusive right to make, use, sell, or offer to sell an invention for a period of time.

- Copyrights: A copyright is a form of intellectual property protection that gives the owner the exclusive right to reproduce, distribute, perform, display, or create derivative works from a creative work.

- Trademarks: A trademark is a word, phrase, symbol, or design used to identify and distinguish the goods or services of one party from those of others.

For example, if a company is being formed and the business operations will be operating on a technology platform developed by one of the partners, that partner's contribution of such platform to the business would need to be valued. Then either the partner would be compensated for the IP, or the IP would be contributed to the business in exchange for equity.

Sweat Equity (time):

Sweat equity contributions are difficult for entrepreneurs to value. In most cases, the business does not have the necessary capital (cash) to pay the fair market value for the services of another, so instead of paying them cash, they offer them equity in the business in trade. Unless the person or company providing the service is a significant future leader in the company, this is often a mistake.

Even worse is when we allocate equity to partners without them contributing anything because we just wanted them to "be a part of the business."

As you will read in future principles in this book, I am a big believer that the executive management teams of every company should have a financial stake in the growth of the business and be treated as intrapreneurs. This equity should be in the form of phantom equity, not real equity.

Equity consists of the units or percentage of shares you hold in the company. For clarity, this section will differentiate between real equity ("equity") and phantom equity.

"Equity" refers to the direct ownership interest in a company. This includes common and preferred shares, as well as any other equity instruments such as options, warrants, and convertible debt. Equity gives the holder the right to vote, receive dividends, and share in the company's profits.

"Phantom equity" is a contractual right to receive a certain amount of future value from a company, usually in the form of a cash bonus for the business's value growth. These bonuses are generally based on certain performance milestones or the achievement of certain financial results of value appreciation. Phantom equity is not considered real ownership in the company. It does not give the holder any voting rights or other rights to the company's assets.

Phantom equity provides an opportunity for an important team member to participate in the business's enterprise value growth without adding more voting members and complications that come with real equity partners. This protects the entrepreneur's equity and their management control in the business.

You do not have to be running your business by yourself. By using a phantom equity instrument, you can build your company with others without complicating the actual equity ownership of the company.

Phantom Equity Example

At ABC Company, Sarah provided an opportunity for her executive management team to participate in the equity growth of the company.

Sarah provided each of the four key management team members with a 2.5% phantom equity instrument in the company (10% total). This phantom equity gave each team member a right to participate in 2.5% of the business's future value *if* the business grew to be valued *over* the minimum threshold of $2M (established by Sarah based on the company's $500K in annual profits).

The employees would need to vest into the phantom equity program over 5 years, with a 3-year cliff.

So, if a team member left the company or was terminated by Sarah within 3 years, the phantom equity instrument for that team member would be null and void. At the 5th anniversary, each team member would be 100% vested in their 2.5% stake.

Due to the hard work and dedication of the entire management team, ABC Company grew to generate $3M in annual profit.

Finally, when Sarah decided to exit and sell the company, the business received a multiple of 4 times its annual *profits*.

The company's total equity value was $12M (4 x annual profit of $3M).

The four management team members were still with the company. Each team member held 2.5% of the phantom equity stake in the business. Together the management team was eligible to participate in a total of 10% of the $10M of value created above the $2M threshold.

The *total* value to be disbursed to the phantom equity holders was $1M (10% x $10M), with *each team member* getting $250K (2.5% of $1M).

Sarah's exit value was $11M ($12M value - $1M in phantom equity bonuses).

Sarah was able to protect her equity, control the direction and decisions of her company, build an executive management team that was vested in the company's success, and handsomely reward the team members for their contributions.

Have you ever had a partner who owned equity in your business but did not provide any real value? Yes, you know what I am talking about! It can get nasty. Terminating relationships with equity partners is painful and costly. A major benefit of using phantom equity instead of real equity is the ability to withdraw from the relationship within a period before the phantom equity begins to vest. In this scenario, if the team member does not add value to the growth of the enterprise, you can terminate the employee, terminate the phantom equity agreement, and move on easily!

2. GROWING YOUR EQUITY INTEREST AND VALUE OVER TIME

Entrepreneurs must develop a long-term plan for increasing the value of their equity and have clarity on their True North Life Plan. What are you trying to accomplish financially in your life? Undoubtedly, growing the value of your equity in your business assets will be the root of this goal.

There are two ways to grow your overall equity value from your business asset. Do both of these simultaneously and you will be heading in the right direction!

- Purchase more equity to grow your percentage interest in the business.

Obviously, the larger percentage of equity that you own, the bigger your ultimate value will become and the smaller you will need to build your business to attain your goals. Building a $10M business at 100% ownership is much easier than building a $100M business at a 10% ownership level! It's a big difference in effort and risk but the same $10M ultimate value for the entrepreneur!

The key here is simple: The more equity you own, the easier it will be to achieve your wildest dreams as an entrepreneur.

If you are fully committed to the company, you must build up your own personal finances and continually seek out opportunities to purchase equity from other partners.

Entrepreneurs need to invest in themselves and the businesses they run. Why invest in a public stock of a company you have no part in when you can purchase more of the business you pour your heart into daily?

- Help the company become more valuable. Commit to growing the value of the equity you have in the business you are invested in. Apply the 7 Principles of Entrepreneurial Success that are in this book, especially the following four:
  - Build your Own Capital (Principle II) to continually reinvest into the business without the need for outside investors who will dilute your equity.
  - Reinvest Smartly (Principle III) to expand and scale your business's products and services and gain increased market share.

- ○ Build a Culture of Intrapreneurship (Principle IV) to build a team devoted to your business's success.

- ○ Protect the House (Principle V) to protect your business against the many existing vulnerabilities.

3. PROTECTING THE POWER OF DECISION-MAKING CONTROL

The equity percentage you own is often a major factor in the determination of decision-making and control of your business.

In most private companies, the majority owner and controlling decision-maker of the business would be the person who owns over 50% of the company. However, this is not always the case. The operating agreement of an organization can be structured to have different voting rights that are not directly tied to the percentage of equity in a business. This can be very dangerous since this area is often overlooked by entrepreneurs but not by sophisticated investors. Many investors seek opportunities to purchase minority interests in a company, amend the operating agreement, and put themselves in control of the business, or at a minimum, retain strong veto rights.

Many decision-making structures can be built into a company's operating agreement, e.g., voting rights, veto rights, and rights requiring a supermajority or unanimous consent. Make sure to consult with an attorney representing *your* rights (not the company's) in negotiating important clauses in all agreements governing the business.

If you are in a current situation where you do not control the decision-making of your organization, you need to ask yourself a series of very serious questions.

- Do I trust the decision-making structure of this business to make decisions that are in the best interests of me, my team, and the business?

- How can I protect my equity while gaining more authority, control, and ownership in this business so that I am not investing every day of my life into something that could be easily taken away from me?

Entrepreneurs must protect themselves at all times, and the best way to do this is to ensure that they can participate in or make critical decisions that impact them and the future of the business that they are investing in.

4. PROPER LEGAL AGREEMENTS IN PLACE TO PROTECT YOUR EQUITY

In business, there are always challenges, and there are always endings. Hopefully, the entrepreneur will persevere through all the challenges to experience a successful ending! Unfortunately, too few prepare in advance for the end.

"How is this going to end?" My first boss and mentor, Jeff, asked me this question at a time when I was not open to hearing the message. It still resonates in my head today.

What about you and your business? If your business partnership, or even your business, was to end today, how would the business unwind? Do you know? Because at some point, it is going to end! It might end well, or it might end poorly, but to avoid a major disaster, you should know precisely how the business would unwind.

Regardless of the size of your equity in the business, it is critically important that you protect your equity stake by thoroughly vetting the legal agreements governing the business. It may be uncomfortable; however, the operating and buy-sell agreements should be carefully negotiated upfront, with the end in mind, among all business partners!

Yes, the end! At some point, there will be an end to your equity stake in this business. You must protect this exit at all times. Way too often, entrepreneurs gloss over these agreements or, worse, do not even have them in place. Then, when things get murky, all hell breaks loose, and the entrepreneur risks losing everything they have built.

- **Operating agreement:** an agreement governing the day-to-day operations of the business, including the roles and responsibilities of each partner, rules and procedures for making decisions, and the distribution of profits and losses.

- **Buy-Sell agreement:** a legal agreement that outlines the terms under which a partner can buy out or sell their ownership stake in the company. This agreement should include essential details such as the buyout price, who will receive the proceeds, and how long the agreement lasts.

Without these agreements in place, it will be a lot more unpleasant for the partners of a business who have a conflict when things do not go as planned. Work with a corporate attorney to draft clear and enforceable provisions that will protect and govern the decision-making mechanisms for your business and the equity interest of all partners.

If Steve Jobs (Apple), Jack Dorsey (Twitter), and many other founders of great companies can get fired from the company they formed, it can certainly happen to you too.

———

The key message in this principle is simple: entrepreneurs must continually seek opportunities to grow their equity percentage ownership in their business while simultaneously growing the overall enterprise's value and protecting their equity interest through the documents governing the business.

Believe in yourself, invest in yourself, and protect yourself!

Action Zone

- What is the total equity value you want to achieve from your ownership in your business?
- With your ownership percentage, what enterprise value does your company need to attain to hit this goal?
- What are 3 actions you can take to grow your equity and influence in your company?
- Do you fully understand the decision-making control you have in your operating agreement?
- Do you have a buy-sell agreement to know how your equity is protected?

———

What is one thing that you will start, stop, and continue based on this principle?

Start? _____

Stop? _____

Continue? _____

Need assistance? Contact us at 100MJourney.com to learn more or for help applying this principle in *your* business!

Scan the QR code below to get access to *The $100M Journey Workbook* and other valuable resources to assist you on your journey!

BUILD YOUR OWN CAPITAL

"You can get by with decent people, strategy, and execution, but not a day without cash!"

— Verne Harnish, *Scaling Up*

If there is only *one* principle in this book that you must master . . . this is it. This principle might save you from facing a business mortality event that many entrepreneurs face. What you will learn from this principle, most entrepreneurs have never learned or mastered. If they had, they would have reached their goals much faster and avoided the many pitfalls of entrepreneurship. Entrepreneurs must build their own capital for growth by generating free net operating cash flow through their business.

Doing so helps entrepreneurs protect and grow their equity (Principle I) and enables them to self-finance their growth rather than rely on external financing sources.

Key Learnings:

1. If you do not build your own capital to grow, external forces will dilute your equity.

2. "Revenue is Vanity. Profit is Sanity. Cash is King and Queen!"

3. Net operating cash flow is your business's most important financial metric.

4. Entrepreneurs need to know their self-financeable growth (SFG) rate.

5. How to develop a 3-year Capital Strategy for your business.

CHAPTER 17

WHY BUILD YOUR OWN CAPITAL?

"We were always focused on our profit and loss statement. But cash flow was not a regularly discussed topic. It was as if we were driving along, watching only the speedometer, when in fact we were running out of gas."

— Michael Dell, founder of Dell

I can attribute most of my business successes and failures to one thing: CASH!

Do you know how much cash your business generated last year? I am sure you know how much revenue and profits you made, but I am asking about cash. Take a minute right now to answer this question: Are you fully aware of how much cash flow your business generates?

The number one reason small businesses fail is due to cash flow. According to a study performed by Jessie Hagen of U.S. Bank, 82 percent of businesses fail because of poor management of cash flow.

There should be no excuses. . . "I am not a numbers person" is no longer a viable excuse for entrepreneurs. To be successful, you must master the measurement and improvement of your cash flow.

Businesses that build their own cash-making machine can reinvest smartly (Principle III) into the company's growth and achieve outstanding results and value. On the other hand, businesses that grow their revenues and simply assume that cash will follow become blindsided and frequently fail to survive.

Cash is a form of capital on a business's balance sheet. The more cash a company has to reinvest in its business, the stronger it is, and the less reliance it will have on external financing (capital) sources.

On a mission to attain their wildest ambitions, entrepreneurs put so much energy into growing their businesses. Yet, they typically have no idea what capital they need to build and reinvest in the business to achieve such goals.

So without this education or knowledge, entrepreneurs put all their hard efforts into growing blindly and putting themselves, and their businesses, at risk.

"Let's build a $100M company!" It is a grand vision, but I painfully learned on two occasions that when a company's full energy is put into attaining that milestone *vanity* revenue number, the business makes very large (and sometimes fatal) mistakes along the way.

In March 2000, I attended an online webinar, "The #1 Method to Boost Cashflow, Value, and Profits," hosted by The Growth Institute and Alan Miltz. Alan's webinar was the most instrumental business finance video I have ever watched! It opened my eyes to what net operating cash flow (NOCF) was and how critical it was to grow a business.

One of Miltz's statements in his opening remarks struck at the core of what is wrong with the entrepreneurial mindset: "Entrepreneurs brag about revenue, very few talk about profit, and rarely or never do they talk about cash!"

Think about it. We, as entrepreneurs, brag about our revenue growth (e.g., "My company grew 20% last year!" or "We did $10 million last year!"). We often hear about how much capital an entrepreneur raised for their business. We rarely hear entrepreneurs bragging about their profits. But we *never* hear an entrepreneur talk about how much cash they made because they either do not have any cash or do not even know how to calculate their net operating cash flow!

This needs to change, and it needs to change now! NOTHING (yes, I am yelling here) is more important than cash; entrepreneurs must manage, track, improve, and master the art of making cash!

Everything got clearer and easier when we realized how vital cash generation was and how we needed to build a self-financing capital strategy for our business. We protected and grew our equity (Principle I), built our own capital (Principle II), and reinvested smartly (Principle III) to grow our business the right way! Do you see how these three principles play into each other?

Miss one of these principles, and you jeopardize everything you have built. This happened to me during my entrepreneurial journey, and I am sure you have either experienced or witnessed this. I chased revenue growth for the sake of building a large company and bragging about how big we were, and as a result, I had no idea if we were making cash or not. Still, we continued to reinvest in the business. Ultimately, the business ran out of oxygen and became weak and vulnerable.

Many entrepreneurs like me cast a large vision—"let's grow to $100M"—because it is sexy, fun, exciting, and challenging. We envision this being an extremely rewarding objective as well. Then we embark on the plan to grow. Unsure of how to build the capital to reinvest in the business to attain our goal, we just start running.

Then inevitably, we run out of oxygen and, without fully understanding how much capital we need to achieve our growth plans, we seek investors to help us grow the business. These investors dilute the entrepreneur's equity and take control of the company.

I have learned the hard way that you cannot embark on a growth plan for your business without clearly planning how much capital you need for your goals and how you will build such capital through your existing operations. You need a capital strategy. You need to know how fast your company can afford to grow without bringing other investors or outside capital into your business.

I wish I had understood—before it was too late—this paragraph in the article, "How Fast Can Your Company Afford to Grow?" (by Neil C. Churchill and John Mullins) in the popular *Harvard Business Review*:

> Everyone knows that starting a business requires cash, and growing a business requires even more—for working capital, facilities and equipment, and operating expenses. But few people understand that a profitable company that tries to grow too fast can run out of cash—even if its products are great successes. A key challenge for managers of any growing concern is to strike the proper balance between consuming cash and generating it. Fail to strike that balance, and even a thriving company can soon find itself out of business—a victim of its own success.

A victim of its own success.

I cannot tell you how painful these words are. Imagine having built a thriving business that fails because it was a victim of its own success. This stems from an entrepreneur's lack of understanding of why cash generation is so much more important than simply growing revenues.

"How Fast Can Your Company Afford to Grow?" by Neil C. Churchill and John Mullins, *Harvard Business Review* (May 2001)

In their article for *Harvard Business Review*, Churchill and Mullins examine how fast a company can afford to grow. They argue that companies must take a measured, strategic approach to growth rather than simply trying to grow as fast as possible. They offer a framework for understanding the costs and benefits of growth and suggest that companies must balance their desire for growth with their need to maintain financial stability and operational excellence. Ultimately, they advise companies to focus on sustainable growth aligned with their long-term vision and goals.

How Fast Can Your Company Afford to Grow?

by Neil C. Churchill and John W. Mullins

Harvard Business Review

Key learnings:

1. Companies need to control their growth and not just aim to grow as fast as possible.
2. Companies must maintain financial stability and operational excellence as they grow.
3. There are costs and benefits associated with growth that need to be carefully considered.
4. Companies must clearly understand their growth objectives and how they fit into their long-term vision and goals.
5. A sustainable approach to growth is essential for long-term success.

"Fortunately, there's a straightforward way to calculate the growth rate a company's current operations can sustain and, conversely, the point at which it would need to adjust operations or find new funding to support its growth."
—Neil C. Churchill and John Mullins,
"How Fast Can Your Company Afford to Grow?"

I am sure you know how much revenue your business made last year, but do you know how much cash your business generated? My guess is that you don't exactly know this answer! This is not a knock on you. According to a case study by Alan Miltz, when asking over 3000 CEOs, he could not find *one* CEO that had a correct understanding of net operating cash flow.

I will never forget Alan Miltz repeating over and over throughout the webinar:

"Revenue is Vanity. Profit is Sanity. Cash is King and Queen!"

He would emphasize that "without cash, all other measures of success for your business are meaningless."

Without cash, your business will die, or you will be forced to severely dilute your equity as you seek investors willing to invest the capital your business needs to survive.

Without cash, your business will die.

Sounds simple, yet we do not respect cash as much as it deserves. It is more important than revenue, more important than profits. It is the prime component of business survival, growth, and sustainability.

These powerful words hit me hard. Sometimes the right message, from the right person, at the right time, can change a life. This is what Alan's words did for me. My lightbulb turned on. It took me 20+ years of building companies to finally figure this out. I heard it this time and hope you hear it clearly as you read this book. Frequently, we understand things cognitively, but until we are emotionally motivated to really understand it, the information passes through the brain without being retained or executed.

Do not ignore this principle! In the next chapter, I will provide tools to help you build your own capital. Make the commitment that you (or somebody on your team) will make cash the most important metric your business will measure going forward.

To achieve your wildest entrepreneurial dreams, you must become a master at generating free net operating cash flow for your business.

Be frugal, collect money owed to you, don't carelessly overspend the cash you generate, and build a minimum cash reserve of up to six months of operating cash as an emergency fund. These are not just concepts for companies. Entrepreneurs should do the same in their personal lives as well! As you do this, your business and personal balance sheets will continue to appreciate in ways you never imagined.

This concept also applies to your personal finances. The more cash you save and build up, the more you can purchase more equity in your business or invest in other assets to build long-term wealth.

In my late 20s, when I read the book *Rich Dad Poor Dad*, there was one statement that the author had written that never fully connected with me until it finally happened in my life.

"The hardest thing an entrepreneur will ever do is make their first million dollars [in net operating cash flow]."

Everything becomes much easier once this incredible feat is accomplished. We are not referring to your P&L showing $1M in profits (although that is also good). We are talking about having $1M in free net operating cash flow.

"Cash is King and Queen!"

The bottom line is that you must build a cash-making machine that generates the capital you need to self-finance your own growth so you do not need to be at the mercy of banks, investors, private equity firms, or any other outlets that will negatively impact your equity (Principle I: Protect and Grow your Equity).

Time is on your side if you compound your business with your own capital; if you reinvest the net operating cash flow smartly back into the business and gradually build up your own capital, your business will benefit from the compounding effect. As your capital increases, your business will have more resources to invest and grow, resulting in higher returns.

Self-Reflection Zone

- Do you know how much net operating cash flow your business generated last year, month, or week? Are you afraid to look?

- What would be possible for your business if your focus was "Cash is King and Queen" rather than chasing revenue?

- How would you feel knowing you had abundant cash flow for growth?

- Who on your team needs to watch the webinar by Alan Miltz or read the "Cash" chapter of the book, *Scaling Up*?

Scan the QR code below to watch a supplemental video about why this principle is so important!

CHAPTER 18

HOW TO BUILD YOUR OWN CAPITAL

"Revenue is Vanity. Profit is Sanity. Cash is King and Queen!"

— Alan Miltz, CASHFlow Story

This chapter will help you understand how to build your own capital and design a 3-year Capital Strategy for reinvesting smartly into your business. You will see how to do this without bringing in capital from outside investors so you can keep your equity in the company.

1. Measure your net operating cash flow.

2. Improve your net operating cash flow.

3. Calculate your self-financeable growth (SFG) rate.

4. Develop your 3-year Capital Strategy.

---

1. MEASURE YOUR NET OPERATING CASH FLOW

Surely, if you are reading this and have a background in high-level finance, this might be elementary to you. However, I have shown Alan Miltz's "The #1 Method to Boost Cashflow, Value, and Profits" webinar to many entrepreneurs of small- and mid-sized companies ranging from $1M–$100M in size. Like me, they have all had their eyes opened to how we *should* measure our business performance.

If we were in a room with 100 entrepreneurs and I asked them to raise their hands if their P&L statement was the primary document they looked at to judge the performance of the business, I suspect that over 90% of the room would raise their hands! Alan Miltz relates this to reading the first chapter of the best murder mystery novel and trying to guess how the story unfolds. That is what we entrepreneurs do every day! Profit from the P&L statement, while essential to measuring success, does not necessarily equate to actual cash flow generated by the business.

For most of my entrepreneurial career, my primary source of financial analysis was the P&L statement. As I gained more sophistication, I graduated to the balance sheet. The balance sheet shows a much clearer picture of the health of a company than the P&L statement. However, we cannot see the full story being told by only looking at these two financial statements.

Alan Miltz said, "The biggest problem with every business is the lack of understanding of cash flow. We have made cash flow too complex. The game of business is to make more cash!" ("#1 Method" webinar).

As I listened to Miltz on the Growth Institute webinar, I was introduced to a simple method of calculating net operating cash flow and why it should be the most important metric an entrepreneur uses to evaluate the financial health of their business. The webinar changed my paradigm for good.

Net operating cash flow focuses on the actual inflow and outflow of cash and the ability of a business to fund its expenses, operations, and investments it needs to grow and achieve its goals. It also helps entrepreneurs understand their future capital needs, a key component to developing a 3-year Capital Strategy. Without it, they cannot plan for the future or determine the business's financing needs.

Net Operating Cash Flow

In this example, the small business generated $10M in revenue in the current year and had a gross margin of $4M after deducting the cost of goods sold. The company also had $3.5M in operating expenses, resulting in a pre-tax net profit of $500K.

The business grew 11% over the prior year and increased its net income. Not bad, right?

Profit & Loss	31-12-2022 12 months	31-12-2023 12 months
Revenue	9,000,000	10,000,000
Cost of Goods	5,400,000	6,000,000
Gross Margin	3,600,000	4,000,000
Overheads	3,150,000	3,500,000
Operating Profit	450,000	500,000
Extraordinary Income/Expenses	0	0
Interest Paid	0	0
Net Profit Before Tax	450,000	500,000
Taxation	180,000	200,000
Net Profit	270,000	300,000
Dividends Paid	150,000	150,000
Retained Profit	120,000	150,000

To answer that question fully, we also need to look at the balance sheet to review the change in working capital and the business's net operating cash flow.

Change in balance sheet accounts over the prior year:

Balance Sheet	31-12-2022 12 months	31-12-2023 12 months
Cash	250,000	250,000
Accounts Receivable	1,200,000	1,600,000
Inventory	1,800,000	2,400,000
Other Current Assets	0	0
Current Assets	3,250,000	4,250,000

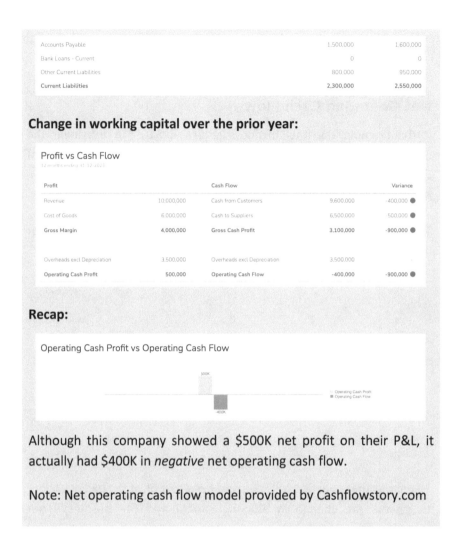

Accounts Payable	1,500,000	1,600,000
Bank Loans - Current	0	0
Other Current Liabilities	800,000	950,000
Current Liabilities	**2,300,000**	**2,550,000**

Change in working capital over the prior year:

Profit vs Cash Flow
12 months ending 31-12-2023

Profit		Cash Flow		Variance
Revenue	10,000,000	Cash from Customers	9,600,000	-400,000 ●
Cost of Goods	6,000,000	Cash to Suppliers	6,500,000	500,000 ●
Gross Margin	4,000,000	Gross Cash Profit	3,100,000	-900,000 ●
Overheads excl Depreciation	3,500,000	Overheads excl Depreciation	3,500,000	-
Operating Cash Profit	500,000	Operating Cash Flow	-400,000	-900,000 ●

Recap:

Operating Cash Profit vs Operating Cash Flow

Although this company showed a $500K net profit on their P&L, it actually had $400K in *negative* net operating cash flow.

Note: Net operating cash flow model provided by Cashflowstory.com

It's worth noting that having negative net operating cash flow isn't necessarily bad, especially if the business is in a growth phase and the owners are consciously investing in new equipment, technology, or marketing efforts. However, negative cash flow can be a warning sign if it continues over an extended period or if the business owners aren't investing in planned growth initiatives.

2. IMPROVE YOUR NET OPERATING CASH FLOW

As an entrepreneur, you must help your management team win at the game of making cash! There are many ways to do this, but it must be a focus for the entire organization. As the CEO of your business, you should make net operating cash flow the #1 metric and report to monitor.

Following are two amazing tools I learned from Alan Miltz that entrepreneurs can use to maximize their company's net operating cash flow. We have invested the time to implement these tools in our businesses, and have found the time investment is well worth it. More of these tools can be found in the book *Scaling Up* or at CashflowStory.com.

Cash Flow Ladder

"If you do not know where you make and do not make money, you are in trouble."—Alan Miltz, CASHFlow Story

The Cash Flow Ladder is a model used to evaluate specific segments of your business by division, industry, product or service, and customer. Instead of measuring your segments by gross margin or gross profits criteria, the Cash Flow Ladder clearly shows the marginal cash flow you make from each segment.

Entrepreneurs usually measure their gross margins correctly, but they do not always consider the cost of overhead or the carrying cost of working capital. This model helps entrepreneurs evaluate opportunities to improve their net operating cash flow. Opportunities may include any of the following:

- Pricing and Gross Margins: Does your company have a strong pricing model that generates strong gross margins with payment terms that are favorable to your business?

- Cash Conversion Cycle (CCC): Do you measure and continually improve the timing differences between the amount of the company's cash that is tied up in working capital before your customers pay for the products sold or services rendered?
    - Get payment terms with your vendors,
    - collect money from customers in advance, and
    - invoice and collect quickly.

A Cash Flow Ladder provides entrepreneurs with a specific view of how certain segments of your business are performing on the following metrics:

- revenue and gross margin
- allocation of overhead to determine net gross margin
- working capital (accounts receivable + prepaid expenses - accounts payable) to determine working capital percentage
- marginal cash flow

In doing this exercise, you may be surprised to find that specific segments or customers you thought were great are actually not good at all.

You may remember me mentioning earlier that it wasn't until we did this exercise for our business that we discovered that for every $1 in revenue we were getting from a particular customer, it would cost us $1.25 of cash flow to perform the business. Ouch!

By force-ranking your products, services, industries, customers, or other business segments on a Cash Flow Ladder, you can mathematically see where you are making cash versus where your cash is being eaten.

Using simple conditional data formatting, you can easily create a Red - Yellow - Green visual scorecard based on your desired key metrics and review the scorecard every month. Doing this will give your management team a tool to help drive net operating cash flow for the company!

Cash Flow Ladder

Segment	1	2	3	4	5
Revenue	4,960,000	3,589,800	1,547,700	159,500	306,090
COGS	3,135,000	2,667,400	1,029,000	122,500	241,370
Gross Margin $	1,825,000	922,400	518,700	37,000	64,720
Gross Margin %	36.79%	25.70%	33.51%	23.20%	21.14%
Overhead Costs	302,000	219,200	268,000	9,700	18,690
Net Gross Margin	30.71%	19.59%	16.20%	17.12%	15.04%
Accounts Recievable	697,000	835,000	149,982	25,830	7,184
Prepaid Expenses	0	250,000	0	0	0
Accounts Payable	269,000	123,000	167,500	11,560	9,924
Working Capital	428,000	962,000	(17,518)	14,270	(2,740)
Average AR Days	51	85	35	59	9
Average AP Days	31	17	59	34	15
Working Capital Days	20	68	-24	25	-6
Working Capital %	8.63%	26.80%	-1.13%	8.95%	-0.90%
Marginal Cash Flow %	22.08%	-7.21%	17.33%	8.17%	15.93%

NOTE: A Segment can be a division, industry, product or service, customer, or any other category you want to evaluate. This model can be used to analyze your business in many different ways.

As you can see from the Cash Flow Ladder example above, not all segments of this company are delivering the same Marginal Cash Flow result to the company.

Segment 1, the company's largest, has a strong Gross Margin % and Marginal Cash Flow %.

Segment 2, however, is costing the company cash. Every time it produces business in Segment 2, the company loses cash strength (demonstrated by the -7.21% Marginal Cash Flow).

The management team should work to improve all segments moving from red to yellow to green by executing the Power of One (more on this coming up) and pulling the various triggers to improve the Marginal Cash Flow %.

Action items may include:

- Improve the Gross Margin % of a segment by increased customer pricing or better-negotiated vendor rates to reduce the Cost of Goods Sold (COGS).
- Become more efficient and reduce the cost of overhead to support the segment.
- Improve the customer's payment terms in a segment to reduce the outstanding accounts receivable (AR) and the average AR days.
- Improve the payment terms with the suppliers to reduce the prepaid expenses the company needs to outlay to earn revenue.
- Or renegotiate payment terms with suppliers or vendors to increase the timing of accounts payable (AP) expenses and average AP days.

Any of these actions, individually or combined, would move Segment 2 from red to yellow to green. If you cannot move the needle and the segment stays in red (or yellow), this segment is bleeding your cash dry and it may be time to make some hard decisions.

Similarly, one may look at the strong Marginal Cash Flow generated by Segments 3 and 4 and develop marketing and sales strategies to increase revenue driven from those segments.

You can build your own Cash Flow Ladder by downloading *The $100M Journey Workbook* at 100MJourney.com/workbook.

Power of One

"By giving the cash flow statement just a little more consideration, and tweaking 7 key financial levers outlined . . . a company can grow considerably faster using its own internally generated cash than by raising or borrowing external capital."—Verne Harnish, *Scaling Up*

Now that you have your Cash Flow Ladder, the next step in maximizing your net operating cash flow is to use the Power of One to improve the marginal cash flow derived from each segment of your business and the net profitability of your entire business. The Power of One is simple, and a more detailed explanation of the theory and model can be found in Verne Harnish's *Scaling Up*.

Too often, entrepreneurs focus on big monumental shifts while tiny 1% shifts can make an incredible difference. Entrepreneurs must work with their finance and management teams to continually seek areas to improve the business's financial health. A small 1% change throughout several financial levers in your business can greatly impact your cash and profitability. This model provides a simple way to evaluate changes you should consider and the impact those changes can have on your net operating cash flow.

The Power of One suggests there are seven levers within a business that you can pull and even small 1% changes can lead to dramatic changes to your cash flow. Over time, these small improvements compound and lead to significant gains in productivity, profitability, and overall business success.

The seven levers are:

Profit Levers

1. Price
2. Volume
3. COGS
4. Overheads

Working Capital Levers

5. AR Days
6. Inventory/Work in Process (WIP) Days
7. AP Days

Power of One

Let's assume the example company sets a goal to improve the following areas by 1% or 1 day over the next year:

- Pricing (increase 1%)
- COGS (decrease 1%)
- Overheads (decrease 1%)
- AR Days (decrease by 1 day)

Here's how these improvements could impact the company's net operating cash flow over one year:

				Net Cash Flow	Operating Profit
Your Current Position				0	500,000
Your Power of One	-	1.0 +	Reset	Impact on Cash Flow	Impact on Operating Profit
Price Increase	-	1.0 +	%	84,000	100,000
Volume Increase	-	0.0 +	%	0	0
Cost of Goods Reduction	-	1.0 +	%	68,000	60,000
Overheads Reduction	-	1.0 +	%	35,000	35,000
Reduction in Accounts Receivable Days	-	1.0 +	days	27,397	
Reduction in Inventory Days	-	0.0 +	days	0	
Increase in Accounts Payable Days	-	0.0 +	days	0	
Your Power of One Impact				↑ 214,397	↑ 195,000
				Net Cash Flow	Operating Profit
Your Adjusted Position				↑ 214,397	↑ 695,000

Over one year, if the company increases pricing by 1%, decreases COGS by 1%, decreases overheads by 1%, and decreases AR days by 1, it has a $195K positive impact on profit! But more importantly, it has a $214K impact on cash!

Note: Power of One model provided by Cashflowstory.com

3. KNOW YOUR SELF-FINANCEABLE GROWTH (SFG) RATE

> *"The self-financeable growth (SFG) rate . . . is the rate at which a company can sustain its growth through the revenues it generates without going hat in hand to financiers."*—Neil C. Churchill and John Mullins, "How Fast Can Your Company Afford to Grow?"

Do you know how fast your company can afford to grow? Do you know your self-financeable growth (SFG) rate?

I never did; I just figured the faster we grew, the better, but I had no clue how fast our company could actually afford to grow. I thought raising capital from investors at a strong valuation was a sign that we were heading in the right direction, only to discover that it might be the worst possible thing to do.

I learned that the more net operating cash flow your business generates (not how much revenue or profits are displayed on your P&L statement), the more your company's SFG rate will grow.

SFG Rate

Neil C. Churchill and John Mullins's article, "How Fast Can Your Company Afford to Grow?" provides a perfect example of an easy way to calculate the growth rate a company can sustain and still fund itself.

Using the same financials from the prior examples in this chapter, we can calculate the SGF rate:

Duration Cash Is Tied Up (in days)

Accounts Receivable	58	AR / (Sales / 365)
Inventory	146	Inventory / (Cost of Sales / 365)
Operating Cash Cycle (OCC)	204	AR Days + Inventory Days
Accounts Payable	97	AP / (Cost of Sales / 365)
Cost of Sales	107	OCC - AP Days
Operating Expenses	102	

Income Statement per Sales Dollar

Sales	$1.000	
Cost of Sales	$0.600	Cost of Sales / Sales
Operating Expenses	$0.350	Operating Expenses / Sales
Total Costs	$0.950	Cost of Sales + Operating Expenses
Profit (Cash)	$0.050	Sales - Total Costs
Tax and/or Distributions	-$0.035	Cash Disbursements
Net Cash	$0.015	Remaining Cash

Amount of Cash Tied Up per Sales Dollar

Cost of Sales	$0.314	Cost of Sales per $1 * (Cost of Sales Days / OCC Days)
Operations	$0.175	Operating Expenses per $1 * (Operating Exp Days / OCC Days)
Cash Required for each OCC	$0.489	Cost of Sales per $1 + Operations per $1
Cash Generated per Sales Doller	$0.015	Sales - Total Costs

SFG Rate Calculations

OCC SFG Rate	3.07%	Cash Generated per $1 / Cash Req for each OCC
OCCs per Year	1.786	Days per Year / OCC Days
Annual SFG Rate (current)	5.47%	OCC SFG Rate * OCCs per Year

In this example, the company can afford to grow 5.47% year over year with its own financing from its operations. It will need funding from a commercial bank or private investors if it seeks to grow more than 5.47%.

Note: SFG model provided by FinancialWing.com

The SFG rate clearly shows the point where the business will need to either adjust or find new funding from outside sources to support the growth it desires.

This is a critical step required to determine your capital strategy. You need to know the rate at which your company can grow through the net operating cash flow it generates (your SFG Rate) without going hat-in-hand to investors or bankers.

If you grow *beyond* your SFG rate, you will grow into a big hole, and trust me, you do not want to be there. Conversely, if you can grow *within* your SFG rate or know precisely what other capital you will need to achieve your growth desires, you can design a 3-year Capital Strategy to accomplish your goals.

It is no wonder we entrepreneurs do not have clarity on our capital strategy. We are not even sure what cash (capital) our business generates or what our SFG rate is.

As an entrepreneur, your eyes are frequently bigger than your appetite. In your attempt to bite off more than you can chew, you put your business and, more importantly, your equity at significant risk.

Knowing your SFG rate is extremely important. If you still are committed to growing more than your SFG rate, that is fine, but you need to have a well-thought-out capital strategy to accomplish this goal, as you will most likely require additional external financing to achieve your growth objectives. This is where the 5 Ps come into play: Proper Preparation Prevents Piss-poor Performance. By knowing that you need capital to attain your growth plans, you can strategically plan for this capital in your 3-year Capital Strategy.

4. DEVELOP YOUR 3-YEAR CAPITAL STRATEGY

A 3-year Capital Strategy outlines how a business plans to invest its capital effectively and efficiently to support its long-term growth and sustainability.

Jeffrey Unger (G2 Capital Advisors) has never encountered a CEO who can answer this important question:

"What is your 3-year Capital Strategy?"

I know I couldn't answer it.

I assumed that if our revenue and profits grew steadily, we could continually reinvest aggressively into our growth and eventually achieve our vision of success. We didn't have a 3-year Capital Strategy! We had a vision to build a large company.

If I had to guess, you do not have a 3-year Capital Strategy either.

Heck, most businesses do not know how much net operating cash they generate or how fast their company can afford to grow (their SFG rate). Without these, how could entrepreneurs have an accurate strategy for managing the capital they need to accomplish their goals?

Unfortunately, most entrepreneurs have never received formal education in creating a capital strategy. I graduated college with a bachelor's degree in accounting and was never taught how to create a capital strategy.

Will you invest it in marketing, sales reps, new systems, machinery, or inventory? What are the best investments to help your business generate more net operating cash flow and further increase your SFG rate? This is the game you are playing now!

The 3-year Capital Strategy begins with a detailed understanding of where the entrepreneur desires their business to be in the future. This step should be clearly articulated within the Strategic Business Plan.

With clarity of where the entrepreneur wants the business to be in the next three years, the entrepreneur must understand clearly where they are currently so that they can identify the gaps between the current state and their desired destination. By doing this, the specific strategies and the capital associated with executing the strategies will be clear.

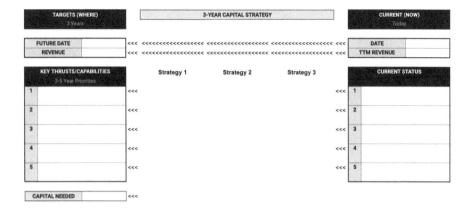

For example, if you aspire for your company to grow to $20M in revenues over the next three years, you need to answer the following questions:

1) What was your revenue in the past year?

2) What specific strategies will you execute to grow the revenues of the business?

3) How much capital will be needed to execute the strategies?

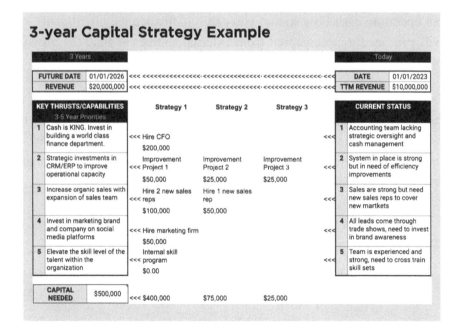

3-year Capital Strategy Example

The company is currently generating $10M of revenue and the entrepreneur believes the business will be able to attain its 3-year growth plan of reaching $20M in revenues through executing the following strategies:

- hire a CFO,
- invest to improve operational systems,
- add 3 new sales representatives,
- engage a digital marketing agency, and
- elevate the skill sets of the current team.

With the strategy on how to attain the 3-year objectives in place, the entrepreneur must estimate the capital requirements needed to fund the growth strategies.

To complete the 3-year Capital Strategy, you need to know how you will finance the investments needed. Does your company generate enough net operating cash flow so that you can self-finance the investments, or will you need to seek capital from external sources to fund the growth plan?

Don't forget that growing faster than your company can afford to grow (SFG rate) is risky and determining how to fund this growth is critical to protecting Principle I: Protect and Grow Your Equity. I strongly advise that you work with your CPA, financial advisor, or other professionals who can guide you through this process.

3-year Capital Strategy and SFG Rate Financial Model

If the owner of the company (from the same examples used in this chapter) that is generating $10M in revenue seeks to grow the business to $20M over the next three years to accomplish its 3-year goal, the owner must develop a capital strategy to finance the investments they cannot self-finance.

The company has an SFG rate showing self-finance growth rate capability of 5.47% in its first year of growth. Using a variety of assumptions purely for illustration purposes, the owner of this company determines that they need $500K of additional capital to finance the company's growth, so they secure a 5-year commercial-bank term loan.

The following model shows how the company would grow, become more profitable, increase its SFG rate, and pay back the loan principal and interest.

Year	SFG Rate From Prior Years Performance	Financed Growth	External Debt Balance	Principal Repayment	Interest Expense	Revenue	Net Income After Taxes and Debt/Interest Payments
1	5.47%	14.53%	$500,000	-$100,000	-$50,000	$12,000,000	$582,000
2	28.03%	0.00%	$400,000	-$100,000	-$40,000	$15,363,971	$797,202
3	35.89%	0.00%	$300,000	-$100,000	-$30,000	$20,878,350	$1,143,579

Again, please note that this is a simplified example with many base assumptions. You should consult with a CPA or financial professional to consider your specific business circumstances.

Remember that if you desire to grow the business beyond your SFG rate, that is ok! You just need to have a strategy in place to get this capital financing. Whether from a bank or an investor, this plan should be carefully laid out and discussed with advisors. And most importantly, be careful not to violate Principle I: Protect and Grow Your Equity.

Proper commercial-bank financing is the best way to access additional capital for your business without selling equity. Using bank leverage to grow your business is undoubtedly a pillar of the American economic system. Using leverage must be done responsibly and with the strongest balance sheet possible.

If not done responsibly, the business becomes overleveraged and you get caught in the Growth Paradox. The only way out of leverage is to grow faster and make more money, which will take more investment. The problems will increase, and inevitably the business will need more money. Then, you'll seek outside investment capital to help you de-lever the balance sheet and help the business grow further, so you'll sell your equity to raise such capital, and so on. . . You get the idea.

———

Building your own capital is a fundamental principle for entrepreneurs to master in order to break through the Messy Middle of business growth.

A world-class team of advisors is essential in helping entrepreneurs generate more capital. It was not until I surrounded myself with solid commercial-banking relationships, a CPA and accounting firm, personal financial-wealth advisors, corporate attorneys, litigation attorneys, estate attorneys, commercial-insurance specialists, captive-insurance experts, and other professionals that I was able to uncover all the ways entrepreneurs can retain even more cash in the business through proper planning. More on that later in Principle V: Protect the House and Principle VI: Access Owner's Liquidity.

With strong net operating cash flows, a growing SFG rate, and a 3-year Capital Strategy, you can maximize the amazing opportunities that will magically start appearing without relying on outside capital. You can keep the outside vultures at bay while protecting and growing your equity (Principle I).

Action Zone

- What was your company's net operating cash flow in the last 12 months?

- Do you know which industries, services or products, customers, or segments generate the most cash for your business?

- How can your company generate enough net operating cash flow to support its growth objectives without overleveraging the company's balance sheet or being at the mercy of banks or outside forces?

- What is your self-financeable growth (SFG) rate?

- What is your 3-year Capital Strategy?

———

What is one thing that you will start, stop, and continue based on this principle?

Start? _____

Stop? _____

Continue? _____

To learn more on how to:

- calculate your net operating cash flow;
- build your Cash Flow Ladder by business segment;
- implement the Power of One;
- calculate your SGF rate; and
- create a 3-Year Capital Strategy,

visit us at 100MJourney.com/workbook.

We are ready to guide and assist you on your journey.

Scan the QR code below to get access to *The $100M Journey Workbook* and other valuable resources to assist you on your journey!

REINVEST SMARTLY

"Growth for the sake of growth is the ideology of the cancer cell."
— Edward Abbey, writer and environmental activist

Any entrepreneur desiring to build a High Performance company must understand the importance of reinvesting smartly, with patient ambition, into their businesses growth. Principle III: Reinvest Smartly, warns of the consequences of making aggressive, careless investments that can lead to wasting cash resources and ultimately losing business control. Entrepreneurs must strategically reinvest their net operating cash flow to increase their ability to self-finance more growth and create the business, wealth, and freedom they deserve.

Key Learnings:

1. Net operating cash flow should be reinvested smartly and strategically to increase the company's ability to self-finance more growth.

2. Entrepreneurs must master patient ambition and remain disciplined with their Strategic Plan in order to avoid careless mistakes.

3. Making aggressive and careless investments chasing shiny objects can lead to the entrepreneur losing control of the business.

4. Attaining the core capital target should be the primary goal of every entrepreneur.

5. Reinvesting to build operational capacity for growth will propel your business forward.

CHAPTER 19

WHY REINVEST SMARTLY?

"Businesses failed, not because of competition or bad business plans, but because they scaled up too quickly."

— Paul Jarvis, author of *Company of One*

If you want to reach your goal of building a High Performance company, Principle III: Reinvest Smartly, cannot be ignored. You cannot "check the box" on Principle I: Grow and Protect Your Equity and Principle II: Build Your Own Capital and be careless on Principle III: Reinvest Smartly without all your great efforts going up in smoke. These principles all have to work together.

We entrepreneurs are not a patient bunch and this impatience can frequently be a significant contributor to our demise.

Can you remember a time when your impatience led to a breakdown in your business? Or maybe your impatience dug you into a hole that you had to climb your way out of? If you take a minute to reflect on your journey, you have most likely encountered something like these experiences several times. Why? Because at the root of entrepreneurship is the drive to succeed and that drive is often fueled by impatience. That same impatience that drives the entrepreneur *away* from "being bossed" to *being the boss* and seeking success on their own terms can also drive the entrepreneur to take unnecessary risks.

My burning desire to succeed as an entrepreneur was so strong that I always tried to grow too fast. I lacked patience and made careless mistakes, reinvesting in opportunities that were not aligned with the core of our business without having a clear strategy or knowing whether we even had the cash to do it in the first place.

I lacked patient ambition. I lacked impulse control. I wanted to grow for growth's sake and it carried the seeds of my own destruction.

Think about the last time a team member came to you excited about a new opportunity for the business to pursue. It was sexy, shiny, and could potentially lift your company to new levels . . . but it was not exactly core to what you did. It *was* a complementary service or product. Would you salivate at the mouth and try everything to maximize this juicy new opportunity for your business? Of course you would! So did I.

The problem is that the impulses we have to jump on these shiny objects are how we get caught—hooked in the mouth. We are ambitious and want to grow and build our businesses as fast as possible. We are not good at waiting patiently and sticking with our core Strategic Plan.

In our personal lives, we know that it is not wise to purchase material, shiny objects that we cannot afford, so we patiently wait (or should wait) until we have the means to splurge on a bigger home or nicer car. In business, we believe so foolishly that everything we do will work and provide us a return on our investment that we invest more carelessly in pursuing our business goals.

Making matters worse, when you lack visibility as to how much net operating cash flow your business generates, and you reinvest too aggressively, you put yourself and the business in a position of needing more financing from outside sources. This, in turn, hurts you through increased interest expenses. Or worse, it costs you your equity.

To build a solid and sustainable company that will break through the Messy Middle, it's very important to reinvest your net operating cash flow into your business wisely, patiently, and strategically—following your 3-year Capital Strategy.

In my 20s, I read the book, *The Millionaire Next Door* by Thomas J. Stanley and William D. Danko, and still to this day all I can think about are my parents. My parents always lived smartly below their means, and my dad is still the cheapest man I have ever met (no offense, Dad!). I say that with the utmost respect because my dad is also the most selfless and generous person I know. He taught me at a very young age how to save and be wise with financial resources. I can only hope to instill these same life lessons in my kids.

As I started to gain traction and experience success as an entrepreneur, this frugal and smart millionaire-next-door mindset started to escape me. I started placing my bets like I was playing with Monopoly money at a casino in Vegas.

As a startup entrepreneur, I was very successful in generating early revenues to get any new business venture off the ground. I am sure my experience in chocolate-bar sales or knocking on doors to sell paint jobs provided a strong foundation for sales. Like most entrepreneurs, my ability to sell the product or service I am passionate about is the easy part.

The hard part is figuring out what to do with the cash that comes into our business. Without knowing how fast we could afford to grow (our SFG rate) or how to develop a 3-year Capital Strategy, I would quickly use the cash our business generated to reinvest into growth, frequently in a careless manner. I would hire new team members, spend more on marketing and sales, upgrade to a nicer office, or start a new business line. As quickly as the cash would come in, it would go back out in my attempt to take the business to the next level.

Not surprisingly, my companies grew, but they always needed more cash (capital) to continue the growth trajectory! So, of course, we would seek to bring in additional revenue or, worse, sell our equity to bring on more cash, and the cycle would repeat.

I wanted our companies to grow rapidly. In order to grow the companies, we needed more cash, and to get more cash, I needed to sell some of my equity.

This sounds sensible, right?

No!

Although our revenues grew and it looked like the company was achieving great success, we were cash poor. We were overinvesting, trying to grow faster than our business could really afford as we did not measure or care about our SFG rate. To make matters worse, we were not investing smartly!

By making aggressive and careless investments in our effort to grow too quickly, our net operating cash flow declined rapidly, violating Principle II: Build Your Own Capital. Then we had to sell equity to bring more cash to the business and violated Principle I: Protect and Grow your Equity.

A more positive outcome would have happened if the reinvestments were made in a strategic, patient, calculated, and smart manner. We would have built our own capital (Principle II) by growing our net operating cash flow and increasing our SFG rate while also growing and protecting our equity (Principle I).

We must grow our businesses with discipline and patient ambition!

Entrepreneurs who do not reinvest smartly cannot continue building their own capital (Principle II) for further reinvestment. They find themselves needing capital investments into their company to sustain their growth path, violating Principle I: Protect and Build Your Equity.

If you fail at any of these first three principles you might still be able to build a nice big business, but you will not own it, you will not control it, and you might eventually be replaced as the leader of that business. Is that what we ultimately want as entrepreneurs? Of course not!

Finding myself exhausted after several years of hard work to build a great company, to then lose it because I did not respect these principles, was the wake-up call I needed to write this book. I hope you take this warning as seriously as I passionately deliver it.

With patient ambition and a commitment to creating long-term wealth and freedom through your business, waiting a few more years to achieve the growth you seek will be well worth the wait. Continue to make smart strategic decisions by reinvesting a portion of your net operating cash flow into the business to steadily increase your ability to self-finance more growth. This is how you will create the business, wealth, and freedom you deserve as an entrepreneur.

Self-Reflection Zone

- How many times were you distracted this week by your impatience?

- Think about the last time you lacked patient ambition and went chasing a shiny object. What were the consequences?

- What controls do you have to protect your business from reinvesting your cash in the wrong areas?

Scan the QR code below to watch a supplemental video about why this principle is so important!

CHAPTER 20

HOW TO REINVEST SMARTLY

"Start up, Scale up, Sc@%w up . . . or Stall out (fail to scale)!

— Verne Harnish, *Scaling Up*

There are four main ways that entrepreneurs should reinvest smartly into their business. Before we review those, we must evaluate other decisions entrepreneurs face when deciding how to best allocate the free net operating cash flow the business generates.

1. Partner distributions

2. Pay down debt

3. Build up reserves

4. Reinvest smartly for growth

    a. Build operational capacity

    b. Marketing and sales

    c. New business segments

    d. Mergers and acquisitions

———

1. PARTNER DISTRIBUTIONS

Entrepreneurs need to be very cautious about extracting cash from the business for the short-term benefit of the partners. You are either committed to reinvesting in your business for long-term wealth creation or you are committed to distributing all free cash flow to the partners for short-term gratification needs, not both—at least not until the business generates north of $1M in net cash flow from operations.

As Robert Kiyosaki says in *Rich Dad Poor Dad*, "To make your first million is the hardest. It sets you off in the right direction. It instills the determination, discipline, and motivation to become financially independent."

Many entrepreneurs distribute some or all of their annual net operating cash flow to the partners of the business so they can enjoy the fruits of their labor. Let's be clear: this is not reinvesting smartly in the business. This is the way you extract cash from the business to pay yourself and other partners today!

Building a business to maximize annual distributions or payments to partners is an easy way to provide short-term rewards for the hard work of building a business. It certainly encourages the entrepreneur to keep building the company's net operating cash flow so they can get paid even more money on an annual basis.

In some cases, these distributions are disguised in the form of high salaries to partners. How often have you seen a friend, family member, or partner with a big title and salary, but everybody knows they are not providing a return to the company? They may not be working at all. This is a form of distribution as well.

If the entrepreneur does not have visions to grow their business beyond its current state, they should enjoy, with pride, the Lifestyle business they have built. But the business might lack oxygen (cash) for any unforeseen emergencies that arise and it will struggle to survive a rainy day.

When cash resources are paid out to partners as distributions, they are usually taxable as income to the business or the entrepreneur. In contrast, if a business reinvests the cash back into the company, the expense is a deduction to its taxable income and no taxes are due for that expense. The business's distribution of capital resources to partners, including the need to cover taxes, should be built into the 3-year Capital Strategy.

As the business grows, there may be additional reasons to distribute more cash profits that are sitting on the balance sheet, but not before the other items on this list are evaluated.

2. PAY DOWN DEBT

> *"Pay off your debt first. Freedom from debt is worth more than any amount you can earn."* —Mark Cuban (qtd. in Musson)

A smart way to use a business's free net operating cash flow is to pay down any outstanding debt obligations. This can help reduce interest expenses and improve the company's financial health. Although leverage is not always bad, it can put restraints on the business in terms of debt covenants, interest payments, principal payback obligations, personal guarantees, and simply the burden of knowing that there is debt.

Banks are always willing to lend you money when you do not really need it, but you will be in trouble if you are highly leveraged with debt and need additional capital for an unforeseen circumstance.

Entrepreneurs who can pay down and eventually eliminate their business's debt will be incredibly empowered with the confidence and ability to reinvest free net operating cash flow into the business.

Leverage Reduction Model

	Debt-to-Equity Ratio	% of NOCF to Paydown Debt	% of NOCF to Build Cash Reserves	% of NOCF to Reinvest
Fully Leveraged	3:1 or greater	90%	5%	5%
Medium Leverage	2:1	75%	10%	15%
Low Leverage	1:1	50%	10%	40%
No Leverage (Debt Free)	0:1	0%	10%	90%

The Leverage Reduction Model provides a matrix to determine how much of your net operating cash flow (NOCF) will be applied to paydown your debt to lower your leverage ratio, build cash reserves, or reinvest into the growth of your business.

NOTE: These leverage ratios and suggested percentages are simply an example and can vary based on business, industry, etc.

How much leverage does your business have? I hope you will say "no leverage" because this is the ultimate position of strength!

Wherever you are on the leverage scale, your goal should be to constantly reduce your debt-to-equity ratio by applying the appropriate amount of net operating cash flow toward the paydown of your debt. As with personal debt, it is very hard to make sizable investments when you have too much business debt building up.

On the other hand, even when fully leveraged, you should always have a small percentage of your net operating cash flow allocated for building up a cash reserve and for reinvesting smartly into the business so that you can, in turn, generate more net operating cash flow to pay down more debt and grow the business.

Unfortunately, some businesses get stuck in a constant state of being fully leveraged and cannot escape because high-interest payments suck up all the excess cash being generated. This further amplifies the need to build your own capital (Principle II). By growing your net operating cash flow, you can escape this trap and break through the Messy Middle.

In *Scaling Up,* Verne Harnish and Alan Miltz discuss the power that comes with attaining the "core capital target," which is defined as a business that has built up two months of operating expenses in cash reserves plus a proper reserve to pay its taxes, and is *debt free*. Hitting this core capital target should be a goal for every entrepreneur. Once attained, everything changes and the entrepreneur is ready to grow their business by reinvesting wisely with their own capital.

Have you ever attained the core capital target in your business? How would things change if you did?

Imagine owning a thriving business that is generating strong net operating cash flow and is completely debt free! And having the ability to apply 100% of your annual net operating cash flow to building up cash reserves and reinvesting smartly into your business's growth! This is where we need to live as entrepreneurs if we want to build the business of our dreams.

3. BUILD UP RESERVES

"Cash combined with courage in a crisis is priceless." —Warren Buffet (qtd. in Schroeder)

Much like every household should have three to six months of living expenses as an emergency fund, your business should also have cash reserves for a rainy day or an unexpected opportunity that may arise. Unfortunately, some businesses manage their cash flow from week to week, creating undue stress on the entrepreneur when a customer payment does not come in on time or a big unexpected expense is incurred. Living this week-to-week grind sucks!

Over the years, I have had countless sleepless nights worried about how I would make payroll, and I am sure you have been there as well. While these challenges have taught me to be resilient and creative, I never want to be there again.

In the book *Great by Choice*, author Jim Collins says that great companies have up to 10X more cash reserves than their competitors. When was the last time your business had excess cash reserves, let alone 2, 3, or 10X more than your competitors?

Great By Choice: Uncertainty, Chaos, And Luck—Why Some Thrive Despite Them All, by Jim Collins and Morten T. Hansen

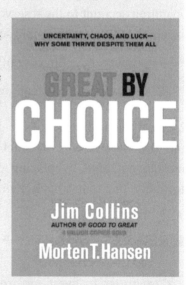

This best-selling book looks at what sets successful companies apart in times of chaos, turbulence, and uncertainty. The book is based on a nine-year study of companies that survived and thrived during chaotic times. Through this study, Collins and Hansen discovered that the most successful companies had a few key traits in common: they embraced disciplined action, engaged in productive paranoia, and had a culture of empiricism.

Key learnings:

1. Stick to your plan and do not deviate from it, even in times of chaos.
2. Constantly practice productive paranoia.
3. Make decisions based on verifiable data, not gut feelings or intuition.

4. Focus on long-term goals and objectives and be committed to learning and experimentation.

5. Luck plays an important role in 10Xers' success, but 10Xers can capitalize on it and make the most out of it.

"The idea that leading in a 'fast world' always requires 'fast decisions' and 'fast action'—and that we should embrace an overall ethos of 'Fast! Fast! Fast!'—is a good way to get killed."
—Jim Collins and Morten Hansen, *Great by Choice*

To start building cash reserves for your business, you should set up a separate bank account (or a conservative investment account) to house a percentage of your annual net operating cash. Many financial planners would encourage you to set up an automatic monthly draw from your operating account to the reserve account. Let it build up. Do not touch it except for these two possible scenarios:

1. Emergency: "In case of emergency, break glass."

2. An opportunity in alignment with your Strategic Plan arises.

As your business continues to generate positive net operating cash flow and the cash reserve account accumulates, you can maximize your earning potential by placing excess funds in a managed investment account rather than a bank savings account (where it earns little interest).

4. REINVEST SMARTLY FOR GROWTH

"Cash is used to invest into growth, or cash is used to fund management-influenced waste."
—Verne Harnish and Alan Miltz, Scaling Up

Think about all the cash your company has burned in "management-influenced" waste (like those listed below) over the years. I get sick to my stomach when I think about it. Do you?

- bad hires
- poorly executed marketing campaigns
- pricing errors
- inventory slippage
- customer refunds
- warranty work
- and so much more

All businesses have waste. Our job is to protect this cash that we have worked so hard to generate and ensure we minimize waste and increase the amount of cash we reinvest into legitimately growing our businesses.

Once we have ensured that our debts are properly managed and paid down and we have built up a discipline for building up cash reserves, we are ready to evaluate the strategic ways to reinvest the net operating cash flow we generate to grow the company and its overall value.

Here are some general categories of reinvestment to consider.

a. Build Operational Capacity

"Entrepreneurs need to identify pathways to grow by getting more revenue and margin from their winners, building their operational capacity, knowing what their formula is to scale, and then creating more opportunities for great people."
—Charlie Chase, CEO of California Closets

This section is not titled "Hire More People!" It's about building operational capacity to make our people, services, and products more efficient. This is very different. Yes, of course, more people may be needed, but in today's workplace, we must seek ways to improve efficiency because this will enable us to generate more net operating cash flow.

An entrepreneur must continually build the capacity for the operational team of the business to produce more volume with better quality. This can include investments in technology, higher-skilled team members, improved processes, better training, additional tools, and more. Entrepreneurs need to perfect their operational delivery model to increase their gross margins and the service they provide to their customers.

Investing to build operational capacity can be tricky. Developing, measuring, and managing KPIs and practicing continuous improvement is essential. Way too many entrepreneurs hire more staff because they have more business but then fail to improve the operational capacity and efficiency of each team member along the way.

If you are not building operational capacity in your business, you risk lagging behind others in your industry that do.

Advances in technology and artificial intelligence are going to change the game, but it is critical to not chase new, shiny-object systems. Instead, be thoughtful and very strategic around any major capital expenditure on technology or system-wide operational changes since they can be incredibly disruptive and expensive. Move slowly—test, validate, and implement the right systems at the rights times— to provide your team with amazing tools and improve productivity.

b. Marketing and Sales

If I told you that every sales representative you hired and trained would cost you $50K but would make your business $200K in net operating cash flow, how many sales representatives would you want to hire? As many as you could get your hands on, right?

It's the same with marketing. If you generated $50K in revenues every time you invested $5K in a specific marketing campaign, how many more of these campaigns would you do? As many as you could, of course!

Investing in the growth of your marketing and sales efforts to scale a winning product or service is critical to the growth of your business. Your operational team, systems, and processes must be ready to handle the volume and you should utilize KPIs to ensure that the investments in people and tactics generate a proper ROI.

If you boil down business growth to its simplest form, you will find some amazing answers. We entrepreneurs tend to overcomplicate our growth strategies when in reality, the answers usually lie in easy mathematics. The format on the next page, taught to me in my first entrepreneurial venture as a College Pro franchisee, is still the simplest way to break down where one must smartly invest to attain their desired target.

Marketing and Sales KPI Report

Desired Revenue Target:	$1,000,000
Average Revenue/Widget:	$2,000
Number of Widgets to Achieve Desired Revenue Target:	500
Success Ratio on Converting Leads to Sales:	35%
Number of Leads Needed to Sell the Number of Widgets needed to Achieve Desired Revenue Target:	1429
Cost per Lead:	$50
Amount That Must Be Invested to Generate the Leads to Generate the Desired Revenue Target:	$71,429

The Marketing and Sales KPI report provides a simple breakdown of how many sales, leads, and investments must be made to generate the desired level of revenue.

NOTE: This model is simply an example and can vary based on business, industry, etc.

The model is so simple, yet very few entrepreneurs break down their goals and KPIs to the simplest form, partly because they do not measure performance.

You don't sell widgets? Your sales process is different? That's ok. This model can be refined for any product or service. You can customize this sales and marketing KPI model for your business. Once in place, you track your performance on all KPIs on weekly, monthly, and quarterly basis and make changes along the way to navigate your sales and marketing strategies to your desired final goal destination.

c. New Business Segments

> *"Place <u>many</u> small bets where your downside risk is small and managed, and the upside outcome could be huge, but do not forget where your bread is buttered. Focus on your core business that generates the margin that drives your company first and foremost and do not chase the shinny objects."*
> —Steve Hearon, President BrandPoint Services

You will discover new opportunities as your business grows. These opportunities will appear very enticing but may not be the best for your business. Evaluating all your business segments using the Cash Flow Ladder from Principle II: Build Your Own Capital can help you assess your customers, industries, divisions, or products and services to ensure you know where your company is winning at making cash.

Diversifying into new business segments can cause major havoc, disrupt your systems, and worse, eat your cash. You must proceed with caution. Often, entrepreneurs chase shiny objects and get caught spending too much of their net operating cash by developing new lines of business instead of focusing on growing and scaling the ones they have mastered. Most new business segments are not as successful as you thought they would be, and you've distracted yourself and your team from the core offerings that are your bread and butter.

Still, expanding your business to new business segments can also be very rewarding and it may propel your business forward in a new direction. Start very slowly, beta test, prove your theory, and only expand once you have proven that this expansion will help you and your business grow its value should you proceed at full speed.

Many companies like Amazon, Google, and others spend an incredible amount of time on research and development, seeking new opportunities for growth. After investing in research, Amazon developed Amazon

Web Services, which is now the most profitable segment of this company that started out as an online bookseller. That investment has proven to be valuable. Conversely, I am sure Kodak regrets not having invested more in becoming a new-age digital company back in the early 2000s.

We do not want our business to stagnate, while at the same time, we do not want to recklessly chase new business segments and blow away our hard-earned cash. Once you have mastered building operational capacity and growing your business with proper sales and marketing KPI management, find areas of opportunity and explore. You never know what you may find!

Like any Startup, the early phases of building a new business segment consume a lot of time and cash. One way to expand your business into a new business segment that you have carefully vetted is through a strategic acquisition.

d. Mergers and Acquisitions

The fastest and riskiest way to exponentially grow your business can be through strategic mergers and acquisitions (M&A). Do not consider this option for growth if your business has a lot of debt or is not generating the net operating cash flow to fund more than 50% of the acquisition with cash. Integration of companies and cultures is very challenging. One bad acquisition can destroy everything you have built, while one great acquisition can help you achieve your business dreams: high risk, high reward. Be careful!

If your business

- has protected its equity (Principle I: Protect and Grow Your Equity);

- is generating significant free net operating cash flow (Principle II: Build Your Own Capital);

- has very low leverage on the business (or is debt free);

- has sufficient cash reserves;

- has built its operational capacity; and

- has invested in sales and marketing to grow its winning products or services,

then investing in a very strategic, tuck-under acquisition might be the move that will propel your business to new heights.

It is critical to carefully vet any potential acquisitions with the help of professional advisors and then integrate those acquisitions cautiously. Do not bite off more than you can chew. It is best to take on bite-size acquisitions that do not pose a big threat to your successful business if the road gets bumpy along the way.

––––

Ultimately, how an entrepreneur decides to reinvest in their business will depend heavily on the Strategic Plan, the vision, the BHAG, the financial health of the business (net operating cash flow, debt, and cash reserves), and the current market conditions. It is important for entrepreneurs to carefully consider all options and seek professional advice to ensure they make the best decisions for their business.

The one common theme that has stuck with me is that all reinvestments must be done with patient ambition! Entrepreneurs who reinvest their annual net operating cash flow back into their business instead of taking distributions out of the company stand to maximize the long-term potential of the business. If they reinvest this capital smartly, they will generate more net operating cash flow and the SFG rate will increase, allowing the business to grow exponentially.

The goal must be to continually focus on building your own capital (Principle II: Build Your Own Capital) by increasing your net operating cash flow. Way too many entrepreneurs reinvest too quickly and too aggressively. Then, when these investments take time to pan out or never pan out at all, the business's net operating cash flow declines rapidly and puts the business in jeopardy.

Making a fast and significant reinvestment decision that does not work will cause a lot of pain and be very difficult to unwind. Often, the entrepreneur is so committed to the reinvestment that they cannot see the forest for the trees and will therefore stick with a bad decision for too long as they try to prove to themselves and others that it was a good decision. Ultimately, when the failure point occurs, the pain and cost harm the business considerably.

Think about how powerfully your business will be positioned if you can get your business to $1M in net operating cash flow and achieve the core capital target of having strong cash reserves and no debt. This is where every entrepreneur should strive to be because once you get here, everything becomes much clearer.

Until you reach this level, you must be extremely frugal with all of your capital and investment decisions. To be frugal and reinvest your net operating cash flow simultaneously, you must make wise, well-thought-out, strategic investments that fit your Strategic Business Plan. Only reinvest in your winning products or services, make small calculated bets that can be unwound quickly (two-door decisions), and do not deviate from your core business.

Entrepreneurs must do everything possible to attain the $1M net operating cash flow milestone as smartly as possible, being very frugal with every dollar until they do. Once they earn more than $1M net operating cash flow, they can accelerate their reinvestment strategy with a dedicated focus on continually growing the annual metric that will drive their growth.

Action Zone

- How much of your net operating cash flow are you distributing to partners annually versus reinvesting in the business?

- What are the 3 best opportunities to reinvest in your business in the next 12 months that will result in your net operating cash flow increasing?

- What 3 investments should you unwind because they decrease your net operating cash flow?

- How many months of operating expenses do you have set aside in cash reserves?

- What is your debt-to-equity ratio?

- What plan should be in place to attain your core capital target?

———

What is one thing that you will start, stop, and continue based on this principle?

Start? _____

Stop? _____

Continue? _____

To learn more on how to:

- create a leverage reduction model;

- build up cash reserves;

- build operational capacity;

- create a Sales and Marketing KPI report; or

- get assistance with mergers and acquisitions,

visit us at 100MJourney.com/workbook.

We are ready to guide and assist you on your journey.

Scan the QR code below to get access to *The $100M Journey Workbook* and other valuable resources to assist you on your journey!

BUILD A CULTURE OF INTRAPRENEURSHIP

"Trust is the one thing that changes everything."

— Stephen M.R. Covey, *The Speed of Trust*

This book aims to help you break through and escape the Messy Middle and create a thriving, High Performance business. To successfully do this, you must create a culture of intrapreneurship within your organization! Embracing a servant and situational leadership mindset will help you unlock a win-win-win dynamic, motivating team members to evolve into intrapreneurs. These dedicated, efficient individuals are pivotal for helping your business achieve enduring success.

Key Learnings:

1. Creating a culture of intrapreneurship within our companies is essential.

2. Situational Leadership is the key to strong skill development among your team.

3. Having a servant leadership mindset is instrumental as you become a mentor.

4. Creating a win-win-win environment is crucial to building a High Performance team.

5. Intrapreneurs should be provided opportunities to participate in the business's success.

CHAPTER 21

WHY BUILD A CULTURE OF INTRAPRENEURSHIP?

"The entrepreneurs who create abundance around themselves—who look to create value for those they work with—are the ones who are truly successful over the long haul."

— Ruth Lund, *True North Advisors*

The biggest and most common problem entrepreneurs face is building a team of committed, productive, efficient team members who treat their role in the business as if it were a business of their own. Imagine solving this problem and building your dream team! How good would it feel to be fully supported by a team that will be there for you and the business through thick and thin?

It is practically impossible for you to build the company of your dreams without talented and committed team members who are willing, able, and ready to go through the good and bad times by your side. There is only one way to do this effectively: create a win-win opportunity for both the team members and the business by developing a culture of intrapreneurship.

We *must* create a culture of intrapreneurship within our organizations to break through the Messy Middle of business growth and build a High

Performance team. An intrapreneur is a leader in your business who acts and feels like an entrepreneur. This is only a possibility if you first provide an environment for this to happen.

Ruth Lund, cofounder of True North Culture Advisors and a trusted advisor and friend, influenced me to discover the type of leader I wanted to become and the culture I desired to create within my companies.

Ruth's message is powerful and opened my eyes to a new way of leadership:

> Few leaders truly understand the power of creating a win-win scenario with their teams. We are conditioned to believe that success means "I win" rather than "I have the power to lift myself and those around me." The entrepreneurs who create abundance around themselves—who look to create value for those they work with—are the ones who are truly successful over the long haul. People want to work with them. Additionally, they sleep well at night and enjoy rich, authentic relationships.

Think about this line again: "The entrepreneurs who create abundance around themselves . . ." How amazing would it feel if you could create success for yourself and your business *and* everybody associated with it! This is the type of leader I wanted to be.

Ruth also taught me the meaning of "servant leadership." A phrase once foreign to me has now become my calling card and a key to developing intrapreneurs. My responsibility is to assist and equip team members to be successful in their roles. If I can assist those around me to achieve their goals and aspirations, not only will I feel a sense of pride for their accomplishments, but I will also feel a sense of purpose for the contribution I was able to make toward their success!

What would it be like to run a team where everyone feels clarity and connection to the same vision and is equipped to own their contribution to the business's success? What do you think the retention and tenure of this team would be?

The world is changing quickly, and we live in a new reality: finding and retaining good people is difficult! When you figure out the secret sauce to creating a win-win environment for team members, you will be rewarded with a world-class team.

This leadership style is no better displayed than in Adam Grant's book, *Give and Take*. Grant, an organizational psychologist and Wharton Business School professor, writes, "Givers end up more successful by building better reputations and more useful networks. Increasingly true as economies shift to collaborative knowledge work."

Give and Take: Why Helping Others Drives Our Success by Adam Grant

Give and Take explores the importance of giving and taking in the workplace. It focuses on the idea that giving is the key to success in any business and that successful people are generous with their time, knowledge, and resources. The book describes how giving can provide a competitive advantage and help create lasting relationships with colleagues and clients.

Key Learnings

1. Giving is essential to success because it helps build relationships and create a competitive advantage.
2. Taking is necessary for learning and growth, and it can help to open up new opportunities.
3. Finding the right balance between giving and taking is important to achieving the best results.
4. Being generous with your time, knowledge, and resources can lead to the most rewarding relationships.
5. You can inspire others to give and take by setting a good example.

"Being a giver is not good for a 100-yard dash, but it's valuable in a marathon."
—Adam Grant, *Give and Take*

Servant leaders focus on giving, and for team members to receive without skepticism, trust is required.

Building a culture where your team members are treated like entrepreneurs, and not like dispensable employees, is a complete game changer. *The Speed of Trust,* by Stephen M.R. Covey, provides a mathematical equation to explain why!

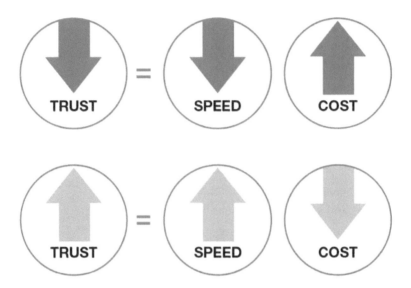

When you build a trusting environment for your team members, where they know that you genuinely desire to create a winning environment, the trust level grows. As the level of trust increases, the speed at which a team can perform increases, and the costs inevitably decrease.

This is a massive win for the business! A massive win for you, the entrepreneur! A massive win for the intrapreneur! And a massive win for anybody associated with your business (customers, vendors, partners, etc.)!

A win-win-win!

The Speed of Trust: The One Thing That Changes Everything by Stephen M.R. Covey and Rebecca Merrill

In *The Speed of Trust*, Stephen M.R. Covey examines the science and psychology of trust, showing why it is essential for successful relationships and organizations. He explains why trust is the single most important factor for achieving success and examines the four core components of trust: integrity, intention, capabilities, and results. He provides practical advice, tools for cultivating trust and strengthening relationships, and strategies for building a culture of trust and transforming an organization. Covey shows readers how to lead with trust and create an environment where trust can flourish. He also helps readers understand how to repair trust when it has been broken. Ultimately, *The Speed of Trust* offers readers a powerful way to increase productivity, reduce costs, and foster collaboration, creativity, and innovation.

Key Learnings:

1. Building trust takes time and effort and requires a sincere commitment to being reliable and honest.

2. When trust is present in an organization, it creates an environment of safety and collaboration, leading to increased productivity and performance.

3. Organizations with high levels of trust outperform those with low levels.

4. Leaders have an obligation to lead by example and set the tone for the level of trust in their organizations.

5. High-trust environments are more resilient and respond better to challenges.

"Trust is equal parts character and competence . . . You can look at any leadership failure, and it's always a failure of one or the other. Above all, success in business requires two things: a winning competitive strategy, and superb organizational execution. Distrust is the enemy of both."
—**Stephen M.R. Covey,** *The Speed of Trust*

My business partner, Mike Hersh, perfectly summarized trust's impact on building and scaling a company: "The entrepreneur should empower their teams to make decisions that will create a strong 'Speed of Trust' with customers, vendors, and partners. Doing so will build incredible loyalty and improve their efficiency of the business."

Consider situations where you have worked for a company or person you did not trust. The opposite happens. Trust levels plummet, team members are unproductive, and the business's costs grow. These businesses ultimately will fail! All due to poor leadership! Or, as author Rande Somma calls (it in his book), "Leadersh!t"!

Leadersh!t: A Look at the Broken Leadership System in Corporate America that Accepts Leaders Who Are Really Good at Being Bad by Rande Somma

Leadersh!t talks about the massive disconnect between workers, management, and top leadership. Somma argues that lowered standards, higher compensation, and increased greed has led to a reliance on financial gain and a lack of integrity. He sees this trend as a pervasive issue affecting companies of all sizes in various industries, and he presents personal anecdotes to support his argument. Somma encourages readers to recognize these challenges and emerge as authentic leaders committed to integrity, authenticity, and real performance.

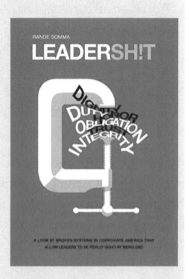

Key learnings:

1. There is a disconnect between workers, management, and C-suite executives, shedding light on lowered standards, increased compensation, and the prevalence of convenience, fraud, greed, and corruption among leaders.

2. The definition of success has shifted toward a focus on financial gain, neglecting the importance of genuine leadership and integrity.

3. This disturbing trend of compromised leadership is not limited to a specific industry but is pervasive across various companies and sectors.

4. "Leadersh!t," a term coined by the author, describes the leadership system that lacks commitment to integrity, authenticity, and real

performance, and suggests the need for authentic leadership solutions.

5. Authentic leaders are committed to integrity, authenticity, and real performance.

"Although it is easy to see that many leaders have lost integrity, I would argue that it is much, much more than that. They have lost their dignity; they have lost our respect; and worst of all, they have lost our trust."
—Rande Somma, *Leadersh!t*

Don't be full of "Leadersh!t"!

Magic happens when you follow your core values, act as a servant leader, and develop intrapreneurs that have a true sense of ownership in your business.

The best way to recruit and retain top talent is to provide for the increasing demand for them to have a sense of purpose beyond a weekly paycheck. Team members treated like intrapreneurs are more committed, work harder, act like business owners, buy into the company's long-term vision, and might one day run the entire enterprise.

David DuPont, founder of TeamSnap, provided a great example of what happens when debating a business issue with his intrapreneurs. He would tell them, "I want to hear your answer as an owner of the company, not as a leader of your function." This compelling statement removed the emotion from the debate and forced the intrapreneurs to think about their role as "an owner of the business," not as individual contributors protecting their roles in the organization.

The goal of an entrepreneur should be to build business assets that will thrive and create income independent of their presence. This means the intrapreneurs you hire, train, develop, and mentor are essential to the long-term success of the business.

Your primary role as the CEO of your company is to replace yourself in all the functions you operate in. You must find intrapreneurs that can do the roles better than you can and provide them with the proper environment for them to act like owners of the business themselves.

Brian Stevenson from Wells Fargo Advisors summed it up best: "An owner of a company can have eight to ten careers within their own business while still maintaining one title: 'Owner.' They need to continuously replace themselves so they can move up the strategic ladder."

What are you doing as an entrepreneur to move up the strategic ladder?

In the mid-2000s, I made one of the best hires of my entrepreneurial career when I hired Mike as a national sales representative for our small business. For years, Mike excelled as a sales representative, bringing large and profitable customers to the company. As the business matured and grew, Mike desired to develop professionally and earned the opportunity to become a key leader in the company. He was an intrapreneur who was motivated to grow within the business. Mike was promoted to vice president of Sales, then general manager, and ultimately he became the company's CEO.

Mike, an intrapreneur, eventually became a full-equity partner and led his team of intrapreneurs to grow the business to a High Performance, $100M enterprise—an incredible feat that would not have been possible if we had not created a culture of intrapreneurship. Mike, along with the company's president, Steve, and their team of dedicated and exceptional intrapreneurs have taken the business to an incredible level and created tremendous value for all.

A true win-win-win!

Self-Reflection Zone

- Does your business have a culture of intrapreneurship? How do you know?

- What 3 changes can you make in your business today to be a servant leader to your intrapreneurs and build the "speed of trust"?

- What 3 roles do you perform today that should be delegated to intrapreneurs?

- Does your business have a succession plan for all key leadership roles?

- What does your dream team look like? Who is on it? What roles do they fill?

Scan the QR code below to watch a supplemental video about why this principle is so important!

CHAPTER 22

HOW TO BUILD A CULTURE OF INTRAPRENEURSHIP

"Train people well enough so they can leave; treat them well enough so they don't want to."

— Richard Branson, founder of Virgin Group

Here are four ways you can create a strong culture of intrapreneurship within your business:

1. Hire for core value alignment.
2. Practice Situational Leadership® and skill development.
3. Provide entrepreneurial authority, freedom, and flexibility.
4. Share in the business's financial success.

———

1. HIRE FOR CORE VALUE ALIGNMENT

To build a culture of intrapreneurship, the core values of your business must align with a culture of entrepreneurship, and you must hire people who align with those core values. We have all done it. We have all chased the sexy résumé, the rock star that we thought would take our business to the next level, only to find that this person did not align culturally with our core values. One bad hire like this can have damaging effects on the culture you are trying to create.

No company does hiring for core value alignment better than FirstService Corporation, the former parent company of College Pro Painters, and the current parent company of CertaPro Painters—one of America's largest and most successful contracting franchise companies. Mike Stone, the CEO of CertaPro Painters, started with the company over 25 years ago as a sales representative selling paint jobs for one of my College Pro franchisees in Iowa. Mike, an intrapreneur looking for an opportunity to prove his value to the organization, now runs the entire CertaPro Painters franchise system. The company's disciplined process in hiring is unparalleled and with their organization's sustained growth, most would say it's rooted in their core values of deliver what you promise, have pride in what you do, respect the individual, and practice continuous improvement.

Small businesses suffer from a lack of expertise in how to perform behavioral interviews to test for core value alignment among their candidates. As a result, small businesses hire based on gut, the likeness of the candidate, or other non-data-driven methodologies, and the resulting effect is a poor hiring record and a weak team.

Conducting a behavioral interview to assess a candidate's alignment with core values involves asking questions that delve into their past experiences and behaviors. Here are some steps and considerations to perform a behavioral interview focused on core value alignment:

1. **Be clear on your core values.** Clearly define the core values that are important to your company. These values should reflect the desired culture and principles.

2. **Ask targeted questions.** Ask behavioral questions that directly relate to each core value. These questions should prompt candidates to provide specific examples from their past experiences that demonstrate their alignment, or lack thereof, with the core

values. Encourage them to provide details about the context, their actions, and the outcomes.

3. **Listen actively.** Pay close attention to the candidate's responses, focusing on their behaviors, attitudes, and decision-making processes. Evaluate whether their past actions align with the core values your organization upholds.

4. **Follow-up with probing questions.** If needed, ask additional probing questions to gain further insights into the candidate's values and motivations. Encourage them to elaborate on their decision-making process and the underlying values that have influenced their actions.

Evaluate how the candidate's values align with your company's culture. Consider how their behaviors and values would contribute to or potentially conflict with the existing team dynamics and values. Behavioral interviews provide insights into past behavior, which can be an indicator of future behavior. It is crucial to consider other factors such as references, cultural fit assessments, and situational judgment tests to gain a more holistic evaluation of a candidate's core value alignment.

If you hire for core values first and you provide your team members with the environment for them to grow, you will quickly find yourself with a team of motivated and driven individuals pushing your company to the next level.

2. PRACTICE SITUATIONAL LEADERSHIP® AND SKILL DEVELOPMENT

Create an environment where you explore and invest in each team member's development as a professional in their area of expertise. Provide your team members with the resources to learn and explore. Challenge them and demonstrate that you care about their professional and personal growth; actions are louder than words.

As the intrapreneurs grow and develop their competency and commitment, your style of leadership should also evolve. Learning how to be a situational leader and how to specifically modify my leadership style as my team members evolved was one of the biggest fundamental learnings I received from my mentors early in my career. Situational Leadership®, a term developed by Ken Blanchard in his book, *Leadership and the One Minute Manager*, means adapting your leadership style to each unique situation or task to meet the team's or team members' needs.

Leadership and the One Minute Manager: Increasing Effectiveness Through Situational Leadership by Ken Blanchard

Leadership and the One Minute Manager is a practical and insightful guide that blends the renowned One Minute Manager principles with Situational Leadership®. Through a compelling story, readers learn about four leadership styles—directing, coaching, supporting, and delegating—and how to adapt them based on team members' development levels.

Revised and Updated for Today's Leaders

Leadership and the One Minute Manager

INCREASING EFFECTIVENESS THROUGH SITUATIONAL LEADERSHIP® II

Ken Blanchard
#1 New York Times Bestselling Coauthor of The One Minute Manager®
Patricia Zigarmi
Drea Zigarmi

Key Learnings:

1. The Situational Leadership® model involves adapting leadership styles based on team members' development levels.

2. Effective leaders diagnose each team member's development level and apply the appropriate leadership style accordingly.

3. Clear communication, goal-setting, and feedback are essential for guiding and empowering team members.

4. Leadership effectiveness is maximized when leaders match their style to the needs of their team members.

5. By leveraging Situational Leadership®, leaders can create a motivated and cohesive team, driving success and productivity within the organization.

"One of the biggest obstacles to high performance in organizations comes from unclear expectations and accountability."
—Ken Blanchard, *Leadership and the One Minute Manager*

In developing a culture of intrapreneurship, you cannot throw your team members to the wolves by delegating all tasks. The intrapreneur is good at many tasks but that does not mean that they are competent for and committed to *all* tasks. I have heard countless entrepreneurs say, "I gave them this big project, gave them authority, freedom, and flexibility to perform it, and they failed. So I am never going to do that again." When entrepreneurs delegate instead of providing the proper direction needed to complete a task, it puts the intrapreneur unnecessarily at risk.

There is no one-size-fits-all leadership style. You cannot just loosely and carelessly assume the intrapreneur has the competence and commitment to complete specific tasks. It is your responsibility as the leader to help them develop their competence and commitment. That is not only Situational Leadership®—that is just plain leadership! Meet them where they are and elevate their game!

Situational Leadership® Model

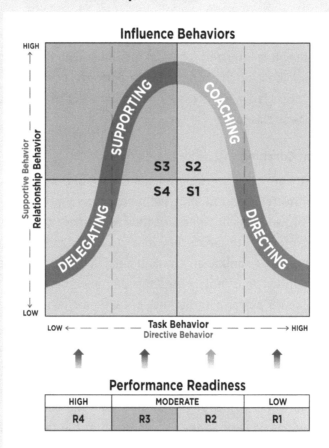

X-Axis: Directive Behavior

The extent to which the leader tells the follower what to do, how to do it, where it needs to be done, and when it needs to be completed.

Y-Axis: Supportive Behavior

The extent to which the leader engages in open dialog with the follower, actively listens, and provides recognition and reinforcement for task-related progress.

S1 Quadrant: Directing

The leader must provide a moderate to a high amount of direction regarding the task and the team member benefits from that knowledge and experience. It is intended for team members with limited (or no) expertise or skill, or lacking confidence to perform such a task. Close oversight by the leader is necessary to develop the team leader for future success on this task.

S2 Quadrant: Coaching

The leader still provides oversight on what, how, and when the team member completes the task but with opportunities for the team member to provide insight to ensure they fully understand the task. This style is intended to create buy-in and understanding from the team member, so encouragement and testing from the leader is encouraged. This style is mostly used for team members with limited (or no) experience performing the task but who are highly motivated and want to learn.

S3 Quadrant: Supporting

S3 is a significant stylistic change from S1 and S2. Instead of being driven by the leader, S3 is driven by the team member. The team member now has developed the skill to perform the task. Still, they have not developed confidence because they have limited experience completing the task. Once this confidence is formed, the leader can move to S4.

S4 Quadrant: Delegating

The team member is ready to perform the task at a high level and is both confident and motivated to do so. The leader can now confidently delegate to and empower the team member to run and complete tasks without supervision but with continued encouragement, praise, and support.

3. PROVIDE ENTREPRENEURIAL AUTHORITY, FREEDOM, AND FLEXIBILITY

As intrapreneurs develop their competence levels and their commitment to their tasks, provide them the authority and freedom to make decisions and *own* their roles and responsibilities within the company. Let them make decisions in line with the company's Strategic Plan, budget, core values, and vision, and demonstrate that you trust them. Allow them to take small, calculated risks, make mistakes, learn, and grow.

As an entrepreneur, your goal should be to evolve from leader to mentor. Invest in the relationship to create a bond with your team members that clearly demonstrates that you care about them beyond their careers. What are their goals (both professional and personal)? What development do they need to attain their goals? What is their True North Life Plan? How can you help them achieve it?

Authority

If the team member has developed high competence and high commitment in a particular task (S4 quadrant), delegate to them and give them the authority to lead it. This can include the authority to own a budget for one of your company's divisions and make decisions without having to ask permission. Provide incentives with the right motivations for accomplishing tasks that are in alignment with the company's objectives but then step away and give them the authority to deliver for the business. As they do, give them more authority.

If they fail at a given task, they might still have high competence but low commitment (S3 Quadrant), so modify your leadership style to support them accordingly.

A favorite question I have learned to ask when a task is not accomplished properly is: "Did you lack the competence, and/or commitment, to get this done?"

It has to be one of these! They either did not have the competence, knowledge, or experience to complete the task correctly or they lacked the commitment, confidence, or willingness to accomplish it. Once you figure this out, you know how to lead them (refer back to the Situational Leadership® style they need from you).

HINT: "I did not have enough time" can be a lack of both competence and commitment.

When you develop a team to have high competence and high commitment (S4 Quadrant) in most of the company's roles, you quickly develop succession within your business. You will quickly identify who may run your company someday.

Freedom

Nothing kills a team member's desire to work hard for a business more quickly than being overseen by a micromanager—someone who always selects a directive leadership style. So concerned with their own job security or need for control, the micromanager has no Situational Leadership® awareness and manages everybody the exact same way, telling them exactly what to do. UGH!

If you have not mastered Situational Leadership®, be aware—maybe you are one of these leaders.

As your team members move along the competency and commitment scale, evolve your leadership style to provide them with more discretion. If you lead a team situationally and administer the proper leadership style, you will be comfortable providing your intrapreneurs with the ultimate flexibility—delegation.

The days of micromanaging your team's hours (unless they are in an hourly job), doctor's appointments, parental duties, or other life obligations or curveballs are over. They do not need you to micromanage this. They can get a better job with another company providing them with more freedom and flexibility.

If you provide the right level of Situational Leadership®, you can also provide your team with more authority and freedom as they develop their talents, which will, in turn, fuel their desire to be an intrapreneur in your business!

In addition to Situational Leadership®, when I fully embraced the meaning of being a "servant leader," leadership became so much easier. To be a servant leader, all you have to do is flip the organizational chart upside down. Your team does not work for you; you work for them. This small paradigm shift can mean the world to your intrapreneurs and simplify leadership.

4. SHARE IN THE BUSINESS'S FINANCIAL SUCCESS

Provide your key intrapreneurs with an opportunity to share in the value appreciation of the company through equity-like incentives—to create a wealth-building mechanism—while treating them like business owners.

Jeffrey Unger suggests that each entrepreneur must have a clear strategy on employee ownership incentives to either:

- share the growth in equity of the company with team members of the business, or

- not share any of the equity with team members.

Much like we discussed in Principle I: Protect and Grow Your Equity, there is never really a need for an entrepreneur to hand out *real* shares of equity in a business. This is where a lot of entrepreneurs go wrong.

Equity is one thing that is very hard to get back once it is given. Protect it with all of your might.

That being said, I am a big proponent of sharing in the value appreciation with the team that contributes to your amazing success day in and day out. This also helps create a culture of intrapreneurship.

Entrepreneurs continually evaluate the ROI they get from each employee. Generally speaking, if an entrepreneur pays an employee $50K per year fully loaded, then they would expect that this employee will generate $75K or more in value to the company, thus netting the company $25K in annual ROI from that employee.

But when do entrepreneurs reverse this script and view it from the employee's viewpoint? What is the employee's ROI for working in your business?

Employees devote their time and sacrifice themselves for the business every day. Don't we entrepreneurs have a responsibility to provide them with an ROI for their commitment to helping our companies grow?

Many may argue, "No, that is what they get paid a salary for!"

If this is your viewpoint, good luck!

The workforce is changing, and they want more. Our responsibility is to provide them with opportunities that will provide them with a strong ROI for their contributions to the company's success.

Entrepreneurs who build their companies with and for their teams and provide opportunities for them to become intrapreneurs within the organization achieve unparalleled results.

Every intrapreneur that works for your company also has a personal balance sheet. Every intrapreneur that works for your company strives to earn a nice living and build a strong financial foundation for their family.

How can we help them achieve these goals while also helping our business achieve amazing results?

There are many forms of equity participation structures, and entrepreneurs should consult their trusted CPA and attorney before choosing which one might be best for their business.

From my experience, the best equity-incentive plan is a phantom equity plan structured around the value appreciation of the business, commonly referred to as value appreciation rights. With this plan, the intrapreneur is granted the right to receive a future bonus based on the increase in the company's value.

Unlike traditional equity or stock options, phantom equity agreements do not require the intrapreneur to write a check to purchase the company's shares at issuance. Rather, the intrapreneur receives the right to receive a monetary reward equivalent to a portion of the increase in the company's growth in value over time, based on several criteria:

- Phantom equity units

    o An entrepreneur will allocate a certain percentage of the business for phantom equity ownership opportunities. Then the phantom equity units are divided among the intrapreneurs selected for the program (e.g., the entrepreneur decides to allocate X percent of the business toward a phantom equity program).

- Value appreciation threshold:

    o Phantom equity programs can come with a minimum threshold of value that the company needs to surpass for the intrapreneurs to be eligible to participate in the program. This protects the entrepreneur if the business does not experience the planned growth it expected (e.g., the entrepreneur is willing to share with the intrapreneurs any growth in value over the minimum threshold of X dollars).

- Vesting period:

    o Unlike real equity, phantom equity allows the entrepreneur to ensure that the intrapreneur remains a contributing member of the organization for a specific period before they vest into the program (e.g., the intrapreneur must be employed with the business for more than X years to be fully vested).

The intrapreneur does not pay taxes or other fees at the time of phantom equity plan issuance. The company does not get a tax deduction for the expense until the intrapreneur earns and is paid the phantom equity bonus in the future.

Phantom Equity Example

There are many variations of phantom equity programs. Here is an example of a model that I have found to work very well.

You hire a new executive and want them to fully buy into the company's success and act like an owner of the business. You want to give them a financial incentive for their long-term commitment to growing the value of the business. You provide this executive with a phantom equity opportunity.

Total phantom equity units available	1000 units (10% of the company)
Phantom equity units awarded to executive	100 Units (10% of the units available)
Estimated value of the company	$5,000,000
Value appreciation threshold	$6,000,000
Vesting period	5 years (3-year cliff)

- The executive is awarded 100 phantom equity units, which is 10% of the total units the entrepreneur has made available to the leadership of the company. Or to put it differently, the executive will participate in 1% (10% of 10%) of the company's total growth in value over the value appreciation threshold of $6M.

- The company's value at the time of the phantom equity award is $5M, and the entrepreneur elects to reward the phantom equity holders if the company grows to be valued over $6M.

- The phantom equity units vest over 5 years, with a 3-year cliff. If the intrapreneur leaves the company within the first 3 years, the phantom equity units are automatically forfeited. After the year 3 cliff, the phantom equity units would be 60% vested; after year 4, they would be 80% vested; and at 5 years, they would be 100% vested.

- If there is a triggering event at any time (e.g., a sale of the company), the phantom equity units would automatically fully vest to 100%.

- If the business grew over time and ultimately sold for $20M, the executive would have earned 1% of the difference between $20M and $6M, which is $14M. This would create a phantom equity bonus of $140K (1% of $14M) for the executive's contribution to helping the company grow.

I understand that's a lot of money. That's the point! If you correctly adhered to Principle I: Protect and Grow Your Equity, you have retained as much real equity as you possibly could in this business while allowing the intrapreneurs to participate in 10% of the value beyond a certain threshold that you established. You get to motivate and reward the leadership that helped you achieve success!

A true win-win-win for the intrapreneur, the business, and the entrepreneur!

Action Zone

- Does your interviewing process include behavioral interviews to test for core value alignment?
- Do you select your leadership style based on the competence and commitment of your team, specific to the task?
- What are 3 improvements you can make to practice leading situationally?
- What 3 ways can your company provide team members with more authority and freedom?
- Are you open to creating a phantom equity incentive plan for your key intrapreneurs so they can participate in the value appreciation of your business?

———

What is one thing that you will start, stop, and continue based on this principle?

Start? _____

Stop? _____

Continue? _____

Scan the QR code below to get access to *The $100M Journey Workbook* and other valuable resources to assist you on your journey!

PROTECT THE HOUSE

"If you don't invest in risk management, it doesn't matter what business you're in, it's a risky business."

— Gary Cohn, Vice Chairman IBM

This principle outlines the importance of the entrepreneur having a productive paranoia mindset to assess the risks to their business. It reminds entrepreneurs of their ethical responsibility to protect the business and those who have invested their lives in helping it grow. It stresses the importance of having a team of advisors to evaluate the business risks and to ask what could potentially harm the business.

Key Learnings:

1. Entrepreneurs must perform vulnerability assessments.

2. Lack of corporate governance and internal processes can cause significant harm.

3. Bringing snakes in suits onto your team can be crippling.

4. You must have a continuous process to manage ongoing customer and operational risks.

5. Make two-door, not one-door, decisions.

CHAPTER 23

WHY PROTECT THE HOUSE?

"Entrepreneurs are constantly playing a game of Whac-A-Mole. Just when you hit 3 in a row, 4, 5, and 6 pop up, and you are behind again."

— Jeffrey Unger, G2 Capital Advisors

You know what the biggest risk is to your business? . . . You! An entrepreneur has an ethical responsibility to protect the company, not solely for the sake of their own personal ambitions and goals, but for the people who invest their lives every day in helping the business grow.

Your business doesn't just pay *your* bills and feed *your* family. As an entrepreneur, one of our greatest contributions is supporting other humans. Your business pays for your employees' housing and puts food on their tables. Your business is so much more than the numbers and the growth. It is imperative that you take care of your house to protect all who are involved.

Nothing is more painful than seeing everything you have built go up in smoke! Unfortunately, I have experienced this tremendous feeling of failure. Although I have gotten back up and learned from these experiences, I am still shaken by them. More notably, I am shaken by how specific decisions I made negatively affected other people.

Albert Einstein has been credited with saying, "failure is success in progress," but when you are in the depths of digesting a failure, you certainly do not feel like you are on a pathway to success. Failure has a great way of bringing an incredible sense of deep humility to a person. This is where the power of introspection becomes an incredible asset. To learn and grow, one must look internally at their contributions to a situation and not take on a victim mindset.

We all know those people in our lives that have a victim mindset. They always seek to blame others when things do not go well, deflecting the spotlight from themselves out of fear that they truly are at fault. The moment you start blaming everybody else for why a failure occurred is the moment you reveal your cards to everybody and show them that you are probably hiding something. You might be the one to blame.

Failure + Introspection = Progress

Ultimately, all decisions along the journey can contribute to a business's demise. I hurt others by not correctly assessing risks and vulnerabilities and making bad, irreversible, one-door decisions. Partners, team members, customers, vendors, and, well . . . everybody is impacted when an entrepreneur does not adequately protect the business. The lost relationships still profoundly impact me today. Your team trusts you to protect the company and them; any failure will affect these relationships at the deepest level.

We must defend everything we have worked for and built by not allowing internal or external forces to throw us and our businesses into a tailspin.

Remember this "Messy Middle" chart from the opening chapter of this book?

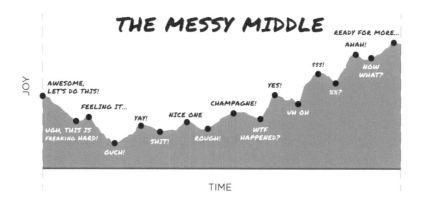

THE MESSY MIDDLE

READY FOR MORE...

AHAH!

JOY

AWESOME, LET'S DO THIS!

FEELING IT...

UGH, THIS IS FREAKING HARD!

OUCH!

YAY!

SHIT!

NICE ONE

ROUGH!

CHAMPAGNE!

YES!

WTF HAPPENED?

UH OH

↑↑↑!

XX?

NOW WHAT?

TIME

Every single "ouch?!" or "shit!" or "WTF happened?!" will give you the constant feeling you're taking one step forward, two steps back. Way too many entrepreneurs are running in quicksand. They are working very hard but sinking.

Ever had that feeling? Of course, you have! We all have. I know I have felt this way hundreds of times.

It is very discouraging to feel like you have done everything right, your business is humming and you're enjoying smooth sailing, and when you least expect it, you get hit by unexpected turbulence. You may have plugged 99 holes in your boat and feel like you are running a tight ship; however, the one hole you did not plug will inevitably become a big problem in the midst of a storm. Sometimes it can be that one hole that sinks your business!

Entrepreneurs need to have a productive paranoia mindset, constantly evaluating risks to the company and making adjustments accordingly. Please note there is a big difference between "productive paranoia" and constant, creepy, "I do not trust anybody" paranoia. The latter will suck the life out of your culture, whereas the former can be used in a positive and effective trust-but-verify manner.

We all know the saying, "entrepreneurs need to work _on_ their business, not _in_ their business!" Unfortunately, this rarely happens because entrepreneurs haven't figured out how to master Principles I–IV, and they essentially just do not "have the time" to work *on* the business. And so . . . they continue working *in* the business, trying to find a way off the hamster wheel.

If you are not protecting the house, who is? The answer is clear: nobody is.

Jeffrey Unger (G2 Capital Advisors) has spent his whole career working with companies and entrepreneurs. He made a comment to me that resonates as so true: "Entrepreneurs are constantly playing a game of Whac-A-Mole. Just when you hit 3 in a row, 4, 5, and 6 pop up, and you are behind again. It is very rare that you find a company that is very tight on corporate governance and paperwork. It is only when something happens to them do they correct the gaps."

Does that feel like you? It sure did resonate with me. The feeling of always chasing your business's goals while ensuring you are running a tight ship to minimize any business risks is not easy.

Unger believes entrepreneurs must "develop a cadence of corporate governance with a team of advisors to evaluate [their] business risks monthly or quarterly and constantly ask [themselves]: 'what is going to pop up that can harm the business?'"

Here are some personal examples of why risk management is so critical:

In 2008, one of our largest customers, who owed us $225K, abruptly filed for bankruptcy. My heart sank to the floor. Our small business could not afford this bad debt write-off.

The recession was hard enough, but now this? "How will we survive this?" I kept asking myself.

Many sleepless nights, doing whatever it took to stay alive to make payroll every week, taught me a valuable lesson. Why did we let this customer rack up this level of credit with our small business? That could *not* happen again!

————

In 2014, our controller received an email from one of our vice presidents asking her to send a $250K wire for an upcoming event. In the body of the email was a made-up conversation between me (the CEO) and the vice president about how important it was for this wire to happen today. The problem was that the email addresses, which looked identical to our company email alias, each had a 1-letter typo. Because the controller did not see the wrong letter in the email addresses (who would have?) and because our company did not have a two-factor authentication system for large transactions and wires, the controller wired $250K that afternoon.

It wasn't until the vice president came into the office the next day, and the controller informed him that she had sent the $250K wire he had requested, that we determined that we had been the victim of wire fraud.

Our business was smack dab in the Messy Middle and could not afford this mistake. Ouch! We never got the money back, and we survived, but it hurt badly. We immediately implemented two-factor authentication controls to make sure this never had a chance of occurring again.

————

You might remember in my entrepreneurial journey, when we were looking to bring investors into the business, my mentor, Jeff, asked me, "So, how are you protected in this business?" and I responded with an air of overconfidence, suggesting that the business could not exist without me.

Well, was I proven wrong on that one. I got fired from the company I had cofounded 15 years prior and was left with nothing to show for it.

Likewise, you can lose everything if you do not ensure the legal documents governing the business also protect you.

Countless stories exist of entrepreneurs reading their operating agreement for the first time only *after* a business partnership turns sour.

———

One of the worst business decisions I ever made was hiring an unknown and unverified executive to join our team. I put them in a critical and visible role and edified them throughout the organization as an executive that would take us to the next level.

Unbeknownst to me, this person had other intentions. In the previously-mentioned book, *Snakes in Suits*, Hare and Babiak appropriately warn of the impacts these individuals can have on an organization. As soon as this person was hired, they infiltrated the organization's culture and used lies to turn team members, trusted partners, and my best friends against me.

I did not realize my error until it was too late . . .

To properly protect what they are building, entrepreneurs should practice being proactive rather than reactive. Yet, entrepreneurs seldom take the necessary time out of their busy schedules to focus on protecting their businesses. Heck, most people claim to not even *have* the time to protect their own personal interests, let alone their business.

When did you last do a comprehensive vulnerability assessment on your business? Do you even know what all your company's vulnerabilities are?

By not developing a routine and strategy around your risk management, you are risking all your equity and all the value you have built within it.

Take action now and protect the business you are building. Make it a top priority.

Self-Reflection Zone

- Think about some of the vulnerabilities you have left exposed in the past and how they have painfully affected you, your team, and your business?

- What are the top 5 risks you believe exist in your business today that scare you?

- When was the last time you performed a vulnerability assessment for your business?

Scan the QR code below to watch a supplemental video about why this principle is so important!

CHAPTER 24

HOW TO PROTECT THE HOUSE

"First rule of business, protect your investment."

—"Etiquette of the Banker," 1775

As an entrepreneur builds their business, they must assess their vulnerabilities and ensure that they limit any areas of exposure that could negatively affect the business. It is an entrepreneur's duty to protect themselves, their team, and their business. Although there are hundreds of possible exposure points, this chapter will review the significant exposure areas that can prevent your business from going off the cliff.

1. Build your team of protectors.
2. Perform vulnerability assessments.
3. Have strong corporate governance and internal processes.
4. Close gaps in your insurance coverage.
5. Minimize customer risk.
6. Implement tight financial controls.
7. Avoid one-door decisions.
8. Beware of snakes in suits.

———

1. BUILD YOUR TEAM OF PROTECTORS

Assembling a robust team of advisors is not just a luxury; it's a necessity. The larger your business grows, the more you need to surround yourself with experts covering all areas of your business and personal affairs.

When forming and starting a business, entrepreneurs tend to be very frugal and avoid incurring hefty professional fees from costly advisors. I get it. I would often do the same thing. But when it comes to growing a business beyond the Lifestyle stage, you must upgrade your team of advisors.

Yes, you will need to pay for it. Like with every other investment, you need to invest in the right advisors. If you do, the investment will generate a strong ROI and you will stop viewing the payments you make as an "expense." Think about it right now. When you pay your professional advisors, do you view it as an expense or an investment? If you view it as an expense, you probably have the wrong advisor. Finding the best advisors may not be cheap, but it will be worth every penny when you make strong returns acting on their guidance.

Stop being penny-wise and dollar foolish.

These advisors will protect you and your business assets from the many dangerous pitfalls while, just as importantly, guiding you and your business to build and protect the wealth you intend to create. Without a world-class team, you can jeopardize your business's growth and stability.

Here is a list of the advisors every entrepreneur should have:

- **Mentor/Coach:** The wisdom of experienced entrepreneurs who've walked the path you aspire to walk is invaluable. These mentors can provide guidance based on firsthand experiences, helping you avoid common pitfalls and offering insights that textbooks cannot provide.

- **Corporate Attorney:** Expert attorneys are your first line of defense against legal troubles. Seek those who specialize in business law, intellectual property, contracts, and other pertinent areas. Their counsel ensures your business adheres to regulations, avoids potential litigation, and safeguards your intellectual property. A comprehensive understanding of your business model and industry is crucial. Corporate attorneys draft ironclad agreements, resolve disputes, and navigate complex legal waters.

- **Litigation Attorney:** A litigation attorney specializes in representing clients in legal disputes and lawsuits. These professionals are skilled in navigating the intricacies of the legal system and advocating for their client's rights and interests. Litigation attorneys handle a wide range of cases, from contract disputes to personal injury claims, aiming to achieve favorable outcomes through negotiation, settlement, or, when necessary, courtroom litigation. Their expertise lies in building strong cases, conducting legal research, presenting arguments, and strategizing to protect the entrepreneurs legal rights in the face of legal challenges.

- **Estate Attorney:** An estate attorney is a legal expert who specializes in matters related to estate planning and management. These attorneys help entrepreneurs and their families create comprehensive plans for the distribution of their assets, properties, and wealth after their passing. Estate attorneys draft essential documents like wills, trusts, and power of attorney documents to ensure that their client's wishes are carried out seamlessly. They provide guidance on minimizing estate taxes, protecting assets, and designating beneficiaries. Estate attorneys play a vital role in preserving family legacies, ensuring a smooth transition of wealth, and minimizing potential conflicts among heirs.

- **CPA:** Financial consultants, including CPAs and tax accountants, offer vital guidance in managing finances efficiently, optimizing tax strategies, and ensuring compliance with tax laws. These financial protectors offer insights that can be the difference between fiscal growth and financial turmoil.

- **Wealth Advisor:** Wealth advisors help manage your personal and business financial goals. They guide you in creating investment strategies, managing assets, and planning for the future, ensuring your hard-earned success extends to the long term.

- **Commercial Insurance Agent:** Commercial insurance advisors serve as your safety net. Their expertise in risk assessment and coverage solutions can shield your business from the financial fallout of unforeseen events, whether it's property damage, liability claims, or other emergencies.

The best way to find these advisors is to network with other entrepreneurs who have built a business like you aspire to build. When selecting advisors, look for individuals with impeccable credentials, a deep understanding of your industry, and a proven track record of success. Beyond expertise, seek advisors who resonate with your vision and values.

Remember, the strength of your team of protectors directly impacts your business's resilience and ability to thrive amid challenges.

2. PERFORM VULNERABILITY ASSESSMENTS

What are your company's vulnerabilities?

If you have not conducted a vulnerability assessment for your business recently (or ever), there is no better time than the present. When entrepreneurs are busy running the daily operations of their businesses, they frequently will overlook the vulnerabilities their businesses may face because they either "do not have the time" to consider them or are simply oblivious to the exposure.

Entrepreneurs must continually assess any possible vulnerability that may exist. If there are 100 possible vulnerabilities a business might face, your role as the entrepreneur is to make sure that *all* of them are addressed in the best way possible and not allow any of them to send your business into a tailspin of risk and back into the depths of the Messy Middle.

One of the best ways to accomplish this is to surround yourself with the best team of advisors possible. This includes attorneys, CPAs and tax accountants, financial wealth advisors, commercial bank relationships, commercial insurance advisors, business advisors and coaches, and other entrepreneurs who have built businesses to the size you envision and dream of.

You must master risk management from all perspectives, so building a risk committee comprising key team members and advisors is always a best practice. This is where the saying "you get what you pay for" really resonates.

Unfortunately, entrepreneurs who do not assess their risks may face situations that jeopardize everything they have built.

Vulnerability Assessment Example

Vulnerability Assessment

- Do you have an updated and accurate Operating Agreement for your business?
- Do you have an updated and accurate Buy/Sell Agreement for your business?
- Do you have copies of your corporate records saved digitally?
- Do you check your business's registration with all the states you are registered in?
- Do you have an employee handbook with sexual harassment, drug, alcohol, vacation and sick leave policies clearly set out?
- Do you have job descriptions for all roles with clear descriptions?
- Do you have an interview procedure with guidelines on what you cannot legally ask?
- Do you use personality tests in your hiring process?
- Does your company do reference checks on all potential employees?
- Does your company do criminal background check on all potential employees?
- Do you confirm citizenship prior to empoyment and retain a copy of the I-9 form?
- Do you have an employee contract that has an arbitration clause for any disputes and that limits your liability?
- Do you have non-compete, non-solicitation, and non-disclosure agreements with your employees?
- Have all signs required by state and federal law been posted?
- Are your salaried employees categorized and paid appropriately under the Department of Labor regulations?
- Do your compensation and benefits comply with discrimination laws, workers' compensation, Family Medical Leave Act, minimum wage, Employee Retirement Income Security Act (ERISA) and Consolidated Omnibus, Budget Recconciliation Act (COBRA) requirements?
- Do you have an employee discipline and separation/termination procedures?
- Do you have a succession plan for your business if you become disabled?

- For corporations or LLCs, are directors and officers insured for liability (i.e., D&O insurance)?
- Do you have your vendor contracts reviewed by an attorney before signing or cancelling them?
- Do you have any personal guarantees on any contracts for your business?
- Does your business have operations procedures written out so it can run without you there?
- Do you do a quarterly assessment of the vulnerabilities of your business and have a proactive plan to deal with them?
- Do you have any personal guarantees on an indebtedness of your company?
- Do you have a monthly financial meeting where you review your year-to-date P&L every month?
- Is your business current on all tax liabilities to the state and federal governments?
- Are you setting aside enough money to remain current on your upcoming tax liabilities?
- Does your business have three months overhead in cash reserve?
- Do you have one customer that is more than 15% of your company's revenue?
- Do you have two people, aside from you, regularly keeping an eye on the billing, deposits, and expenses?
- Do you have premises liability coverage for all locations your business operates?
- Do you have written leases for all property your business uses including any you personally own?
- Have you assessed the dollar value of the risks associated with your business with an insurance agent and attorney?
- Do you complete an annual insurance checkup with your agent to assess your coverage for the extent of your risk and obtain quotes?
- Do you have regular employee reviews?
- If your company uses any independent contractors, do you have contracts with them that make it clear they are not employees?

Consult with your corporate attorney, commercial insurance agent, CPA, and other advisors to ensure that you are properly reviewing all the vulnerabilities your business may encounter.

Note: Example vulnerability assessment questions provided by www.DavisBusinessLaw.com

3. HAVE STRONG CORPORATE GOVERNANCE AND INTERNAL PROCESSES

It is mind-boggling how many entrepreneurs do not have clear and updated operating agreements, buy-sell agreements, and other fundamental corporate legal agreements needed for the governance of their businesses. Of course, these become a big deal when something happens and these documents could have helped resolve a dispute.

My lack of attention to this area has proven very costly in the past. I was always focused on building the business and assuming everything would work out if we continued to grow. I did not make the proper effort to read the 50+ pages in the legal documents, nor did I want to pay for proper legal counsel to protect my interests.

If you do feel like you have your corporate governance agreements in place, do you understand them? Can you articulate how your business is governed by your operating agreement? Does your business have a buy-sell agreement? Most don't.

If your corporate legal documents are not tight, you are probably just as loose with other written contracts that are essential to managing the business. To protect your business, it is critical to spend the time upfront to make sure all the corporate governance documents, customer contracts, vendor contracts, employee agreements, and all other legal documents are written clearly and contain the proper legal oversight.

Have you ever been sued by an employee? It sucks! And it is becoming a big problem. The American legal system provides an environment for any employee to file a suit against a company for any reason, and the number of law firms prospecting for these frivolous cases is numerous. For any entrepreneur facing a former-employee lawsuit, not having tight documentation and processes around everything related to onboarding and managing your team can result in a legal disaster and cause major harm to the business.

Whether you are right or wrong in the specific situation is not really the issue here. Of course, it helps to be right. Still, most complaints filed by employees are settled out of court by insurance companies, with some measure of financial reward for the employee and their attorney. The law firms and the employees they represent see this as a reward for filing a claim, and the cycle repeats itself.

There are two ways to prevent these lawsuits and subsequent losses from happening:

1. Create an amazing culture of intrapreneurship (Principle IV), which attracts excellent talent and increases retention, and

2. protect your business with tight documentation and human resources processes. Without proper legal processes and paperwork, businesses are vulnerable to discrimination claims, wrongful termination, and other employee rights that employees feel are violated.

The lack of tight human resources processes can open the door to many legal issues for entrepreneurs, so it is a priority to put the proper protocols in place from the outset to protect the business from any potential legal vulnerabilities.

4. CLOSE GAPS IN YOUR INSURANCE COVERAGE

I do not think you will be surprised to know that there are many coverages that your typical commercial insurance policies simply do not cover. You should know what those are upfront and then consult annually with your trusted commercial insurance agent to ensure you are properly covered with the policies they can provide.

Do you know what your commercial insurance does not cover?

Did you know there are other ways to get insurance coverage that can further protect your business and provide certain advantages?

I didn't know until I surrounded myself with the best advisors.

Have you ever heard of a business having a captive commercial liability insurance program?

Larger companies have long understood the benefits of this structure, as a captive can allow them to self-insure their own business and build up reserves to effectively manage their risk and protect themselves against large catastrophic losses.

But this is also a tool for small- to medium-sized businesses earning strong net operating cash flow.

By forming a captive insurance company, a small business can access *extraordinary* coverages that a traditional commercial liability insurance program will not cover, thus providing more coverage to the business. Also, captives allow entrepreneurs to tailor coverage to suit their specific needs and operations while providing access to larger coverage limits than they can obtain through traditional insurance policies.

If that is not enticing enough, there are also numerous tax advantages to starting a captive insurance company. Entrepreneurs can deduct the premium their business pays to their captive company as a business expense for income tax purposes, reducing the overall cost associated with operating a captive and reducing the business's taxable income. I have been amazed at the benefits a captive program can provide a business.

A few years ago, we lost a large customer that had generated $500K in annual gross margin. This was covered under our captive policy, and we received a $500K claim payment. Imagine having an insurance policy that further protects your business in the cases of the loss of a key customer, key employee, or key supplier, or workplace violence, cyber attack, and other non-traditional incidents not otherwise covered.

Most importantly, you own a captive insurance company! An incredible tool so few entrepreneurs know about. If you are interested in pursuing a captive insurance company and program, it is very important that you consult with your professional advisors and strictly work with proven administrators who can manage the captive on your behalf.

5. MINIMIZE CUSTOMER RISK

Entrepreneurs frequently have a catalyst customer that helps their business surge to higher levels. Although this is a great problem to have, the risk of too much business coming from one customer or a small group of customers is real. This risk is particularly serious if any single customer represents a large portion (20% or more) of the revenue stream.

Entrepreneurs should constantly strive to diversify their customer base to reduce this risk. Having customers who are geographically spread out, are in different industries, or have different revenue sources can help reduce the potential impact of losing a large customer. Having too much business from a single customer or concentrated group of customers puts entrepreneurs at the mercy of demands made by such customers.

When providing customers with credit terms, businesses must make the necessary risk assessments to ensure that the customer can properly and promptly pay their invoices. When they do not, you must have a mechanism to cease performing your services because you will be at risk.

The larger the credit you are extending a customer, the greater level of due diligence your business needs to perform. This includes a heightened level of precaution when monitoring customer payments and creditworthiness and assessing the customer's risk profile and industry trends.

6. IMPLEMENT TIGHT FINANCIAL CONTROLS

Growth can lead to many growing pains and challenges as your internal controls try to keep up with the ever-changing needs of managing the operation. Way too often on my entrepreneurial journey, I did not upgrade the accounting function's resources, systems, and team members fast enough.

Way too often, entrepreneurs focus on sales and marketing first, operations to produce what they have sold second, and accounting last. The pain and suffering that can result from not maintaining tight financial controls is crippling. If you truly aspire to build a High Performance business, the company's finance department needs to be equipped for the task.

What your business needs is very different in each stage of the Entrepreneurial Journey:

- Startup and Struggle stages: As the entrepreneur strives to keep their costs low, the accounting function is typically handled by either an in-house or outsourced bookkeeper.

- Lifestyle stage: As the business stabilizes, the entrepreneur begins to build a small accounting department with an accounting manager.

- Messy Middle stage: As the journey to cross the chasm between Lifestyle and High Performance begins, it is essential that the business brings on a qualified controller to manage the accounting function and ensure tight control of the business.

- High Performance stage: At this stage, the business needs a fully functioning accounting department led by a CFO who strategically guides the direction of the business.

Outsourcing to a firm providing fractional accounting and finance services is one way businesses navigate these various stages. Fractional firms provide the right amount and level of support for your business and can often save your business money over hiring someone in-house.

7. AVOID ONE-DOOR DECISIONS

Any one-door decision—a significant decision that is irreversible—needs to be evaluated in incredible depth and with all advisors present. As an entrepreneur, you have your family and employees' families in your hands. Any major mistake you make by not protecting your business or making irreversible, bad decisions will affect them.

You must avoid any decision that can create a possible business mortality event!

One way to do this is to make sure that you make two-door decisions. In a one-door decision, you have no way out, whereas a two-door decision provides the entrepreneur with an *out*.

For example:

- Instead of giving your key employees *real* equity in the company (very hard to reverse), give them phantom equity that must be vested over time and can be voided if the employee leaves the company.

- If you cannot build your own capital, instead of bringing an investor into your company, try to find opportunities to obtain a loan that allows you to repay over time and retain your equity.

- Build a partner divorce clause into your operating agreements *now*, not when you have a dispute years from now.

- Give all new employees a 90-day trial period, and if they are not performing to your expectations, part ways before it is too late.

Quite simply, avoid making one-door decisions. Always give yourself and the business an executable option so you'll have an escape hatch to get out of a bad situation.

If you find yourself in a situation where you are contemplating a one-door decision, you should invite all of your professional advisors to contribute their experience and guidance to ensure you are considering all angles. We have implemented a process in our business where we seek unanimous "sign-off" from all advisors on one-door decisions before proceeding.

8. BEWARE OF SNAKES IN SUITS

This can happen on day one! Have you ever partnered with somebody in a business and come to find out that it was not a good partnership? How painful was it to terminate the relationship?

We must better vet the partners, investors, and team members we bring into our business.

Although employees can be terminated if they are not a good fit for the business, it is common that bad hires—and in some cases, bad people—can really be a cancer in your business's culture. They can cause incredible, sometimes irreparable, damage if they stay too long. These individuals pose a massive risk of destructive activity; falsifying information, improperly using company resources, and other financial fraudulent activities can occur.

Once again, I recommend all entrepreneurs and small-business owners read *Snakes in Suits: When Psychopaths Go to Work*. Reading it may help entrepreneurs to identify the traits of psychopaths that may be trying to enter the company or may already be in the company. In addition, the book contains valuable insights into the implications these psychopaths can have on workplace culture and operations.

Snakes in your organization can be incredibly adept at manipulating people and taking advantage of the weaknesses of their colleagues. They can potentially cause major disruption in your culture. Entrepreneurs must be aware of the signs and implications of psychopathic behavior when recruiting and managing their team and of the potential effects that psychopathic behavior can have on their business.

Imagine bringing somebody like this into your business as a partner or investor. Unlike an employee, they are very hard to get rid of and can cause massive disruption, not only to the business but to you and your mental health and happiness.

These bad actors must be rooted out *before* you bring them into your company. This is best accomplished by establishing a track record with individuals before bringing them into your business, performing proper diligence on them and their history—discounting their résumé and the references *they* line up for you to call and doing your own deep research—and having a trial period or way out.

————

There are many potential risks. This is not an exhaustive list of business vulnerabilities but highlights the ones that have caused me the most harm as an entrepreneur. You only need to learn some of these lessons the hard way once to realize how critical risk management is to everything you build.

Entrepreneurs must also perform risk management assessments in their own personal matters. Many entrepreneurs do not have personal liability coverage, living trusts, irrevocable trusts, wills, and other critically important estate planning and protection components so that they are fully protected in their own lives.

Please take a moment and complete the vulnerability assessment checklist by accessing *The $100M Journey Workbook* at 100MJourney.com/workbook. Use this checklist to assess your business and personal vulnerabilities and identify areas that need immediate attention. Do not wait!

Any one of these risks could send you right back into the depths of the Messy Middle, or worse, drive your business off the cliff!

Action Zone

- What are the top 3 risks your business is facing today?

- What can you do to mitigate your risks and protect your business?

- What ongoing risk management protocol can you put in place to ensure that your business risks are being overseen continually?

- Do you have all of the necessary advisors on your team?

- What 5 advisors sign off on any one-door decision you are considering?

———

What is one thing that you will start, stop, and continue based on this principle?

Start? _____

Stop? _____

Continue? _____

Scan the QR code below to get access to *The $100M Journey Workbook* and other valuable resources to assist you on your journey!

ACCESS OWNER'S LIQUIDITY

"Money is multiplied in practical value depending on the number of W's you control in your life: what you do, when you do it, where you do it, and with whom you do it."

— Timothy Ferriss, *The 4-Hour Workweek*

In this principle, we discuss the various ways that entrepreneurs can access the liquidity that is stuck within their business's balance sheet. We discuss the importance of understanding that small businesses are illiquid by nature since cash must remain on the balance sheet for the business to stay solvent. But there are ways for entrepreneurs to access liquidity without selling their equity—they are just not widely known or maximized.

Key Learnings:
1. Small businesses are illiquid by nature.

2. Too often, entrepreneurs pay themselves last.

3. The biggest trap in entrepreneurship is when a great company is built, and the entrepreneur feels like they *need* to take the opportunity to monetize their hard work by selling equity.

4. If you have a strong business and have implemented Principles I–V, you do not need to sell your equity.

5. Understand how to access liquidity without selling your equity.

CHAPTER 25

WHY ACCESS OWNER'S LIQUIDITY?

"Entrepreneurs do not create wealth running their businesses; they create wealth when they are able to access the liquidity within it"

— Jeremy Harbour, owner of The Harbour Club

I had grown several companies over my 20 years of being an entrepreneur, but yet I found myself having very little to show for it. Sound familiar? Think of all the times you have worked so hard on a business or project only to end up with nothing. Unfortunately, this comes with the territory of being an entrepreneur, but it still stinks.

Your business has grown yearly, you are profitable, and you feel like the next few years will finally start paying off, yet you continue to find that all you are doing is paying more in taxes to the government and increasing overhead costs as the company balloons in size. You continue to wonder when you will finally get a big payday.

Has this ever happened to you? "Maybe next year will be the year I can finally get a big dividend from this business!" you delusionally tell yourself, half believing what you are saying.

Way too many entrepreneurs work tirelessly to grow their businesses, only to find out that all the wealth they have created is tied up in the company's balance sheet. They simply cannot access it!

As an entrepreneur, you have the ability to control your financial success in a way others don't. That opportunity also comes with the risk of not knowing how to access and protect your hard-earned profits. Unfortunately, this big payday never arrives for some entrepreneurs. Whether it be a sudden pandemic, shifts in consumer behavior, an unanticipated challenge, or a market decline in desire for your product or service, if you wait too long to finally enjoy the fruits of your labor, it may one day all be gone!

Many entrepreneurs seek to build a Lifestyle-sized company so they can generate high annual income for their families. This is great! But if you are an entrepreneur seeking to build a High Performance business, you need to keep capital on the balance sheet as working capital to reinvest in the company's growth. You cannot extract all the cash earned on an annual basis to increase your personal income and lifestyle.

So, if the capital must remain on the company's balance sheet, how can entrepreneurs building a High Performance business ever get paid? How can they access the liquidity that is building up on their business's balance sheet?

In order to unlock this liquidity, we first must understand that unlike public companies, where you can rapidly sell the shares you own on the stock market, private businesses are illiquid by nature! In addition to not being able to redeem your shares in a private business, in most cases, the business needs cash to remain on the balance sheet to stay solvent and provide the working capital needed to continue to fund growth initiatives. The more you grow, the more cash you need! As you begin to earn profits, taxation starts to eat up a large portion of your liquidity. And the cycle repeats itself.

Entrepreneurs can certainly access the value they have built up in a business when they *sell* their equity. However, as mentioned in Principle I: Protect and Grow Your Equity, this might not be the best option. Consider the impact of selling your equity:

1. SELLING A MINORITY INTEREST

An entrepreneur can access liquidity by selling a minority interest in the business to another party while still maintaining a controlling stake in the company.

If you really believe in your business, why would you do this? Go back to Principle I: Protect and Grow Your Equity. Unless you or your business is desperate for cash, selling *any* equity is a big mistake. Equity is the one thing you cannot get back. Even if you retain the ultimate control of the business by only selling a minority of your interest, you will have somebody else to answer to. This is not an ideal way to access the liquidity that you have built up in your business.

*NOTE: Speaking from painful experience, I, like most entrepreneurs, had linked majority ownership with control. This is not always correct. Most sophisticated investors have developed methods to usurp control over a company, even when owning a minority stake in the business. They do this by implementing restrictions within the company's operating agreement, wherein no actions can occur without their consent. This can be crippling to an entrepreneur, so be careful.

2. SELLING A MAJORITY INTEREST

The entrepreneur should only consider selling a majority interest in their business to another party, and giving up management controls, when the entrepreneur cannot build or secure the necessary capital to grow their business on their own and must seek new investors to take the business forward.

Reread the above paragraph again, and again. . . It is a critical lesson that entrepreneurs need to learn! *When the entrepreneur cannot build or secure the necessary capital to grow their business on their own . . .*

Go back to Principle II: Build Your Own Capital. Do you now see how this principle is a major factor? If you build your own capital and can self-finance your growth, you may never need to sell a majority interest in your business to another party and subsequently lose control.

You either believe in your business and yourself, or you do not. If you do, keep control and build your own capital for reinvestment and growth. If you do not, sell 100% and get out!

3. 100% SALE (EXIT)

The decision to sell 100% of the equity you own in a business is a big entrepreneurial decision that you should only explore when you are confident that the sale will provide greater returns than continuing to operate the business.

Why sell if you have a strong business and have properly implemented Principles I–V? You have built something rock solid that can continue to grow and appreciate.

Beyond retirement, there are two core reasons entrepreneurs want to sell all of their equity:

1. The entrepreneur is getting tired of running the day-to-day operations of the business and, even though they love the business, they do not want to run its operations 60+ hours a week.

2. Or, the entrepreneur wants to get a return on everything they have put into growing the business and is afraid that if they do not take their chips off the table now, they may not get another chance to monetize their efforts.

Before selling all your equity for either of these two reasons, consider the following two alternate ideas:

1. Why are you running the day-to-day operations of your business anyway? If you have properly applied Principles I–V, especially Principle IV: Build a Culture of Intrapreneurship, you should have intrapreneurs in your company who would love to step up and take on a bigger role in your business. Quite frankly, you are probably not the best person to run and grow your business anyway. It might be time for you to move from active CEO to passive chairperson of your business (see Principle VII: Move from CEO to Chairperson).

2. Entrepreneurs need to learn how to access the liquidity in their businesses *without* selling their equity. Too often, entrepreneurs pay themselves last. If you have a successful business that is generating positive net operating cash flow, how can you start building your wealth beyond your annual compensation? Let's explore this further. . .

Entrepreneurs find themselves in a pretty big dilemma once they have built a great company that is generating strong net operating cash flow. They are suddenly faced with incredible opportunities to monetize some or all of their hard work and efforts. They may not be ready to sell, but they feel like they *need* to. They may have pressure from their spouse to finally get that vacation home or a boat. They may be wondering, "If I do not sell my business now, will I ever get a big payday?" But mostly, they simply do not see other ways to access the owner's liquidity in their business without selling equity. So they sell.

Think for a minute about how and why companies are bought. In a traditional business, an entrepreneur can sell their equity for a multiple of EBITDA (earnings before interest, taxes, depreciation, and amortization). There are certainly other valuation methods, but for now, let's just use this one as an example.

Why would an investor pay 5X your company's EBITDA for your equity?

The answer is simple: because in five years, assuming the business stays flat, they will have paid for the investment and now own the business into the future, earning themselves an ROI. Note that they are certainly not buying your business to keep it flat. If they can grow it, the timeline to pay off the original investment shrinks, and the ROI increases.

Well, what if you could hold your equity for five more years, then sell it for 5X the EBITDA? Simple math would indicate that this would earn you closer to 10X the sale price, or in other words, 2X more than if you sold your equity today for 5X your company's current EBITDA.

Where will you put the money if you take chips off the table now? You will either purchase material luxury items or invest in paper assets like mutual funds or stocks. The first violates the principles from *The Millionaire Next Door,* and the second makes no sense. Why on earth would you invest in a public corporation, where you have zero control, when you can continue to control (or at least have a say in) your own business?

Business owners simply do not know that there are very creative ways to have their cake and eat it too—by accessing liquidity on the balance sheet without selling equity.

Imagine being able to protect and retain all of your equity (Principle I) and continue to build your capital (Principle II), all while growing your business and accessing your liquidity to pay yourself very nice dividends on an annual basis in a way that is also *beneficial to the company* in many ways. Yes, you can amplify Principles I–V and build a wealth engine by being smart here!

You cannot keep sucking your balance sheet dry by making owner distributions every time you make a profit. This will kill your business.

What happens when there is a problem in the business or a big recession? If this happens, you are now in a bind. You need to raise more capital by selling equity, getting a bank loan . . . and the cycle repeats.

I spent 15 years building a company and never got anything from it because I did not follow the 7 Principles of Entrepreneurial Success. Do not let that be you! By following the principles in this book and understanding how to access the owner's liquidity, you will understand how to best maximize your equity and be wise with every dollar on your balance sheet.

Self-Reflection Zone

- Have you ever grown a business and not gotten rewarded for your efforts in the end? What could you have done differently?

- When did you last pay yourself a profit dividend from your business without selling equity?

- If you were able to pay yourself a healthy owner dividend every year, above and beyond your compensation, why would you ever sell your equity?

- Do you execute any strategies to reduce your taxable income and help you keep more capital in your business?

Scan the QR code below to watch a supplemental video about why this principle is so important!

CHAPTER 26

HOW TO ACCESS OWNER'S LIQUIDITY

"As your business grows, owners can use liquidity in the business balance sheet and put it in tax-efficient vehicles that provide immediate and long-term benefits to the business and its owners."

— Vince Pastore, CPA, HBK Advisors

There are several ways to access liquidity that is tied up in your business's balance sheet while still maintaining your full ownership. Many are unknown to small-business entrepreneurs because their business does not make enough net operating cash flow, and they have never been exposed to these incredible opportunities. In this chapter, we will review the traditional method of making distributions to partners versus employing tax-efficient vehicles that enable owners to access liquidity from their companies while also helping the businesses themselves.

1. Dividends or distributions to owners

2. Implement a safe harbor 401(k) and cash balance profit-sharing plan.

3. Form a captive insurance company.

4. Build new business assets with a Series LLC holding company.

WARNING: If you are not currently working with high-level business advisors, including an experienced CPA, and you are still using the independent, mom-and-pop CPA that managed your taxes before you built your business (who does not have the sophistication to guide your growth), you must find an experienced, small- to medium-sized-business CPA.

I know it is hard to invest in these professionals, but shame on you if you are not taking advantage of the current tax laws. The U.S. government (and other governments) have provided entrepreneurs access to different taxation tools as motivation and incentive to grow small businesses. Most importantly, you will never be able to unlock the liquidity in your business if a large percentage of your earnings and cash gets eaten up by taxes.

When it comes to tax planning, tax efficiency is paramount. It is not how much you make, it's how much you keep. You can think of this as revenue protection. Reduction of tax liability is critical for you as an entrepreneur because it will create opportunities for your business to have increased cash flow for reinvestment in growth (something the government also wants businesses to have). You can also extract liquidity from your business for your hard-earned effort. The issue is that most business owners are not aware of the more advanced concepts beyond just regular deductions, business expenses, and asset depreciation. There are several wealth-creation tools that I've learned by surrounding myself with the best-in-class professionals including CPAs, financial advisors, insurance agents, legal counsel, and business mentors. I had no clue these incredible, tax-efficient tools existed until I could build a business the right way and surround myself with the best advisors. If I had not learned about these tools and had simply taken all the money we were earning to make owner distributions, a large portion of our cash flow would have been going to pay taxes, and we would not have been able to reinvest in the company's growth.

There are ways to keep your company's balance sheet strong, reinvest in the company's growth, provide financial incentives to your team, provide stronger risk management, and fuel your growth.

———

1. DIVIDENDS OR DISTRIBUTIONS TO OWNERS

If your goal is to build a High Performance company, paying dividends or distributions to owners before the business has achieved a net operating cash flow of over $1M is not ideal. Better strategies can be executed to create a stronger win-win for the business and the entrepreneur.

Of course, when a business has excess cash on the balance sheet, you can distribute profit to owners and take the cash off the balance sheet. This is simple, but is it the right thing to do?

First, any earned or distributed profits will most likely be taxable to the business or the owners. The ordinary income tax rate (at the time of this writing) is 24–37% for federal taxes (for U.S. residents); this does not include state tax rates. So, if you are in a high tax-rate bracket and earn over $200K annually, the tax on profits could be around 40%.

As an example, if you earn and distribute $1M, the owners could be taxed up to $400K, netting the owners $600K in cash. Meanwhile, the balance sheet was weakened, the business lost $1M in cash, and there was no tax benefit to the business or the owners.

Some entrepreneurs own a business specifically to earn a high annual income so they can purchase the material items they desire for their lifestyle. Others build businesses to create long-term wealth for themselves and their families.

This can be compared to the stories of professional athletes who have earned tens of millions of dollars during their playing careers but are now bankrupt. Between taxation and maintaining a luxurious lifestyle, they spend the money as quickly as they earn it; whereas those who have earned a lot less in their careers have figured out ways to amass an abundance of wealth. Which one do you want to be?

Vince Pastore, CPA at HBK Advisors, advises his clients to use proper leverage as the company grows its balance sheet so that the owners do not have to fund the company's continued reinvestment growth strategy. This allows the owners to access some of the company's liquidity.

A bank loan based on the strength of the business can allow the business to borrow money to provide the business with the proper working capital it needs so that the owners can pay themselves a proper dividend with free cash flow.

In some cases, where the company has an incredibly strong balance sheet, a bank loan can be secured solely for the purpose of providing a dividend or distribution to its owners. This type of loan can give entrepreneurs access to the liquidity within the company's balance sheet while maintaining full ownership and control of the business. The business then repays the bank loan over time (typically 5–7 years) with interest, while the entrepreneurs can use their dividends for other investments, thus diversifying their holdings.

This strategy is perfect for a business that has mastered Principle II: Build Your Own Capital and is generating significant positive net operating cash flow.

The typical amount of leverage a bank will allow a business to have depends on the size of the business, the purpose of the loan, and the business's creditworthiness. Generally, banks will allow businesses to leverage 3–4 times their net worth, or up to 80% of the assets being financed.

So as an example, if your business had a balance sheet net worth of $1M (and a strong credit history), and your business did not have any debt, you might be able to find a bank that will loan you $2M for a dividend recap to owners. In this case, the owners would receive $2M, the business would pay back the $2M loan in time (5–7 years) with interest, and you would still own 100% of the business!

It's great, but there is a reason most entrepreneurs cannot do this:

- They do not properly execute Principles I–V.

- They make a conscious decision to fund the working capital of their business with their own cash because they are averse to incurring any debt.

- They do not *know* they can do this.

- They have too much leverage on their balance sheet as it is.

- They would rather reinvest any leverage the business can access into their business growth (not a bad idea if reinvested smartly— Principle III), and the growth strategy is sound.

2. IMPLEMENT A SAFE HARBOR 401(K) AND CASH BALANCE PROFIT-SHARING PLAN

There is a great way to impact and change the financial well-being of your employees while also benefiting you and your company. By providing your team with profit-sharing opportunities in their retirement plans, you may be eligible to put up to 10X the maximum limit into your own 401(k) plan as an owner of the company (see IRS.gov[1] in "References"). And all the cash your business would contribute to the 401(k) profit-sharing plan for you and your employees would also be a tax-deductible expense to your company, minimizing your taxable income!

Let me repeat the punch line: you may be eligible to put up to 10X the maximum limit into your own 401(k). Do I have your attention now?

As an owner providing a safe harbor 401(k) and cash balance profit-sharing plan to your employees, you can put a significant amount more than the IRS maximum ($22,500 in 2023) into your own 401(k) cash balance (see IRS.gov[2] in "References").

- Safe harbor allows employers to make additional matching and/or nonelective contributions for their employees.

  - This plan is designed to help employers meet their fiduciary responsibilities under ERISA (Employee Retirement Income Security Act) while providing additional retirement benefits for their employees.

  - The plan is considered a "safe harbor" plan because it automatically meets the requirements of ERISA, which requires that employers make certain contributions on behalf of their employees to qualify for certain tax benefits.

    - These contributions are typically made in the form of matching contributions or nonelective contributions.

    - For example, our company elected to provide each employee with a contribution of 3% of their payroll to the employee's 401(k) plan (not a match, just a simple "everybody gets 3%").

- Cash balance profit sharing is a type of retirement plan combining features of a defined benefit plan with a defined contribution plan.

- The employer makes profit-sharing contributions for each eligible employee, credited to the employee's account. Combined with a safe harbor 401(k), the employer may also make profit-sharing contributions to the employee's account based on a fixed formula of profits.

- This program typically comes with a vesting period for employees where they fully earn the employer's contributions over time. This slowly builds a nest egg for your employees and encourages them to stay with your company for more years of profit-sharing and growth.

The safe harbor 401(k) and cash balance profit-sharing plan allow the business to provide incredible retirement benefits to their employees while allowing them to share in the company's success (a huge competitive advantage), and reduce the annual taxable income of the company itself.

Business owners who implement a safe harbor 401(k) and cash balance profit-sharing plan reduce the company's taxable income, control how the money is invested, attract and retain quality employees, and receive a significant dividend and distribution in their own retirement accounts.

Safe Harbor 401(k) and Cash Balance Profit-Sharing Plan Example

A business earning $1M a year in net income would most likely distribute or pay up to $400K (40% estimate) in taxes. This would net the company $600K in cash.

But if you set up a safe harbor 401(k) and cash balance profit-sharing plan to share some of the profits of your company with your employees and maximize your personal 401(k) as an owner, you might be able to place $450K into the 401(k) plans of you and your employees (heavily weighted toward you as the owner—consult with your CPA to learn more).

The company would then receive a $450K expense deduction, reducing its taxable income from $1M to $550K, for which the company would then pay $220K (40% estimate) in taxes. That's a tax saving of $180K that, instead of going to the government for taxes, has been used to reward the employees (and owners) of the company.

This program blew my mind! Sure, this is post-tax 401(k) income that should not be touched until age 59 1/2 (minimum age in 2023) to avoid early-withdrawal penalty, but what a way to extract liquidity from your company without needing to sell equity!

So net/net:

- The company gets the tax deduction in the current year.

- You are helping build your employees' personal balance sheets.

- And the owners get to invest significant company profits into their own 401(k) plans and defer taxes on such proceeds.

Entrepreneurs should implement a safe harbor 401(k) and cash balance profit-sharing plan when their business has attained significant annual profitability and is generating strong, positive, annual net operating cash flow.

3. FORM A CAPTIVE INSURANCE COMPANY

Ever consider owning your own insurance company? Maybe you should!

A captive insurance company, established and owned by the owners of a business, provides supplemental insurance coverages for the business and affiliated entities they own.

Not only can a captive insurance policy reduce the overall cost of traditional commercial insurance coverages but it can also provide the business with coverages not normally covered by traditional commercial policies, providing increased risk management protections (Principle V: Protect the House). Coverages such as loss of key customers, loss of a key employee, loss of key suppliers, supply chain interruption, workplace violence, cyber attack, and much more would be cost prohibitive under traditional means.

If there is an extraordinary event that needs insurance coverage to protect the business, the claim is spread among the hundreds of other companies in the captive pool, greatly minimizing the risk of self-insuring your business. Not only can a captive insurance program reduce the cost of premiums, deductibles, and other insurance-related expenses, it also provides improved risk management for the business. It gives the owners greater control over the terms and conditions of their coverage.

The best part is that your business pays the captive premiums to *your* captive insurance company! *You* are the insurance company.

Just as importantly, a captive insurance program can help to reduce the business's overall tax liability. When a business purchases a policy through a captive insurance company, the expense to the business is tax deductible (up to $2.6M in 2023), thus decreasing the business's taxable income. The profits generated through the captive, which you own, are subject to capital gains tax treatment, which is lower than the ordinary income tax treatment you would get with traditional profit distributions. So, not only does your business have a lower taxable income, but the owners (through the captive) also receive better tax treatment.

The business wins (lower taxable income and more protection), the captive insurance company wins (earning significant premiums with large group pools to protect against claims), and the owners win (building significant cash on the captive balance sheet that will be taxed at lower capital gains rates).

Captive Insurance Example

An operating business makes $1M in taxable income, and the owners purchase a $250k insurance policy from their own captive insurance company. The operating business's taxable income would then be $750k.

The operating business would get increased risk-management protection against any extraordinary event.

The captive would receive a $250K premium (minus management fees to the captive manager), and the captive balance sheet should receive the net earnings from the premium (usually around 90%, assuming your business does not have any major claims). So, the captive now has retained earnings of $225K.

When distributed to the owners, the captive profits would be taxed at capital gains rates (15–20%) rather than ordinary income tax rates (35–37%) if the operating business distributed the profits to owners from the business itself.

So net/net:

- The company gets the tax deduction in the current year.

- The company gets additional insurance coverage above and beyond the typical commercial coverage policies.

- The owners get to build a strong balance sheet within the captive insurance company.

- Upon distribution of captive proceeds, the owners will receive capital gains tax treatment rather than ordinary income tax treatment.

Captive insurance companies are highly scrutinized and should always be set up and managed by a professional management company specializing in captive insurance programs and following all of the proper regulations.

4. BUILD NEW BUSINESS ASSETS WITH A SERIES LLC HOLDING COMPANY

If your goal is to access liquidity from your existing business asset so that you can diversify and invest in other business assets (something Rich Dad tells us to do), then there is no better way to do this than with a series LLC holding company.

> A series LLC holding company is a type of company that allows for the creation of separate legal entities within a single holding company. It provides the same benefits as a traditional holding company but with additional flexibility, tax advantages, and legal protections (Principle V: Protect the House).

Instead of distributing profits to the owners, which will be taxed, a series LLC holding company can be formed to manage your desired investments into other businesses. Holding multiple businesses as one larger company has some great benefits.

Series LLC holding companies are more tax efficient because each series company is treated as a separate entity for tax and legal purposes. This means that the income and losses of each series are tracked separately so that each series can claim the appropriate deductions and credits without being affected by the tax liabilities of the other series. This helps to reduce the overall tax burden on the company and its owners.

The businesses within a series LLC holding company have distinct legal identities providing risk protection. This can benefit entrepreneurs looking to reduce risk and liability and make it easier to manage multiple business ventures. Additionally, series holding companies are more tax efficient and provide greater asset protection, making them an attractive option for their owners.

Series LLC Holding Company Example

The owners form a series LLC holding company for the purposes of diversifying their ownership of business assets.

As their primary business generates $1M of taxable income, the owners, through their series LLC holding company, form a new series Limited Liability Company (LLC) to purchase another business asset.

With counsel from their CPA, this newly acquired business asset will provide the opportunity to take advantage of accelerated depreciation.

"Accelerated depreciation is any method of depreciation used for accounting or income tax purposes that allows greater depreciation expenses in the early years of the life of an asset. Accelerated depreciation methods, such as double-declining balance (DDB), means there will be higher depreciation expenses in the first few years and lower expenses as the asset ages. This is unlike the straight-line depreciation method, which spreads the cost evenly over the life of an asset." —Alicia Tuovila, *Investopedia*

In addition to accelerated depreciation, any investments made in this new business will reduce the taxable income of the series LLC holding company.

In essence, instead of claiming $1M of taxable income and paying up to 40% ($400K) in taxes, the entrepreneur can significantly reduce their taxable income for that given year and start building a new business asset.

So net/net:

- Entrepreneurs can reinvest profits into other business assets through a series LLC holding company.

- A series LLC holding company will provide tax efficiencies and proper legal protections for all entities.

- Entrepreneurs can diversify their ownership into other business assets through a series LLC holding company.

Please consult with your CPA and corporate attorney to discuss the pros and cons of setting up a series LLC holding company for your business assets.

———

Too many entrepreneurs distribute cash out of their business as soon as they start making money. This drains the business of cash, is taxed at the highest rates, and does not help the entrepreneur further build the business. There are many tax-advantaged ways to access the owner's liquidity in a business that provide a win-win-win for the business, the employees, and the entrepreneurs. These strategies are not well-known by most CPAs, so how can we even expect entrepreneurs to know about them? With this lack of knowledge, entrepreneurs pay a large percentage of their profits to the government, their companies fail to grow because they lack cash flow, and the business risks going on life support.

Example of How These Strategies Can Work for Entrepreneurs

Suppose your company made $1M in taxable income last year.

Instead of paying taxes on $1M of taxable income, which would be estimated at $400K, you may be able to reduce your taxable income in a tax-advantaged manner.

- Set up a safe harbor 401(k) and cash balance profit-sharing plan to share some of the profits of your company with your employees and maximize your personal 401(k) as an owner. You place $450K into the 401(k) plans of you and your employees (heavily weighted toward you as the owner). When filing taxes, the company will then claim a $450K expense deduction, reducing its taxable income from $1M to $550K.

- Then, you purchase a $250K insurance policy from your own captive insurance company. The operating business's taxable income would then be lowered to $300K.

- Then, you purchase a new business asset through your series holding company and take advantage of accelerated depreciation and any investments made in that business to reduce your taxable income to $0.

All of a sudden, your company's $1M taxable income has become $0 (saving approximately $400K in taxes).

By doing this, you and your employees are rewarded as you have generously funded everybody's retirement accounts. This is such a huge, competitive advantage.

Your captive company balance sheet has $250K in cash (minus captive fees), and the business is further protected with extraordinary insurance coverages for risks such as workplace violence, cyber security attacks, loss of key customers, key employee loss, director and officer's liability, computer and software disruption, and more.

If a catastrophic claim on your business met the captive insurance underwriting policy criteria, the coverage would be put into a pool with hundreds of other companies that would assist in covering the claim.

In the future, any distributions from the captive insurance company would be taxed at capital gains rates versus ordinary income rates. As the funds on the balance sheet of the captive insurance company continue to grow, you would hire an investment advisor to invest those funds in equities so they can appreciate every year.

And last but not least, you have added a new business asset to your portfolio.

These tax-advantaged vehicles significantly impact all the principles in this book.

- You do not have to sell any equity (Principle I: Protect and Grow Your Equity).

- You keep more cash in the business (Principle II: Build Your Own Capital).

- You pay down debt, build up cash reserves, and reinvest to grow the business (Principle III: Reinvest Smartly).

- You reward your employees with profit-sharing in their retirement plans (Principle IV: Build a Culture of Intrapreneurship).

- You protect the business with increased insurance coverages (Principle V: Protect the House).

- You can access the owner's liquidity that you have worked so hard to build (Principle VI: Access Owner's Liquidity).

- You can spend more time strategically overseeing the business as you diversify into new business assets (Principle VII: Move from CEO to Chairperson).

There are too many horror stories of entrepreneurs, like me, who built their companies for 10, 15, or 20+ years only to bring in additional investors and lose everything because they did not know how to access the owner's liquidity they had in their business. Do not do this!

If you want to sell your equity for liquidity reasons, I strongly advise that you consider a full exit. Just get out!

If you need cash badly and it's an emergency, then selling a portion of your equity for cash might be necessary. However, additional precautions must be taken if you are giving up control of your company. That is a one-door decision that you cannot reverse. You must exercise extreme caution.

If you do not need the money, and I mean NEED with capital letters, why are you selling your equity? Do you not have confidence in your company? Are you scared? Are you trying to take advantage of a high valuation? Why?

If you are tired of running your company operationally but are profitable and generating positive net operating cash flow, and you are able to access some liquidity from your business, then proceeding directly to Principle VII: Move from CEO to Chairperson may assist you in really extracting the value from your business.

However, if you must sell now, consider selling 100% of your equity in the company and fully exiting the business. Unfortunately, 90% of potential purchasers will attempt to pay you with your own money using seller notes with long terms of payment. This is highly risky. Selling a small business is very difficult, heart-wrenching, stressful, and risky. This process distracts all involved, and you may ultimately not achieve your desired outcome. If you can successfully exit your business and accomplish your dreams in exiting your business, congratulations! You should be extremely proud of this incredible feat. However, you do not need to sell your business to become a passive, long-term investor in the business asset class.

What if you have appropriately accomplished Principles I–VI so you can now extract yourself from your company's current operations and become your business's strategic chairperson? This allows you to create an annual annuity from this business as you diversify your talents into other ventures. More on that next.

Action Zone

- How much taxable income does your business have each year?

- Have you investigated strategies with your CPA to reduce your taxable income?

- How much liquidity would you like to access from your company over the next 3 years?

- How would your lifestyle change if you could pay yourself annual dividends from your company beyond your compensation?

———

What is one thing that you will start, stop, and continue based on this principle?

Start? _____

Stop? _____

Continue? _____

Scan the QR code below to get access to *The $100M Journey Workbook* and other valuable resources to assist you on your journey!

MOVE FROM CEO TO CHAIRPERSON

"If your business depends on you, you don't own a business—you have a job. And it's the worst job in the world because you're working for a lunatic!"

— Michael Gerber, *The E-Myth Revisited*

Imagine what it would be like to move from CEO to chairperson of your own company and be 100% focused on improving and monitoring the Strategic Business Plan and the 7 Principles of Entrepreneurial Success. This principle will review why and how you should work to replace yourself as CEO and promote yourself to chairperson so that you can have a business asset that can continue to grow and mature while you invest your time building other business assets.

Key Learnings:

1. You are not the best person to run your business.

2. Develop succession with intrapreneurs to replace yourself as CEO.

3. Diversify your time and resources into other areas of interest and asset classes.

4. Build multiple business assets to create true wealth and freedom as an entrepreneur.

5. Use a strategic versus operational approach to entrepreneurship.

CHAPTER 27

WHY MOVE FROM CEO TO CHAIRPERSON?

"The 10X Rule ensures that you think and act big, push yourself beyond what you previously thought possible, and create explosive results in every area of your life."

— Grant Cardone, *The 10x Rule*

Imagine the possibilities. . . What if your company operated without you? What if you could stop working for the business and start owning a business that works for you?

How would it feel to build a business that was self-sustaining, creating opportunities for those that helped you build it while also providing you with the freedom to rise above the business and remove the shackles? Would this allow you to spend more time with your family, build deeper relationships, travel more, or build new business assets?

It's time to stop being the "chief cook and bottle washer." If you apply the 7 Principles of Entrepreneurial Success, you do not even need to work in your business anymore. Your company should run on its own. The management—your intrapreneurs—should take over the business, improve it, grow it, and make it even more profitable.

In his book, *The E-Myth Revisited,* Michael E. Gerber describes the three stages of business as infancy, adolescence, and maturity. It is in the maturity stage that a business has become self-sufficient, systemized, and can operate without the entrepreneur's constant involvement. The entrepreneur has established a strong team capable of executing the vision of the company and can spend their time working *on* the business rather than *in* the business. This means that they can focus on growth, development, and strategy rather than getting bogged down in day-to-day management. In essence, an entrepreneur that builds a company to the maturity phase has built a business that can thrive and grow without their constant presence and has created a system that allows the business to operate smoothly and efficiently.

The E-Myth Revisited: Why Most Small Businesses Don't Work and What to Do About It by Michael E. Gerber

The E-Myth Revisited is a business book exploring the common challenges and pitfalls small-business owners face. Gerber introduces the concept of the "E-Myth"—the mistaken belief that entrepreneurs are primarily motivated by their technical skills when, in fact, they need to be equally skilled in managing a business. Gerber outlines a framework for creating a successful business, including developing a clear vision, creating systems and processes that can be replicated, and building a strong team. The book offers practical advice and tools for small-business owners looking to build a business that can grow and thrive over the long term.

Key Learnings:

1. Entrepreneurs motivated by their technical skills need to be equally skilled in managing their business.

2. To succeed, small-business owners must focus on creating systems and processes that can be replicated and refined rather than relying solely on their technical skills.

3. Developing a clear vision for the business is crucial, and this vision should be communicated clearly to all stakeholders, including customers, employees, and partners.

4. Business owners should focus on identifying and attracting top talent and empowering and motivating them to achieve the company's goals.

5. Business owners must learn to work *on* the business rather than *in* the business. This means focusing on strategy, growth, and development rather than getting bogged down in day-to-day operations and tasks. By doing so, they can build a self-sufficient business that can operate without their constant involvement.

"The purpose of your life is not to serve your business, but that the primary purpose of your business is to serve your life."
—**Michael E. Gerber,** *The E-Myth Revisited*

As you move from CEO to chairperson, you can oversee the creation and manage the execution of the Strategic Plan, receive annual liquidity from the business, and have the time and energy to diversify your talents into other areas of interest. You can spend more time with your family, go on vacation whenever you want, and wisely invest your liquidity into other asset classes. Isn't this what we dream of as entrepreneurs?

Hopefully, this is why you are reading this book!

As a chairperson of your own company, you can be 100% focused on the Strategic Business Plan and the 7 Principles of Entrepreneurial Success and ensure your company's long-term success.

I have learned that the entrepreneur that founded and built the company from the ground up might not be the best person to lead the company on its future growth path, but unfortunately, they stay stubbornly in the way, preventing their business and the intrapreneurs from growing!

You might be surprised to learn that your business may expand exponentially when you, as the owner, move out of the way!

If you are an entrepreneur stuck in the Messy Middle right now, I know the feeling. It is tough. It's a grind. Too often, we do all the heavy lifting, pay ourselves last, and feel like we are running in thick quicksand going nowhere! We need to *stop* this!

Believe me, you are not the best person to run your business! Find that person—the intrapreneur—who is!

When I first heard this idea, it was hard for me to accept it. The reality is, as entrepreneurs, we are usually overconfident. "Nobody can do what I do!" we tell ourselves. It sounds silly to hear it now, but I certainly believed it at times.

If we had the mindset that our sole responsibility was to build a business and replace ourselves as the operator of that business, we would be a lot more successful, happy, and wealthy.

Yes, wealthy . . .

I'm sure somebody would like to challenge me on that, and I would have also challenged myself. However, remember that if you are the best person to run your company, you are a business operator, not a business owner!

Don't you want to be a business owner rather than a business operator?

You should be able to lead and develop your intrapreneurs to run your company, and chances are they will bring new dimensions and talents to the business that exceed your wildest expectations.

One of the best outcomes of becoming the chairperson of your business is the ability it gives you to diversify your time into other interests. Imagine having a mutual fund of businesses that you own. You can focus on all the businesses strategically, spread your talent and impact, and help other intrapreneurs and entrepreneurs create wealth for themselves and their families.

You can also diversify your time into other personal interests, like spending more time with family and friends, traveling, enjoying your favorite hobbies, or completing items on your bucket list. That is freedom!

Most importantly, you can diversify your time and talents to make an impact in your community and the world around you.

I did not write this book for successful entrepreneurs who have already built and sold their companies for millions of dollars. I want to help the entrepreneurs who battle for years through the ups and downs of growing a business, trying to break through the Messy Middle. I aim to help entrepreneurs avoid catastrophic events and overcome their business growth challenges by following a Strategic Business Plan and the 7 Principles of Entrepreneurial Success.

This is my "why." What is your "why"?

Is it to run your company as an operator until it is time to retire? At this point, do you hope to sell your company to somebody else who wants to purchase it for a high valuation in an all-cash transaction and let you go off into the sunset? It does not always work out like this.

You need to know your specific "why"—your True North—and have a Strategic Plan for achieving it through your business asset.

Bill Gates has been credited with eloquently saying, "Most people overestimate what they can do in one year and underestimate what they can do in ten years."

So, what do you dream of achieving in the next 10 years, and what steps should you start taking now? Think big, dream big, and challenge your thought process.

Your "why" might be to spend more time with your family; your "why" might be to be a captain on a yacht someday; your "why" might be to make an impact in the world and help others. It doesn't really matter *what* your "why" is, but unless your "why" is to be a stressed-out entrepreneur operating a business 80 hours a week for the rest of your career, then these 7 Principles are essential in helping you become the chairperson of your own company and achieve your wildest entrepreneurial dreams.

Robert T. Kiyosaki said it best. You must build four assets to achieve financial wealth.

1. Businesses
2. Real Estate
3. Papers (bonds, notes, stocks, etc.)
4. Commodities (gold, silver, bitcoin, etc.)

Those who seek to achieve wealth do not buy one real estate property or one stock, or even one commodity, so why should you only own one business? For example, consider a real estate investor. They don't buy one building, become the manager of that one building, and become wealthy. They accumulate multiple buildings over time, hire management companies to operate them, and hire maintenance groups to maintain them, all while they collect the checks every month (and they may not even do that themselves). Why don't more entrepreneurs own several business assets? Well, if you desire to have multiple businesses as an asset class, you cannot be running around operating them all.

How many businesses can you be the full-time, focused CEO of? One? You certainly can build and sell (flip) one company at a time, but that takes a long time and is not the ideal way to build true wealth—unless one of them is an absolute unicorn.

But how many businesses can you be the chairperson of? Many!

Imagine having several profitable, debt-free, positive net operating cash flow companies that you are the chairperson of. That is entrepreneurship!

By replacing yourself as CEO and promoting yourself to chairperson, you now have a business asset that can continue to grow and mature. At the same time, you can invest your time building other business assets.

Now we are talking!

The best way to achieve incredible wealth and freedom is to have multiple business assets that you own and can build strategically as a chairperson while accessing the owner's liquidity within them as they prosper.

You can make your business a High Performance asset and a passive investment by establishing Principles I–VI, then use your strategic talents to oversee your company's continued growth and protection while diversifying your time into growing other businesses by employing the skills you have learned.

When you build assets (like a business) that can generate income for you without you working for the asset on a full-time basis—this is how you create true wealth and freedom!

This strategic versus operational approach to entrepreneurship was a complete game changer for me. This is how you work *on*, not *in,* your business.

Self-Reflection Zone

- Review your True North Life Plan. How would your life change if you could elevate yourself and become the chairperson of your business?

- What would you be able to do in your personal life if you no longer had a day-to-day operational role in your current business?

- What would you do with your free time if your business was a passive investment generating strong liquidity? Would you build other companies? Do more community service?

- Who are the intrapreneurs you are developing to take over your business? Is there a specific succession and development plan in place?

Scan the QR code below to watch a supplemental video about why this principle is so important!

CHAPTER 28

HOW TO MOVE FROM CEO TO CHAIRPERSON

"If you don't have big dreams and goals, you'll end up working for someone that does."

— Unknown

Without a doubt, I have learned that the best and maybe the only way to move from CEO to chairperson of your business is to follow the Strategic Business Plan and the 7 Principles of Entrepreneurial Success outlined in this book. Let's revisit them one more time.

- Your True North and Strategic Business Plan

    - Your True North

    - Your Strategic Business Plan

- 7 Principles of Entrepreneurial Success

    - Principle I: Protect and Grow your Equity

    - Principle II: Build Your Own Capital

    - Principle III: Reinvest Smartly

- Principle IV: Build a Culture of Intrapreneurship

- Principle V: Protect the House

- Principle VI: Access Owner's Liquidity

- Principle VII: Move from CEO to Chairperson

———

YOUR TRUE NORTH AND STRATEGIC BUSINESS PLAN

Your True North is where it all starts.

What are you trying to accomplish in your life? You need to know where you want to go and what you want to do before you should even start forming your business strategy.

Your Strategic Business Plan outlines the short-term and long-term goals and the specific actions and KPIs that must be accomplished to hit such goals.

The Strategic Plan of your business needs to align with what you are trying to achieve in Your True North Life Plan! If it doesn't, you are on the road to nowhere. You should stop now and recalibrate before wasting any more time.

7 PRINCIPLES OF ENTREPRENEURIAL SUCCESS

How do you move from CEO to Chairperson?

Master the principles in this book!

By properly implementing Principles I–VI, you can begin the process of replacing yourself and becoming the chairperson of your business. This move will turn your business asset into a passive investment.

This is where wealth is built. If you can stop running your business and be a true business owner, you can create a business that generates incredible cash flow with amazing entrepreneurial benefits.

If your business is not ready for you to transition from CEO to chairperson, one of the principles has not fully matured yet, or one of the principles was ignored or missed. Go back to the start of the journey and master each principle in your business. It's that simple. Have patient ambition!

Principle I: Protect and Grow Your Equity

Entrepreneurs must build and protect their equity and control their own businesses as much as possible. This is where your wealth will be created. One mistake here and you can lose complete control of your business and everything you have built. Seek to grow your equity stake and continually work to increase the value of your enterprise.

Principle II: Build Your Own Capital

Entrepreneurs must build their own capital through their business by generating strong net operating cash flows. Entrepreneurs relying too heavily on bank debt or external investment to grow will violate Principle I: Protect and Grow Your Equity. By building your own capital and increasing your net operating cash flows annually, you build a massive layer of protection for your business while also building value.

Principle III: Reinvest Smartly

Entrepreneurs that succeed in Principle I: Protect and Grow your Equity and Principle II: Build your Own Capital must reinvest wisely and patiently into their growth in order to build a High Performance business. Mistakes here will roll back downhill and affect the principles before it. Entrepreneurs must stick to their Strategic Plan, control their impulses to expand and grow beyond their ability, and have patient ambition to focus on the areas of the business that, with reinvestment, will continue to help the business build more capital through generating additional net operating cash flows.

Principle IV: Build a Culture of Intrapreneurship

Entrepreneurs must fully engage their leadership teams and provide them the situational leadership, authority, and freedom to grow within the

business. Providing key intrapreneurs with the ability to participate in equity value appreciation of the business further cements their commitment to the long-term vision of the business. Your role as an entrepreneurial leader is to continually seek to replace yourself in this business. Your intrapreneurs are the key to this happening.

Principle V: Protect the House

Entrepreneurs must strategically assess and manage internal and external risk factors that can harm the business. Miss a major risk factor here and all the principles before it can be severely affected. As the entrepreneur of the business, you have a responsibility to protect all stakeholders from risk. Hiring the right advisors and continually performing vulnerability assessments on the business is essential.

Principle VI: Access Owner's Liquidity

Entrepreneurs must continually build the strength of their balance sheet and be diligent to not suck the cash from the business for short-term gratification. Entrepreneurs must use smart, tax-efficient ways to access the business's liquidity without harming the business's strength. Entrepreneurs that can access this liquidity while still building and growing the business will enjoy the fruits of their labor without the need to sell their equity in the business.

Principle VII: Move from CEO to Chairperson

Entrepreneurs must replace themselves operationally so they can strategically rise above the business. The goal of an entrepreneur should be to own the business, not run the business. By executing Principles I–VI, the entrepreneur is now ready to turn their business into an incredibly valuable asset.

Read on for a fun short story that illustrates these principles from the two sides of my entrepreneurial journey: the one side where I did *not* apply these principles, and the other side where I *did* apply them.

Action Zone

- When would you like to promote yourself out of your current role and responsibility so you can be the strategic chairperson of your business?

- Which Principle (I–VI) do you need to improve to provide the framework for you to move from CEO to chairperson?

————

What is one thing that you will start, stop, and continue based on this principle?

Start? _____

Stop? _____

Continue? _____

Scan the QR code below to get access to *The $100M Journey Workbook* and other valuable resources to assist you on your journey!

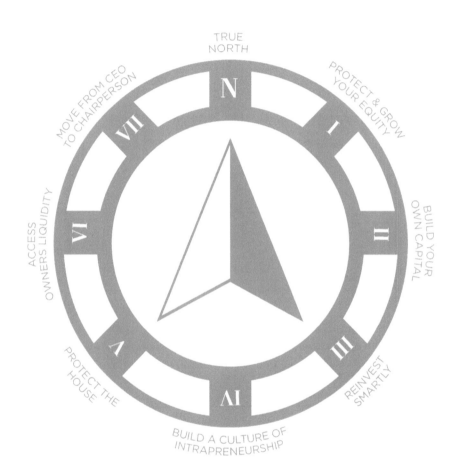

THE ENTREPRENEURIAL SHORT STORIES OF JEKYLL AND HYDE

"Here's to the crazy ones. The misfits. The rebels. The troublemakers. The round pegs in the square holes. The ones who see things differently. They're not fond of rules. And they have no respect for the status quo. You can quote them, disagree with them, glorify or vilify them. About the only thing you can't do is ignore them. Because they change things. They push the human race forward. And while some may see them as the crazy ones, we see genius. Because the people who are crazy enough to think they can change the world, are the ones who do."

—Apple Inc. "Think Different" ad campaign

Entrepreneurs are a special breed. Some of us are creative, some of us can see trends before others, some of us can build things, some of us love numbers, and sometimes we are all of these in one person, but one thing is for sure . . . we are all crazy! We have split personalities. We can be the CEO, the customer service representative, the sales representative, the IT manager, and the janitor, all on the same day.

We put all our chips on the table to pursue our goals and dreams. Yet, we are usually inadequately educated or trained on how to accomplish everything we dream of achieving. And so we learn from trial and error. We take the beating, get back up, and try again.

Over the years, I developed a split personality between my work life and my personal life. In my work personality, I would move into serious mode—on calls and in meetings non-stop, with little time for fun. I was focused, busy, stressed, and, yes, boring. In personal life mode, I would let my hair down, get a little crazy, smile, laugh, dance, and be a completely different person, and yes, sometimes even fun!

As a result of this split personality behavior, my neighbor once gave me the nickname Jekyll and Hyde, depending on the personality I was displaying. This nickname has stuck over the last 20 years. My wife still uses it today to differentiate between the "all-too-serious" John and the "let's-have-some-fun" John.

In summarizing the key messages in this book and the learnings of my entrepreneurial experiences, I thought we could have some fun by telling two short stories through the eyes of my two personalities, Jekyll and Hyde. These two short stories summarize the massive pain and joy I have experienced through entrepreneurship. Just like Dr. Jekyll and Mr. Hyde in Stevenson's book represent the duality of human nature, entrepreneurs often have to balance competing interests, such as risk-taking and caution, ambition and humility.

Do you see yourself in these characters?

Strange Case of Dr. Jekyll and Mr. Hyde by Robert Louis Stevenson

This 1886 Gothic novel by Scottish author Robert Louis Stevenson is one of the most famous pieces of English literature. The novel has also had a sizable impact on popular culture with the phrase "Jekyll and Hyde," frequently interpreted as an examination of the duality of human nature, usually expressed as an inner struggle between good and evil.

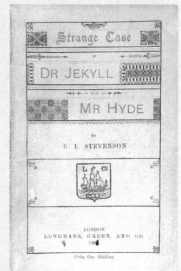

Dr. Jekyll is a "large, well-made, smooth-faced man of fifty with something of a slyish cast" who sometimes feels he is battling between good and evil within himself, leading to the struggle between his dual personalities of Henry Jekyll and Edward Hyde. He has spent much of his life trying to repress evil urges that were not fitting for a man of his stature. He creates a serum, or potion, to separate this hidden evil from his personality. In doing so, Jekyll transforms into the smaller, younger, cruel, remorseless, evil Hyde. Jekyll has many friends and an amiable personality, but as Hyde, he becomes mysterious and violent. As time goes on, Hyde grows in power. After taking the potion repeatedly, he no longer relies upon it to unleash his inner demon—his alter ego. Eventually, Hyde grows so strong that Jekyll relies on the potion to remain conscious.

Mr. Hyde is the id which is driven by primal urges, instincts, and immediate gratification; the superego is represented by the expectations and morals of Victorian society; and Dr. Jekyll is the rational and conscious ego which acts as a balance between the id and superego. When Jekyll transforms into Hyde, the ego is suppressed, and the id is no longer held back by either the ego or the superego.

"Jekyll had more than a father's interest; Hyde had more than a son's indifference."
—**Robert Louis Stevenson, *Strange Case of Dr. Jekyll and Mr. Hyde***

CHAPTER 29

THE SHORT STORY OF HYDE

Hyde was a typical entrepreneur with a never-say-die attitude, always eager to take risks and try to make things happen quickly. He was a person of action, but unfortunately, he did not take the time to fully understand what he was ultimately trying to accomplish in his life. He did not have a deep sense of purpose, was unclear on his "why," and assumed that entrepreneurial success would drive him to achieve his goals in life.

Hyde did not have a solid Strategic Plan for his business. He would often jump on any shiny object that caught his eye without thinking it through carefully. He was so eager to be successful that he would diversify his services and products, trying to be the best at everything.

Hyde's ambition was admirable, but his lack of thoughtful strategy was his downfall. His ego was out of control. He was so focused on his vision of being the biggest and best that he didn't take the time to consider the practicalities of achieving such a feat.

He lacked the discipline and patient ambition to focus on one thing and make it great instead of chasing after the next big thing. Ultimately, this misguided strategy cost him dearly.

Principle I: Protect and Grow Your Equity

Hyde was determined to grow his company quickly and make it a success. Thinking it would be the "right thing to do," he surrounded himself with other passionate entrepreneurs and asked them to partner with him on the venture, giving them significant equity interests in the company.

Unfortunately, this was not the best move. Hyde was giving away much of the equity in and control of his company without fully considering the implications.

As time passed, Hyde focused more on raising capital for growth than he did on protecting and growing his equity and eventually found himself with a very small ownership stake in the company.

Though he was succeeding in his mission to grow the company rapidly, this rapid growth meant he was losing control of the wheel. He now had to bring about 10 times the growth to attain what he could have achieved if he had retained 100% of the equity in his company from the start.

Principle II: Build Your Own Capital

Hyde was obsessed with revenue, believing it was the most important thing for success. He planned to rapidly grow the company to reach $100M in revenue as quickly as possible. However, he was burning through cash quickly in pursuit of this goal.

The strategy of chasing revenue for growth's sake led to a scattered approach in the business, with many different products and services being offered. As a result, more capital was needed to hire more people and implement new systems.

Unfortunately, Hyde found himself in a difficult position, with little cash left to grow the business. Without access to adequate capital, not only would his plans for rapid expansion not be realized but the company's continued success and ability to reach all its goals would be put at risk.

It was possible the company could even struggle to stay afloat. Hyde was forced to raise outside capital. He gave up even more equity in his company in exchange for the funds. This significantly reduced his ownership stake in the company and led to a reduced position of control.

Principle III: Reinvest Smartly

The problem with Hyde is that he was unable to create positive net operating cash flow, which made it difficult to reinvest any capital into the growth of the business.

In an effort to try and create more net operating cash flow, Hyde took every opportunity available to diversify the business lines of the company trying to capture increased margins, but these only further distracted the company and consumed more capital than it generated.

The lack of cash flow and the inability to reinvest in the growth of the business was an ever-present problem for Hyde. Hyde could not hire the necessary personnel or implement the necessary systems to ensure the continued growth of his business. Without the necessary capital, he could not properly grow and manage the company, leaving it vulnerable.

Principle IV: Build a Culture of Intrapreneurship

Hyde had a great vision for his business and was determined to make it a success. He saw potential in his team and was determined to reach his goals by driving the employees of the company to achieve strong annual growth targets.

Hyde failed to recognize the patience needed to foster intrapreneurial growth and development that would help his team members elevate to higher levels of management. As the business continued to grow, it failed to develop intrapreneurs within the organization at the same pace. It was unable to grow beyond the existing team's capability.

This situation forced Hyde to take on too many of the management responsibilities himself, leading to a lack of focus on the business's overall strategy. Hyde was spread too thin.

Principle V: Protect The House

As the business grew, Hyde faced the challenge of trying to grow beyond the company's capabilities.

With a desire to keep growing the business aggressively, he decided to hire an unproven and unverified executive to support the growth of the business and help the business raise additional capital.

Hyde was so eager to get the new executive onboarded that he didn't take the time to properly vet the track record of the individual. This proved to be a devastating mistake. The new executive did not fit in with the core values or culture that the company was built on.

Hyde tried to correct the situation, but it was too late. The executive had infiltrated the team and brought new investors into the business to provide the capital the company needed to further its growth.

Ultimately, the company terminated Hyde and replaced him with the very executive Hyde had hired to help grow the business. He was devastated. He had worked so hard to build his business only to have it destroyed by his own carelessness.

The executive, now the new CEO of the company, proceeded to destroy the company's culture and caused the business to spiral out of control.

Principle VI: Access Owner's Liquidity

Hyde had devoted 15 years of his life to building the business but was left with nothing from all of his efforts.

When the company was in its early days, Hyde wanted to be the biggest and best in the industry. He wanted to expand as quickly as possible without looking at the long-term implications. He went on a hiring spree, bought up companies, and expanded operations without a proper strategy for managing the associated costs. This created a situation in which the company spent more cash than it brought in. Hyde could not generate enough cash flow to keep up with the demands of the business.

Hyde was now unable to enjoy the fruits of his labor. He was stuck in a situation where he could not extract any liquidity from the company for himself or his investors. It was a hard lesson to learn and a tough pill to swallow.

Principle VII: Move from CEO to Chairperson

Hyde never became the chairperson of his business! He failed! He failed hard!

He had learned a valuable lesson: to always protect his equity, build his own capital, reinvest wisely into the business, build his team of intrapreneurs, and of course, always assess the risks of the business to ensure that his companies cannot be exploited.

CHAPTER 30

THE SHORT STORY OF JEKYLL

Jekyll was a visionary entrepreneur with patient ambition. He had clarity on his life's purpose and goals. Starting with his "why," he created a True North Life Plan that provided him with a vision for what he wanted to accomplish throughout the next 30 years and clarity on how being an entrepreneur and building business assets could align with his True North.

He focused on creating a clear, multi-year Strategic Plan for his business with a strong vision, mission, and BHAG. He knew why his company existed and what he and his team sought to achieve.

Jekyll knew that he must have a solid strategy to achieve his company's goals. He and his team worked together to develop a detailed plan that laid out the specific tasks and milestones that had to be achieved quarterly to move the business forward.

He was laser-focused on executing his Strategic Plan and never let any shiny object distract him or his team.

Principle I: Protect and Grow Your Equity

Jekyll had several strategies in place to protect and grow his equity value in the company he was leading.

The first strategy was to never sell his equity unless absolutely necessary. He knew that selling equity would dilute his control in the company and could potentially prevent him from running and building the company the right way.

The second strategy was to purchase more equity in the business as opportunities arose. If he was going to invest in himself, he wanted to own as much of the equity in the business as possible.

Originally starting with a minority equity ownership in the company, Jekyll grew his ownership stake over the years until he became a majority equity owner. He amplified his equity value as the company grew and became more valuable.

By believing in himself and the company, he was able to take control of his destiny and ensure that he could remain in charge of the company for the long term.

Principle II: Build Your Own Capital

Jekyll focused on generating strong net operating cash flow from operations and reinvesting the capital back into the company so it could flourish. He was frugal and disciplined in his spending habits, investing only in the core components of his business that would generate additional cash flow.

The strategies Jekyll employed to ensure his business was successful included setting a sound pricing and profitability model, investing in sales and marketing, and improving cash flow.

He also worked to build a strong balance sheet with cash reserves to ensure he could weather any storm and take advantage of any opportunities that presented themselves.

By growing the net operating cash flow, Jekyll could use the capital the company had generated to expand his business, invest in new technologies, hire more staff, increase sales and profits, and create a positive return on investment for his shareholders.

Principle III: Reinvest Smartly

Jekyll was committed to smartly reinvesting the profits back into the company instead of extracting the earnings to pay large dividends to partners. This provided more fuel for the company to flourish even further over time.

Although he believed that reinvesting in the business was the key to success and growth, he used his net operating cash flow to first pay down any incurred debt and then to build up emergency cash reserves.

He didn't chase after shiny objects but focused on growing the most profitable products and services with strong gross margins.

His willingness to pay a little more upfront for the right systems to manage and govern the business gave his team the proper tools to customize operational processes.

Through these smart investments, Jekyll was able to generate additional net operating cash flow, giving his company the capital it needed to flourish.

Principle IV: Build a Culture of Intrapreneurship

Jekyll invested heavily in his team, offering them training, competitive salaries, and incredible benefits to ensure they were motivated and productive. He was a servant leader who believed that the best way to build a strong team was to lead situationally and provide his team with the authority and freedom to make the best decisions for the company. This empowered the team to act quickly on any ideas or opportunities they discovered, increasing the business's success.

Jekyll opened the door to intrapreneurship within his organization. He saw the potential for his employees to take ownership of their own projects and, in turn, help the company grow.

To that end, he offered each of his executive team members a stake in the company in the form of phantom equity which gave them a stake in the company's valuation growth.

In addition to this, he was passionate about succession planning and the idea that everyone must be ready to replace themselves in their respective roles.

As a result, his team was always looking for ways to improve the business and move forward. This gave them a sense of security and career growth potential, leading to a strong retention rate among his key executives.

Principle V: Protect The House

Jekyll strategically focused on risk management to protect his business from any possible events that could harm it.

He was surrounded by a team of expert advisors, including a CPA, financial wealth advisor to manage his finances, corporate attorney, litigation attorney to handle legal issues, and commercial insurance broker to add extra layers of protection in case of catastrophes. He also had a peer group of other successful CEOs that he could turn to for advice and guidance.

Jekyll was very risk-averse yet still bold in his decision-making, always looking for creative ways to diversify his business while also making sure that any potential risk he was taking was well thought out.

He even set up a captive insurance company to help cover potential extraordinary losses and provide tax advantages to further protect his business.

To further safeguard against potential risks, Jekyll invested a lot of time and effort in assessing vulnerabilities within his business and setting up effective processes.

Through his strategic risk management approach, Jekyll protected his company, allowing him to pursue his entrepreneurial goals without worrying about any possible events that could hurt it.

Principle VI: Access Owner's Liquidity

Jekyll implemented a series of creative tax-efficient strategies to ensure that he could pay himself dividends and distributions as his company prospered.

He first established a safe harbor 401(k) profit-sharing plan for all his employees, and funded the employees' retirement plans annually with 3% of their salaries so they could benefit from tax-deferred returns. This allowed him to reduce his company's taxable income while providing himself and his employees with a retirement savings option.

Next, he established a captive policy that provided his business with additional, extraordinary insurance coverage, paying the premiums to his own insurance company. This allowed Jekyll to build a new business asset in a tax-advantaged manner while also protecting his business.

As the company continued to generate strong net operating cash flow, he secured an annual annuity for himself. This enabled him to keep a steady income stream while maintaining ownership of the business.

By taking advantage of the various strategies available, Jekyll could successfully pay himself in a tax-efficient manner while also helping to grow his business. He created a win-win situation for himself and his company, providing the company with the resources to continue expanding and improving.

Principle VII: Move from CEO to Chairperson

Jekyll sought a way to elevate his business beyond its current scale. He decided that the best way to do this was to replace himself as the CEO and promote an intrapreneur who had proven their abilities to take the role.

Realizing he may not be the best person to grow the business further, Jekyll determined it was time for his team to take the reins.

He was able to replace himself as the operator of his business and elevate himself to a more strategic level where he could help the company even more.

This move also allowed Jekyll to diversify his interests into other businesses and asset classes and build wealth for himself, his partners, employees, and any entrepreneurs he worked with.

Through his investments, he could make well-informed decisions and grow his businesses.

Jekyll continued to apply the Strategic Plan and 7 Principles to scale his business assets in ways he had never thought possible. He committed to helping entrepreneurs learn from his experiences and help them achieve their version of entrepreneurial success!

IT'S TIME!

"There are people that make things happen. There are people that watch things happen. And there are people that say 'What just happened?'"

—Anonymous

The entrepreneurial journey is full of challenges, failures, and successes. It is said that life brings us challenges and tragedies so that we can pass on our learnings to others to help them avoid the same challenges. Well, that is my hope in writing this book.

Aren't you sick and tired of being sick and tired, trying to grow your business to the next level and getting your butt kicked?

Well, enough is enough!

If you are still here, reading this epilogue, you must have a burning desire to achieve your entrepreneurial dreams.

In my entrepreneurial journey, I had the opportunity to grow two outstanding companies to greater than $50M in revenues (each) over a period of 15+ years. Unfortunately, in one instance, I lost everything! Not only did I not properly execute the 7 Principles of Entrepreneurial Success, but I did the complete opposite of the principles. I lacked patient ambition. I wanted to succeed and grow so badly and so quickly that I made fatal errors. I was growing the business the wrong way and for the wrong reasons. This was one of the most painful experiences of my life, and many people were hurt in the process.

I do not want this to ever happen to you!

Luckily, I learned valuable lessons and developed the 7 Principles by applying these learnings. My incredible partners and I implemented the 7 Principles, broke through the Messy Middle, overcame the Growth Paradox, and built a High Performance company.

You can do this too! But only if you believe you can; only if you know exactly what you are trying to ultimately accomplish in your True North Life Plan; only if you design a Strategic Plan for your business with a vision and BHAG that excites you; and only if you implement the 7 Principles of Entrepreneurial Success to ensure that you protect everything you are building as you grow.

Do you want your True North badly enough?

Being an entrepreneur is HARD! You are often faced with difficult decisions and uncertain outcomes. It can be overwhelming, daunting, and lonely. Often we find ourselves in a place of unknowns. When we try to grow our businesses from Lifestyle to High Performance, we encounter the Messy Middle and the Growth Paradox. It is a time of disruption, doubt, and pain that can prevent you from ever achieving success. It is when you feel overwhelmed, exhausted, and unsure of your future. You may feel like you're in a never-ending cycle of frustration and lost opportunity.

Private equity companies prey on good companies with entrepreneurs who have broken their backs (and bank accounts) over the years to grow their businesses but lack the skills and knowledge to get their companies through the Messy Middle of business growth. Private equity firms invest in companies in this stage so they can skip the ever-painful startup years and, using their resources and expertise, take the business the final mile where it creates incredible value. Meanwhile, the entrepreneur, who either lacked the confidence or ability to achieve this value on their own, has likely relinquished their equity and control to the private equity firm. Unfortunately, the entrepreneur allowed their business to become vulnerable and is unable to maximize the benefits of what they built.

Do you have the grit that it takes to persevere through this period? Do you have the discipline to design your True North Life Plan, your Strategic Business Plan, and implement the 7 Principles of Entrepreneurial Success?

If not, finding a way out will be very challenging, and you might risk *everything* and then lose it all . . . just like I did.

Through this book, we have walked through some major sections. Let's recap.

Your True North and Strategic Business Plan

As Napoleon Hill said in *Think and Grow Rich*, "Whatever the mind can conceive and believe, it can achieve."

What do you want to achieve in your life? What is your True North? You need to know this because it also should direct your business strategy and your company's Strategic Plan.

Before you know where your Strategic Plan will take you, you must know where you are! In this section, we reviewed the stages of business:

1. Startup
2. Struggle Zone
3. Lifestyle
4. Messy Middle
5. High Performance

Once you know where your business is on its entrepreneurial journey, you must have a very clear plan for what you are trying to accomplish with your life and business. Without a Strategic Plan of where you want to go and how you will get there, your business will just be going through the motions.

This book has focused explicitly on how entrepreneurs can successfully overcome the dangerous Messy Middle to ease the transition from Lifestyle to High Performance. Being clear and intentional about designing a strategy, vision, and BHAG for your businesses will help guide you and your leadership team through implementing quarterly, annual, 3-year, and 10-year Strategic Plans to help your business achieve its goals.

7 Principles of Entrepreneurial Success

Along with your True North Life Plan and your Strategic Business Plan, the 7 Principles, applied correctly, will help you and your business avoid the massive pitfalls and trouble areas you may experience in trying to grow to a High Performance size.

When implemented, these 7 Principles can provide the structure to break through the Messy Middle, overcome the Growth Paradox, protect your business, and eventually help you achieve your definition of entrepreneurial success.

———

Congratulations! You've made it to the end of this incredible journey with me! You know exactly what it takes to succeed in the entrepreneurial world and build a High Performance business.

Success is a game of attrition. You must stick around, learn, and grow to pursue your Strategic Plan and achieve your True North goals. You have the tools, you have the knowledge, and you have the power to create the success you've always envisioned.

With tenacity, discipline, and patient ambition, you can take action steps to break through the Messy Middle and never be stuck there ever again.

If you have a burning desire to achieve freedom and financial wealth through entrepreneurship, then it is time, right now, to change the way you think and approach your business. Stop procrastinating, stop making excuses, and start taking massive action. Some decisions may be hard, but you must make them so you can achieve your dreams.

Don't wait for tomorrow or for the perfect moment. The perfect moment is now!

It's TIME to stop draining yourself of time, energy, and resources and take the necessary steps to achieve your goals.

It's TIME to download *The $100M Journey Workbook* at 100MJourney.com/workbook and use it as your guide.

It's TIME to take the entrepreneurial world by storm, become the best version of yourself, and make it happen once and for all—for you, your family, and the team you are leading.

It's TIME! Go out and make your entrepreneurial dreams come true! Believe in yourself and never give up. Your success awaits you!

Scan the QR code below to get access to *The $100M Journey Workbook* and other valuable resources to assist you on your journey!

"Building the Bridge"
by William Allen Dromgoole

An old man going a lone highway,
Came, at the evening cold and gray,
To a chasm vast and deep and wide.
Through which was flowing a sullen tide
The old man crossed in the twilight dim,
The sullen stream had no fear for him;
But he turned when safe on the other side
And built a bridge to span the tide.

"Old man," said a fellow pilgrim near,
"You are wasting your strength with building here;
Your journey will end with the ending day,
You never again will pass this way;
You've crossed the chasm, deep and wide,
Why build this bridge at eventide?"

The builder lifted his old gray head;
"Good friend, in the path I have come," he said,
"There followed after me to-day
A youth whose feet must pass this way.
This chasm that has been as naught to me
To that fair-haired youth may a pitfall be;
He, too, must cross in the twilight dim;
Good friend, I am building this bridge for him!"

*Thank you to Kellan Fluckiger for helping me structure the story arc of this book and sharing this great poem with me.

ACKNOWLEDGMENTS

My entrepreneurial journey has been fueled by the collective support, guidance, and love of countless individuals who have touched my life in profound ways. As I reflect on my experiences with all of the following people, I am reminded of the profound impact each person has had on my path as a person and an entrepreneur.

To my wife, Amy, the love of my life, your unwavering belief in me and my entrepreneurial journey has been full of loving support. You have given me the strength to rise from the challenges and to continue building our dream life together. For all the times you have been my short-fused wrecking ball, my rock, my confidante, and my partner in this incredible journey, I am eternally, profoundly grateful.

Maxim and Danick, although you may have been too young to fully understand the turbulent nature of entrepreneurship, you provided me with the smiles, laughs, and drive to be present in all that you do. I can only hope that I have been, and will continue to be, a role model to give you the confidence to accomplish your dreams in life.

Mom and Dad, your values and love have been the grounding of my aspirations. You provided me with the opportunity to chase my dreams, even knowing that this would bring physical distance between us.

Tracey and Rob, and Patricia, your support and love is forever present and felt in my heart. Sharon and Dennis, Kelly and Brad, and Brian—the extended family bond has added richness to my journey.

To Alexandra, Michael, Zachary, Caleb, Leila, and Luca—you are the future of our family, and I hope my pathway will in some way inspire you on your journey.

Michael, Steve, and the BrandPoint intrapreneurs, the accomplishment of Project 100 was an incredible feat to which this book pays honor. We have built an amazing team and business together and I cannot wait to see what the future has in store for us.

Jared, Shannon, Laura, Jason, Travis, Erika, and all the intrapreneurs working every day to build great companies, I appreciate your leadership at IOI, Pellucid, Financial Wing, and World Hockey Group and look forward to watching your companies prosper.

Rich, my co-host on the *Entrepreneurs United Podcast*, your longtime friendship and camaraderie has added depth through my entire entrepreneurial journey. To the EU podcast guests and listeners, your insights and enthusiasm have fueled my continued passion to grow and learn.

Travis, Skipp, Atul, Chet, Kurt, Chris, and the leadership in Exeter, thank you for being more than partners—for being great friends and having my back.

To our team of advisors: Vince and the team at HBK Advisors; Brian, Jay, and the team at Wells Fargo Advisors; Chris at United Insurance; Rick at Ropka Law; Chris and Dan at Hinckley Allen; and all the additional advisors that have guided me and our businesses over the years, thank you for protecting and guiding us.

Jeff, Eric, Charlie, Ron, and all the other business mentors that were there to help me on my journey, your guidance has shaped my leadership, perspective, and choices.

To all the former partners, bosses, colleagues, and team members of the past, thank you for your contributions to our ventures, collective learnings, and growth. I have been extremely fortunate to have built such amazing relationships across the globe with you all and will always be there for each and every one of you.

Stefano, and all my childhood and school friends back on the south shore of Montréal, our shared memories remind me of the importance of authentic relationships and I miss you all.

To Sean, Vince, Marisa, and our North Hampton besties: Joe and Cheryl, Tim and Jarrett, Chris and Laurie, thank you for grounding me and reminding me of life's simple joys (there are many).

To all my lifelong friends from Maine, Chicago, Philadelphia, and New Hampshire, you've made every chapter memorable. Thank you.

To Keira, my publisher; Kellan, for my Story Arc; Mindy, for editing; Tally, for creative work; IOI for marketing; Wendy Freedman Photography for headshots; and Rumble Tree for video—your belief in this book's message and pushing me to be more vulnerable and bold has been invaluable.

To all those I interviewed for this book—your insights have added depth and wisdom.

And to everyone who has stood by me through thick and thin, your unwavering support is a testament to the strength of human connections.

You've all provided wisdom, inspiration, and love to my journey. This book stands as a tribute to each one of you, and I am forever grateful.

With heartfelt appreciation,

John

REFERENCES

Abbey, Edward. *A Voice Crying in the Wilderness*. New York: St. Martin's Press, 1990.

Aesop. "The Hare and the Tortoise." *The Fables of Aesop: Selected, Told Anew, and Their History Traced by Joseph Jacobs*. New York: MacMillan, 1926.

Apple Inc (formerly Apple Computer, Inc). "Think Different" ad campaign script with major contributions from Ron Siltanen and Lee Clow. 1997–2002.

Babiak, Paul and Robert Hare. *Snakes in Suits: Understanding and Surviving the Psychopaths in Your Office*, Revised Edition. New York: HarperBusiness, 2019.

Belsky, Scott. *The Messy Middle: Finding Your Way through the Hardest and Most Crucial Part of Any Bold Venture*. New York: Portfolio / Penguin, 2018.

Blanchard, Ken. *Leadership and the One Minute Manager: Increasing Effectiveness Through Situational Leadership*. New York: HarperCollins, 1985.

Branson, Richard (@richardbranson). "Train people well enough so they can leave; treat them well enough so they don't want to." X (formerly Twitter.) March 27, 2014, 10:23 a.m. https://twitter.com/richardbranson/status/449220072176107520?lang=en

Brueckmann, Alex. *Secrets of Next-Level Entrepreneurs: 11 Powerful Lessons to Thrive in Business and Lead a Balanced Life.* Hoboken: Wiley, 2023.

Buffett, Warren. qtd. in Dan Anderson, *Corporate Survival: The Critical Importance of Sustainability Risk Management.* Bloomington: iUniverse, 2005, 138.

Canadian Charter of Rights and Freedoms:

Section 23 of the Canadian Charter of Rights and Freedoms states that: "(1) Citizens of Canada whose first language learned and still understood is that of the English or French linguistic minority population of the province in which they reside have the right to have their children receive primary and secondary school instruction in that language in that province. (2) Citizens of Canada of whom any child has received or is receiving primary or secondary school instruction in English or French in Canada, have the right to have all their children receive primary and secondary school instruction in the same language."

Cardone, Grant. *The 10X Rule: The Only Difference between Success and Failure.* Hoboken: John Wiley & Sons, 2011.

Chase, Charlie. Unpublished interview with John St.Pierre.

Churchill, Neil and John Mullins. "How Fast Can Your Company Afford to Grow?" *Harvard Business Review*, May 2001. https://hbr.org/2001/05/how-fast-can-your-company-afford-to-grow.

Churchill, Winston. Widely attributed. Source unknown.

Cloud, Henry. *Necessary Endings: The Employees, Businesses, and Relationships That All of Us Have to Give Up in Order to Move Forward.* New York: HarperCollins, 2010.

Cohn, Gary. qtd. in Christine Harper, "Goldman's Cohn Says Firms Burned by Poor Controls, Not Products." *Bloomberg*, Sept. 25, 2011. https://www.bloomberg.com/news/articles/2011-09-25/goldman-s-cohn-says-companies-burned-by-poor-risk-management-not-products

Collins, Jim. *Good to Great: Why Some Companies Make the Leap and Others Don't.* New York: HarperCollins, 2001.

Collins, Jim and Jerry Porras. *Built to Last: Successful Habits of Visionary Companies.* New York: Harper Business, 1994, p.127.

Collins, Jim and Morten T. Hansen. *Great by Choice: Uncertainty, Chaos, and Luck—Why Some Thrive Despite Them All.* New York: HarperCollins, 2011.

Covey, Stephen M. R. and Rebecca Merrill. *The Speed of Trust: The One Thing That Changes Everything.* New York: Simon & Schuster, 2006.

Cramer, Jim. Interview with Ann Curry. *The Today Show*, October 6, 2008.

Cuban, Mark. qtd. in Brian Musson, "DEBT DEBT DEBT most of us have it." LinkedIn, November 11, 2015. https://www.linkedin.com/pulse/debt-most-us-have-brian-musson/.

Cunic, Arlin. "How to Develop and Practice Self-Regulation."
Verywell Mind, May 2023.
https://www.verywellmind.com/how-you-can-practice-self-
regulation-4163536#citation-5.

Delfino, Devon. "The Percentage of Businesses that Fail—and How to
Boost Your Chances of Success." LendingTree, May 8, 2023.
https://www.lendingtree.com/business/small/failure-rate/

Dell, Michael. qtd. in Peter Lynch, "LBO Model: The Cash Flow
Statement." A Simple Model (ASM).
https://www.asimplemodel.com/financial-curriculum/lbo-case-
study/projected-period/the-cash-flow-statement.

DeLoe, Rona, "What Noncitizens Need to Know about Filing an LLC."
LegalZoom, May 2023.
https://www.legalzoom.com/articles/what-noncitizens-need-to-
know-about-filing-an-llc.

Disney, Walt. qtd. in Hedda Hopper, "Hedda Hopper's Hollywood,"
The Lima News. Lima, Ohio, July 15, 1957, p. 11

"Dot-com bubble." Wikipedia. https://en.wikipedia.org/wiki/Dot-
com_bubble.

Dromgoole, William Allen. "Building the Bridge." *Rare Old Chums*.
Boston, 1898.

Drucker, Peter. *The Effective Executive: The Definitive Guide to
Getting the Right Things Done*. New York: HarperCollins,
1967.

Dupont, David. Unpublished interview with John St.Pierre.

Einstein, Albert. Widely attributed. Source unknown.

"Etiquette of the Banker." 1775. Authors unknown.
https://www.scribd.com/document/358449797/Etiquette-of-the-Banker-1775-PDF

Ferriss, Timothy. *The 4-Hour Workweek: Escape 9–5, Live Anywhere, and Join the New Rich*. New York: Crown Publishers, 2007.

Gates, Bill. Widely attributed. Source unknown.

Grant, Adam. *Give and Take: Why Helping Others Drives Our Success*. New York: Penguin Books, 2014.

Gerber, Michael. *The E-Myth Revisited: Why Most Small Businesses Don't Work and What to Do About It*. New York: HarperCollins, 2009.

Gillebaart , Marleen. "The 'Operational' Definition of Self-Control." *Frontiers in Psychology*, July 2018. https://www.frontiersin.org/articles/10.3389/fpsyg.2018.01231/full; Qtd. in Cunic, Arlin. "How to Develop and Practice Self-Regulation." Verywell Mind, May 2023. https://www.verywellmind.com/how-you-can-practice-self-regulation-4163536#citation-5.

Hagen, Jessica. qtd. in Alexander Huls, "The Key to Managing Profit and Cash Flow for Your Small Business and Knowing the Difference Between the Two." *The Hartford*, May 24, 2023. https://sba.thehartford.com/finance/managing-profit-cash-flow/

Harbour, Jeremy. Unpublished conversation with John St.Pierre.

Harbour, Jeremy and Callum Laing. *Agglomerate: From Idea to IPO in 12 Months*. Norfolk, United Kingdom: Rethink Press, 2016.

Harnish, Verne. *Mastering the Rockefeller Habits: What You Must Do to Increase the Value of Your Growing Firm*. New Delhi, India: Dreamtech Press, 2007.

———. *Scaling Up: How a Few Companies Make It . . . and Why the Rest Don't*. Ashburn: Gazelles Inc., 2015.

Hearon, Steve. Unpublished conversations and unpublished interview with John St.Pierre.

Hersh, Mike. Unpublished conversations and unpublished interview with John St.Pierre.

Hill, Napoleon. *Think and Grow Rich: The Landmark Bestseller—Now Revised and Updated for the 21st Century*. New York: Penguin Publishing Group, 2005.

Inverted Pyramid (Chapter 22, p.172) :

https://www.trig.com/tangents/leadership-and-the-inverted-pyramid

IRS.gov[1]. "Retirement Topics - Defined Benefit Plan Benefit Limits." https://www.irs.gov/retirement-plans/plan-participant-employee/retirement-topics-defined-benefit-plan-benefit-limits. *Note: more information can be found here: https://www.cadenceretirementgroup.com/business-owners.htm, click on "2. Multiple Retirement Plans for a Business" to see an informational pdf from Wells Fargo.

IRS.gov[2]. "Cash Balance and Other Hybrid Defined Benefit Pension Plans: Notice 2007-6." https://www.irs.gov/pub/irs-drop/n-07-06.pdf. *Note: more information can be found here: https://www.cadenceretirementgroup.com/business-owners.htm, click on "2. Multiple Retirement Plans for a Business" to see an informational pdf from Wells Fargo.

Jarvis, Paul. qtd. in Josh Pollock, "Small is the New Big: An Interview with Paul Jarvis." *Torque Magazine*, November 8, 2018. https://torquemag.io/2018/11/small-is-the-new-big-an-interview-with-paul-jarvis/.

Keller, Gary and Jay Papasan. *The One Thing: The Surprisingly Simple Truth Behind Extraordinary Results*. Portland: Bard Press, 2013.

Kiyosaki, Robert and Sharon Lechter. *Rich Dad Poor Dad: What the Rich Teach Their Kids about Money – That the Poor and Middle Class Do Not!*. Brentwood: Warner Books, 1997.

Laing, Callum. Unpublished interview with John St.Pierre.

Lund, Ruth. Unpublished email to John. St.Pierre.

Ma, Ted. Unpublished email to John. St.Pierre.

Miltz, Alan. CASHFlow Story. AlanMiltz.com

———. "The #1 Method to Boost Cashflow, Value, and Profits – even in tough times" webinar. The Growth Institute, https://info.growthinstitute.com/cash-profit-value-replay-5-27-20?utm_campaign=CASH%20Master%20Business%20Course&utm_source=hs_email&utm_medium=email&utm_content=88628092&_hsenc=p2ANqtz--SlLa-vK1AAmEs5QnDInIT9nVgkJTGj6KPnNsa8LubEOayRgMybKE6LRMvoB4_CJruLGpqEuo9nS7vgkyGJikl5IQeOQ&_hsmi=88628092

Mitchell, John. Unpublished interview with John St.Pierre.

NAICS Association. "Market Research: Detailed Business Counts." Acquired August 18, 2023. https://www.naics.com/market-research/

Pastore, Vince. Unpublished interview with John St.Pierre.

Ravikant, Naval. qtd. in Tim Ferris, *Tools of Titans: The Tactics, Routines, and Habits of Billionaires, Icons, and World-Class Performers*. New York: Houghton Mifflin Harcourt, 2016.

Robbins, Anthony. *Personal Power!: A 30-Day Program for Unlimited Success*. San Diego: Robbins Research International, 1993.

Schlessinger, Laura (aka Dr. Laura) qtd. in James L. Harmon (ed.). *Take My Advice: Letters to the Next Generation From People Who Know a Thing or Two*. New York: Simon & Schuster, 2010.

Sinek, Simon. *Start with Why: How Great Leaders Inspire Everyone to Take Action*. New York: Portfolio / Penguin, 2009.

Smith, Revr. Andy, Investopedia Team. "What Is Capitalism: Varieties, History, Pros & Cons, Socialism." *Investopedia*, March 2023.

https://www.investopedia.com/terms/c/capitalism.asp.

Somma, Rande. *Leadersh!t: A Look at the Broken Leadership System in Corporate America that Accepts Leaders Who Are Really Good at Being Bad*. Saint Petersburg: BookLocker.com, 2016.

Stanley, Thomas J. and William D. Danko. *The Millionaire Next Door: The Surprising Secrets of America's Wealthy*. New York: RosettaBooks, 1996.

Stevenson, Brian. Unpublished interview with John St.Pierre.

Stevenson, Robert Louis. *Strange Case of Dr. Jekyll and Mr. Hyde*. London, 1886.

St.Pierre, John. *You 2.0: Find Your Purpose & Kick Some Ass*. Unpublished.

The Martian. Directed by Ridley Scott. Written by Drew Goddard and Andy Weir. Featuring Matt Damon, Jessica Chastain, and Kristen Wiig. 2015, 20th Century Fox.

Tuovila, Alicia. "Accelerated Depreciation: What Is It, How to Calculate It." Investopedia, October 28, 2020. https://www.investopedia.com/terms/a/accelerateddepreciation.asp#:~:text=Accelerated%20depreciation%20is%20any%20method,the%20life%20of%20an%20asset.

Unger, Jeffrey. Unpublished interview with John St.Pierre.

Vilante, Tom. qtd. in Bill Carmody, "Only 0.04 Percent of Companies Reach $100 Million in Annual Revenue. Here's the 1 Thing Driving YapStone's Explosive Growth." *Inc.* https://www.inc.com/bill-carmody/only-0-04-reach-100-million-in-annual-revenue-here-s-the-one-thing-driving-yapst.html.

Wooden, John. Widely attributed. Source unknown.

Ziglar, Hilary "Zig." Heard by the author at *The Success 1997 Business Conference*.

JOHN ST.PIERRE

John St.Pierre is an entrepreneurial executive with 25 years of business leadership experience who has cofounded and grown two companies to over $50M in revenues each.

While he was a college student in 1995, John began his entrepreneurial career as a franchisee for College Pro Painters. Upon graduating with a Bachelor of Science in Accounting from the University of Southern Maine, he continued to develop his entrepreneurial skills as a general manager for College Pro. In 1998, John joined other prominent College Pro entrepreneurs as a VP of Sales for HandymanOnline.com, a venture capital-backed platform connecting homeowners with vetted contractors. After the dot-com crash in 2001, John took a role as president of WorldAtMyDoor, an e-commerce platform for small businesses, which was successfully sold in 2002.

In 2003, John cofounded two companies: Selects Sports Management (which was rebranded Legacy Global Sports) and Rhombus Services (which was rebranded BrandPoint Services).

Legacy Global Sports, a global youth sports management company, rapidly rose to $50M+ in global revenues before John was replaced as CEO in 2018.

Meanwhile, BrandPoint Services, a national commercial contracting and project management firm, is a $100M+ company where John serves as chairperson.

John is also the chairperson of Rhombus Group, a private holding company formed in 2020 comprising several small businesses run by extraordinary entrepreneurs. His mission is to help entrepreneurs and their companies to achieve their goals and dreams by building a solid foundation based on a clear and concise Strategic Business Plan and following the 7 Principles of Entrepreneurial Success in his book, *The $100M Journey: Your Guide To Growing The Business Of Your Dreams Without Going off The Cliff!*

In 2020, John and his cohost, Rich Hoffmann, started the *Entrepreneurs United Podcast*, which can be found on YouTube, Apple podcasts, Spotify, Amazon, and other outlets, including EntrepreneursUnited.us.